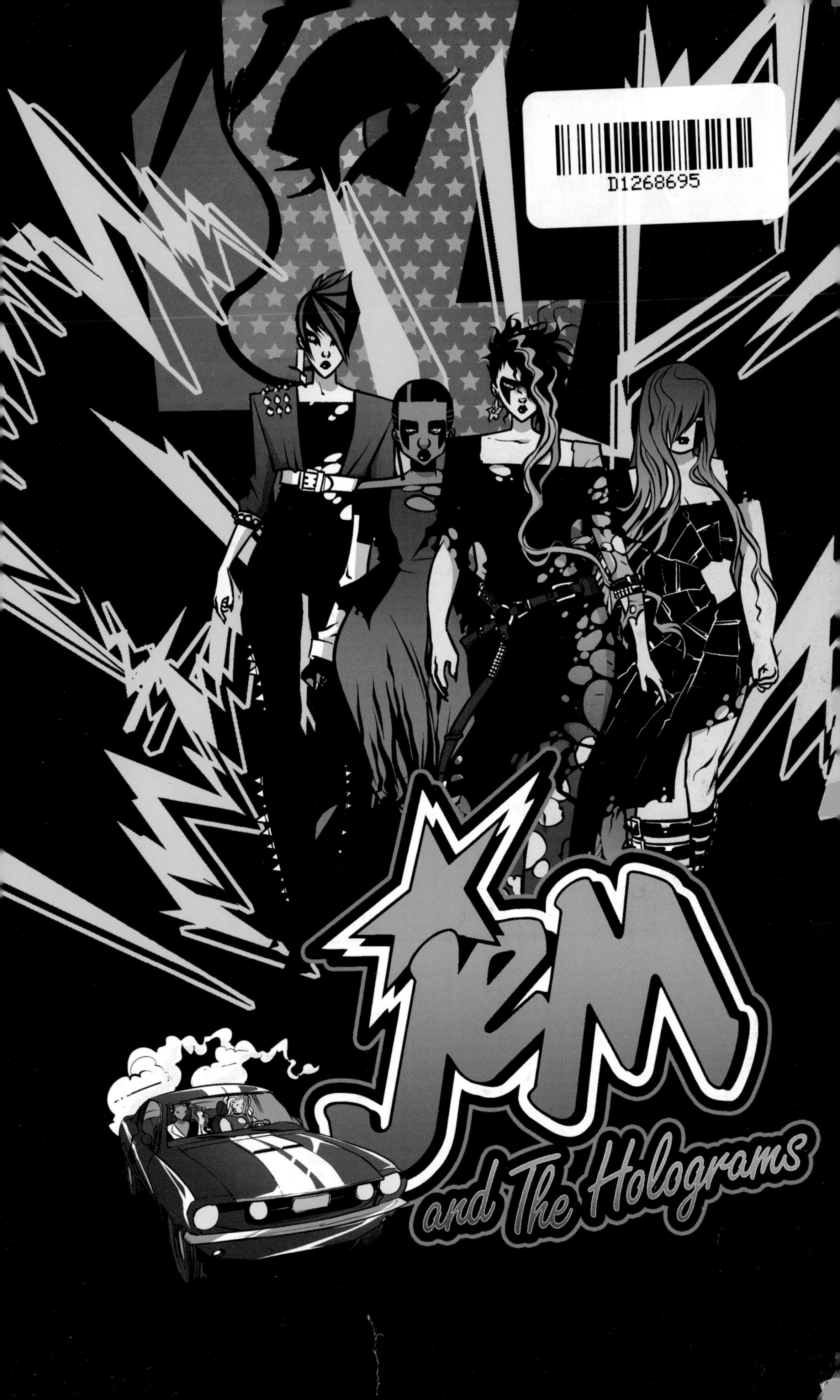
Jem
and The Holograms

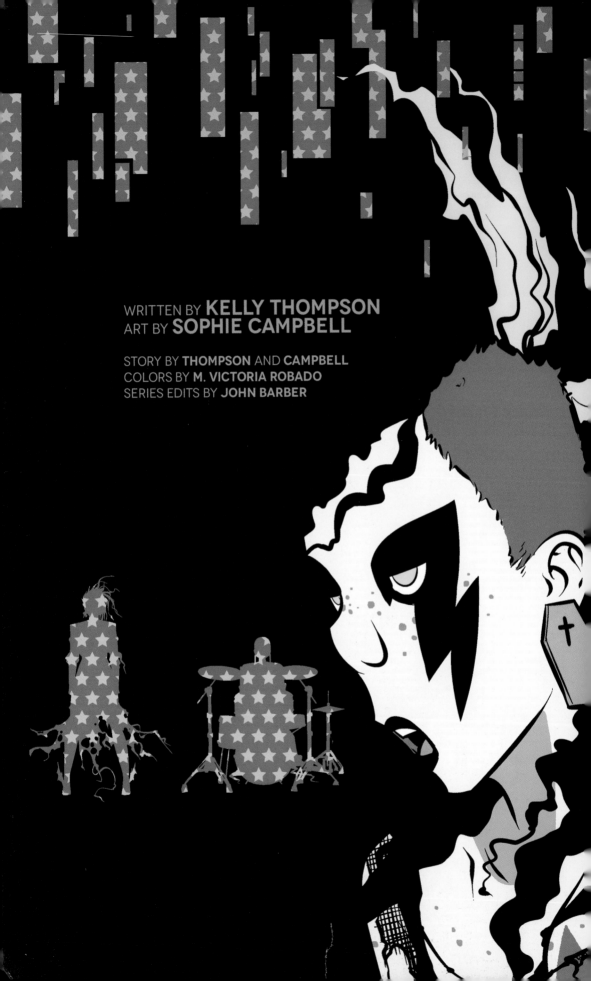

WRITTEN BY **KELLY THOMPSON**
ART BY **SOPHIE CAMPBELL**

STORY BY **THOMPSON** AND **CAMPBELL**
COLORS BY **M. VICTORIA ROBADO**
SERIES EDITS BY **JOHN BARBER**

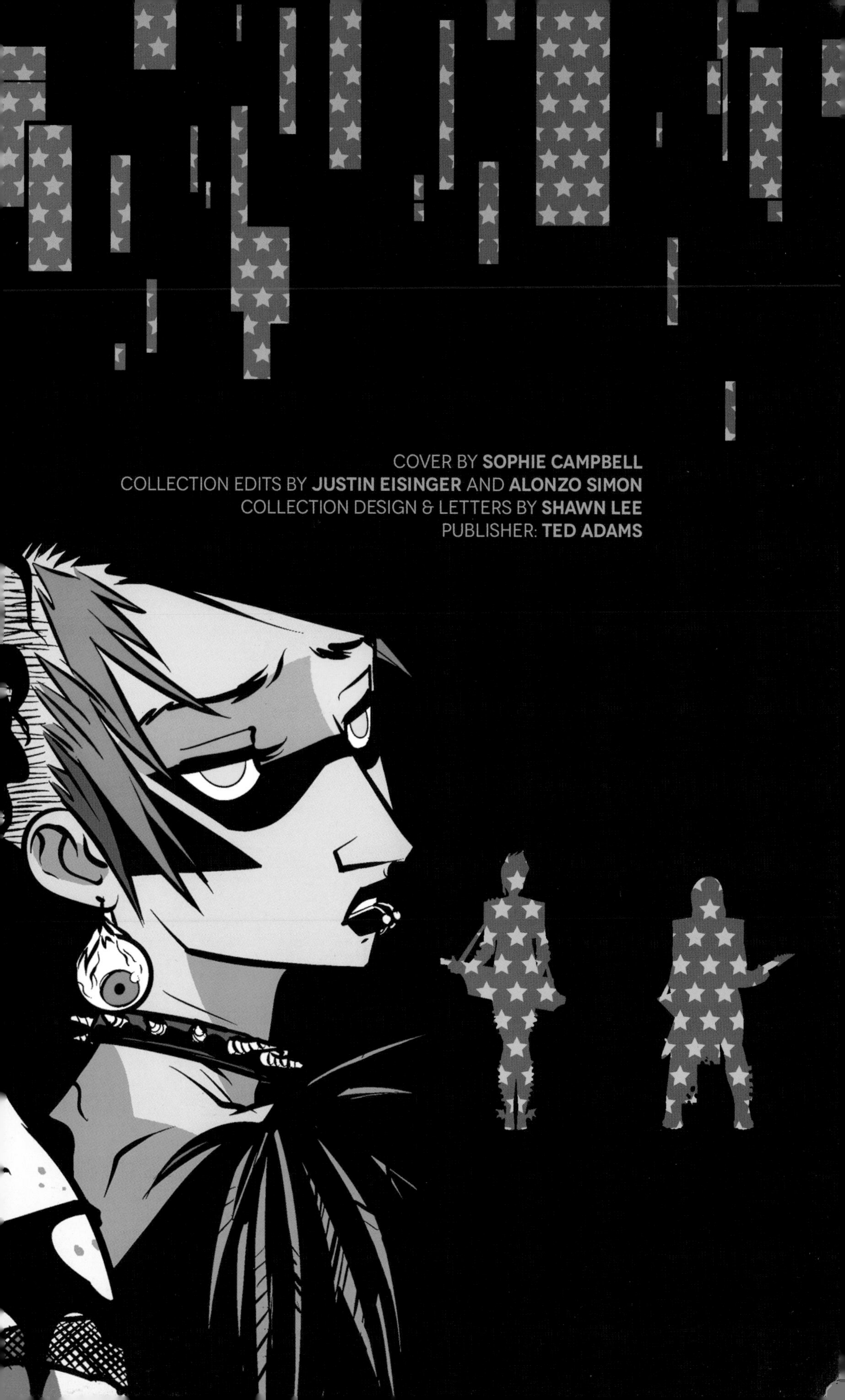

COVER BY **SOPHIE CAMPBELL**
COLLECTION EDITS BY **JUSTIN EISINGER** AND **ALONZO SIMON**
COLLECTION DESIGN & LETTERS BY **SHAWN LEE**
PUBLISHER: **TED ADAMS**

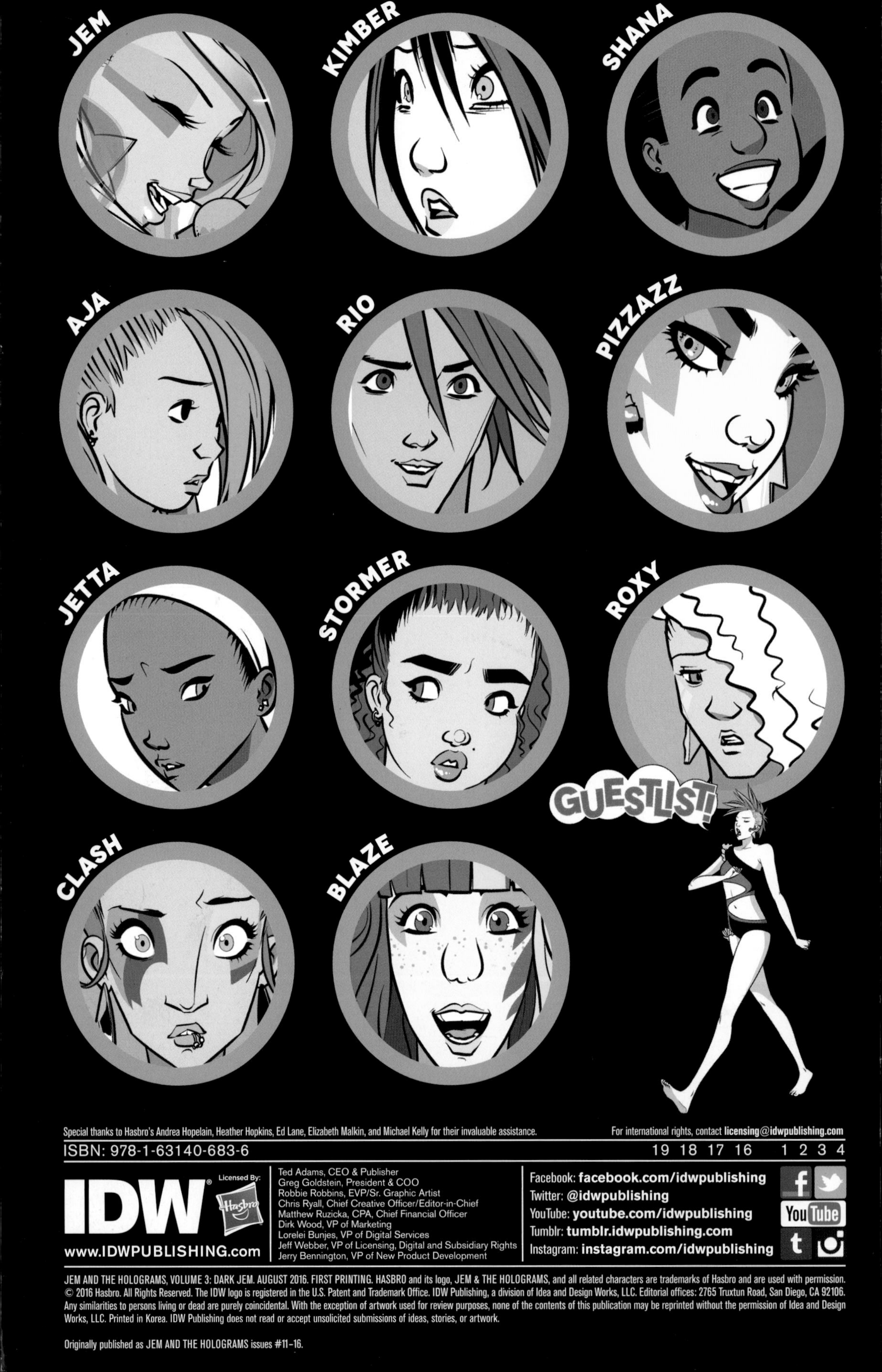
JEM
KIMBER
SHANA
AJA
RIO
PIZZAZZ
JETTA
STORMER
ROXY
GUESTLIST!
CLASH
BLAZE

Special thanks to Hasbro's Andrea Hopelain, Heather Hopkins, Ed Lane, Elizabeth Malkin, and Michael Kelly for their invaluable assistance.

For international rights, contact licensing@idwpublishing.com

ISBN: 978-1-63140-683-6

19 18 17 16 1 2 3 4

IDW Licensed By: Hasbro

www.IDWPUBLISHING.com

Ted Adams, CEO & Publisher
Greg Goldstein, President & COO
Robbie Robbins, EVP/Sr. Graphic Artist
Chris Ryall, Chief Creative Officer/Editor-in-Chief
Matthew Ruzicka, CPA, Chief Financial Officer
Dirk Wood, VP of Marketing
Lorelei Bunjes, VP of Digital Services
Jeff Webber, VP of Licensing, Digital and Subsidiary Rights
Jerry Bennington, VP of New Product Development

Facebook: facebook.com/idwpublishing
Twitter: @idwpublishing
YouTube: youtube.com/idwpublishing
Tumblr: tumblr.idwpublishing.com
Instagram: instagram.com/idwpublishing

Originally published as JEM AND THE HOLOGRAMS issues #11–16.

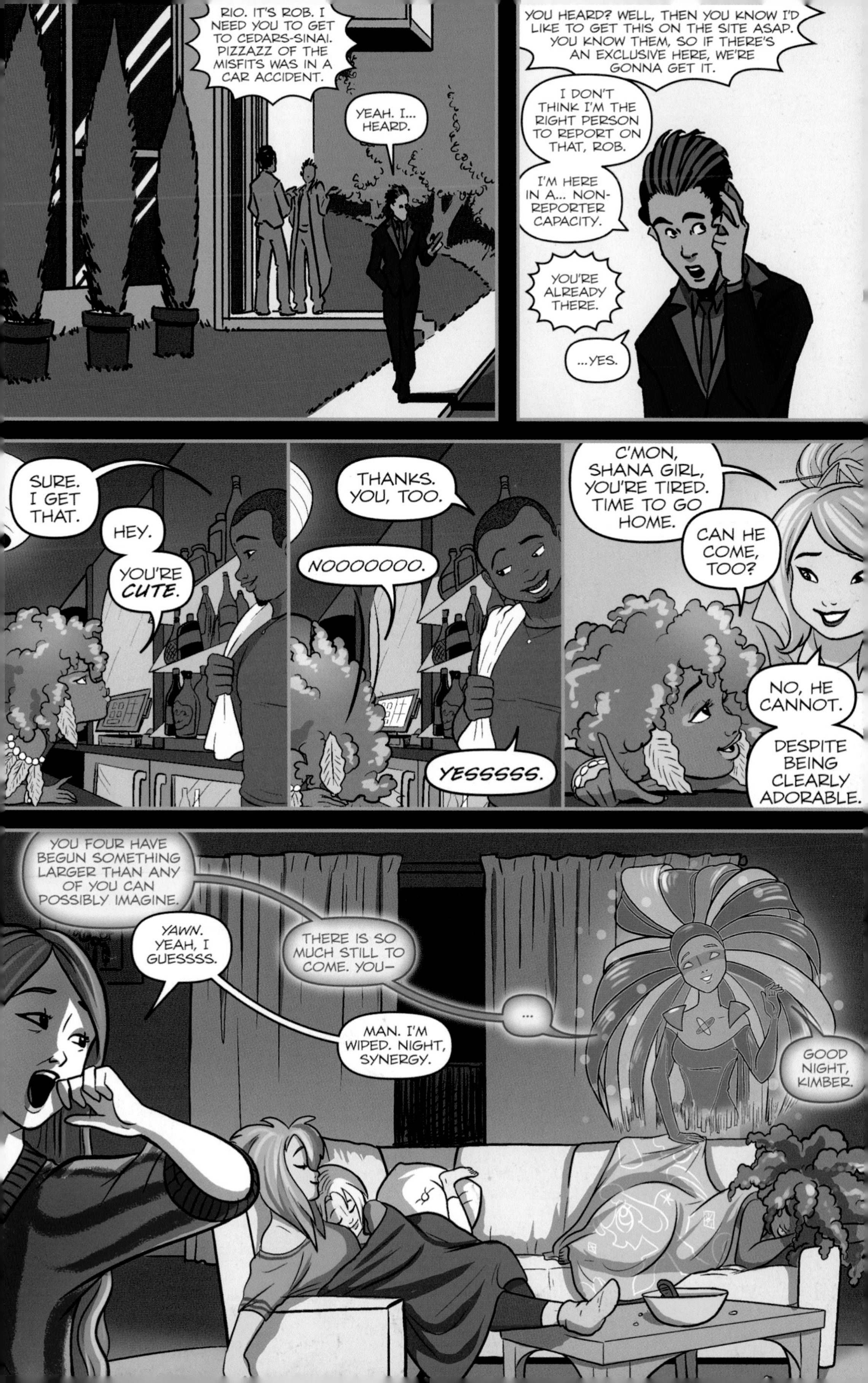
RIO. IT'S ROB. I NEED YOU TO GET TO CEDARS-SINAI. PIZZAZZ OF THE MISFITS WAS IN A CAR ACCIDENT.
YEAH. I... HEARD.
YOU HEARD? WELL, THEN YOU KNOW I'D LIKE TO GET THIS ON THE SITE ASAP. YOU KNOW THEM, SO IF THERE'S AN EXCLUSIVE HERE, WE'RE GONNA GET IT.
I DON'T THINK I'M THE RIGHT PERSON TO REPORT ON THAT, ROB.
I'M HERE IN A... NON-REPORTER CAPACITY.
YOU'RE ALREADY THERE.
...YES.
SURE. I GET THAT.
HEY.
YOU'RE CUTE.
THANKS. YOU, TOO.
NOOOOOOO.
YESSSSS.
C'MON, SHANA GIRL, YOU'RE TIRED. TIME TO GO HOME.
CAN HE COME, TOO?
NO, HE CANNOT.
DESPITE BEING CLEARLY ADORABLE.
YOU FOUR HAVE BEGUN SOMETHING LARGER THAN ANY OF YOU CAN POSSIBLY IMAGINE.
YAWN. YEAH, I GUESSSS.
THERE IS SO MUCH STILL TO COME. YOU—
...
MAN. I'M WIPED. NIGHT, SYNERGY.
GOOD NIGHT, KIMBER.

1 ART BY **SOPHIE CAMPBELL**

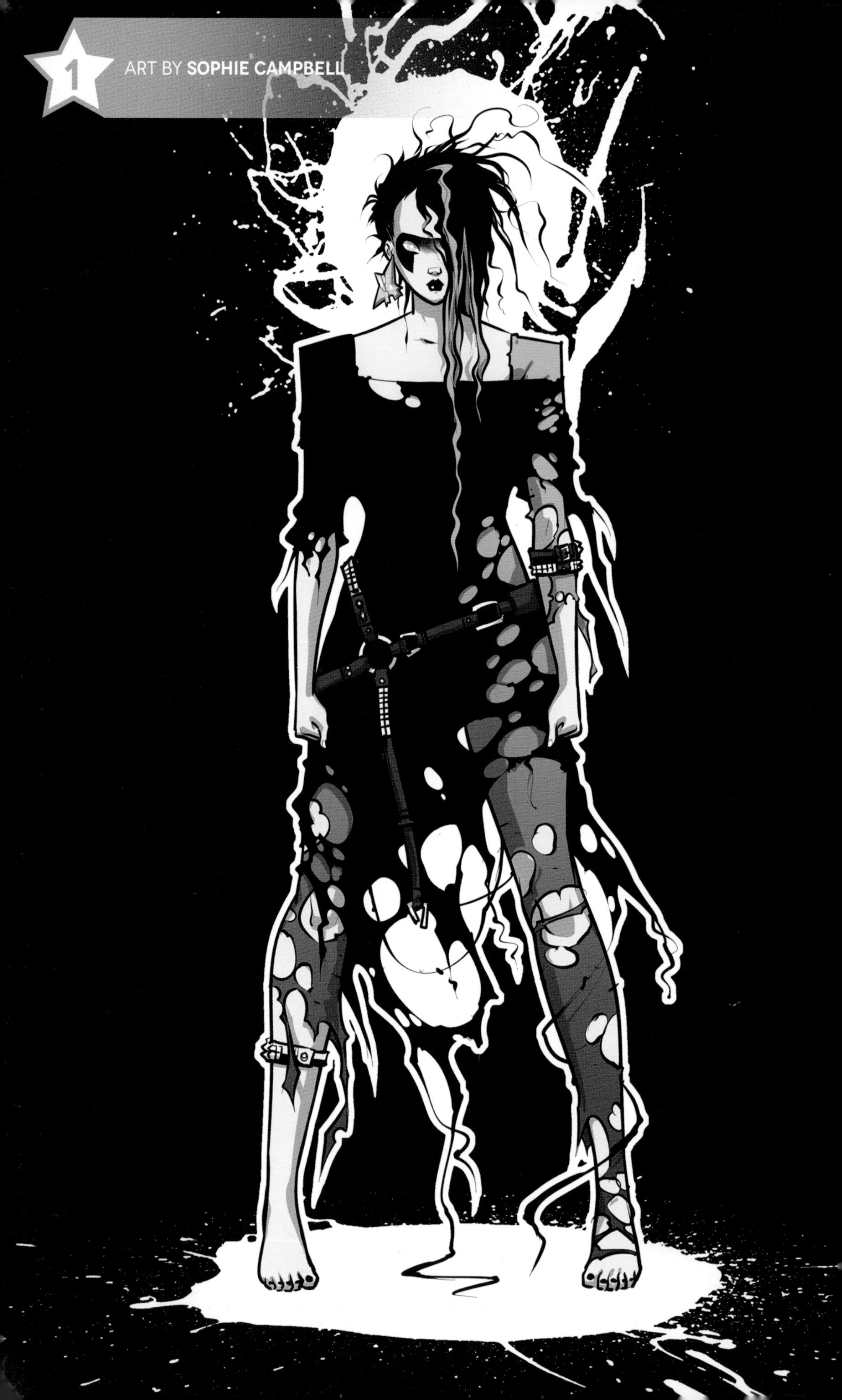

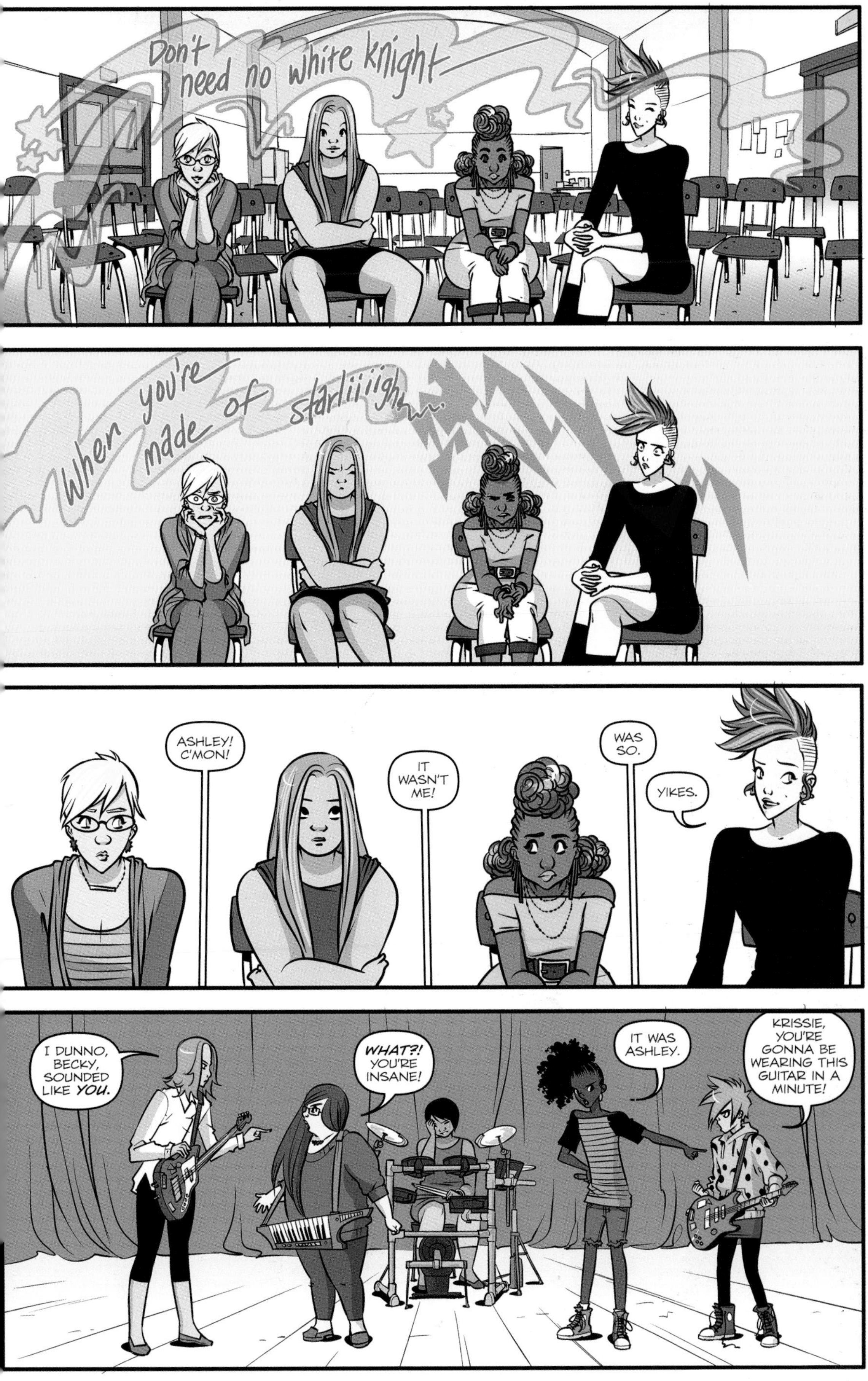
Don't need no white knight
When you're made of starliiiiigh...
ASHLEY! C'MON!
IT WASN'T ME!
WAS SO.
YIKES.
I DUNNO, BECKY, SOUNDED LIKE YOU.
WHAT?! YOU'RE INSANE!
IT WAS ASHLEY.
KRISSIE, YOU'RE GONNA BE WEARING THIS GUITAR IN A MINUTE!

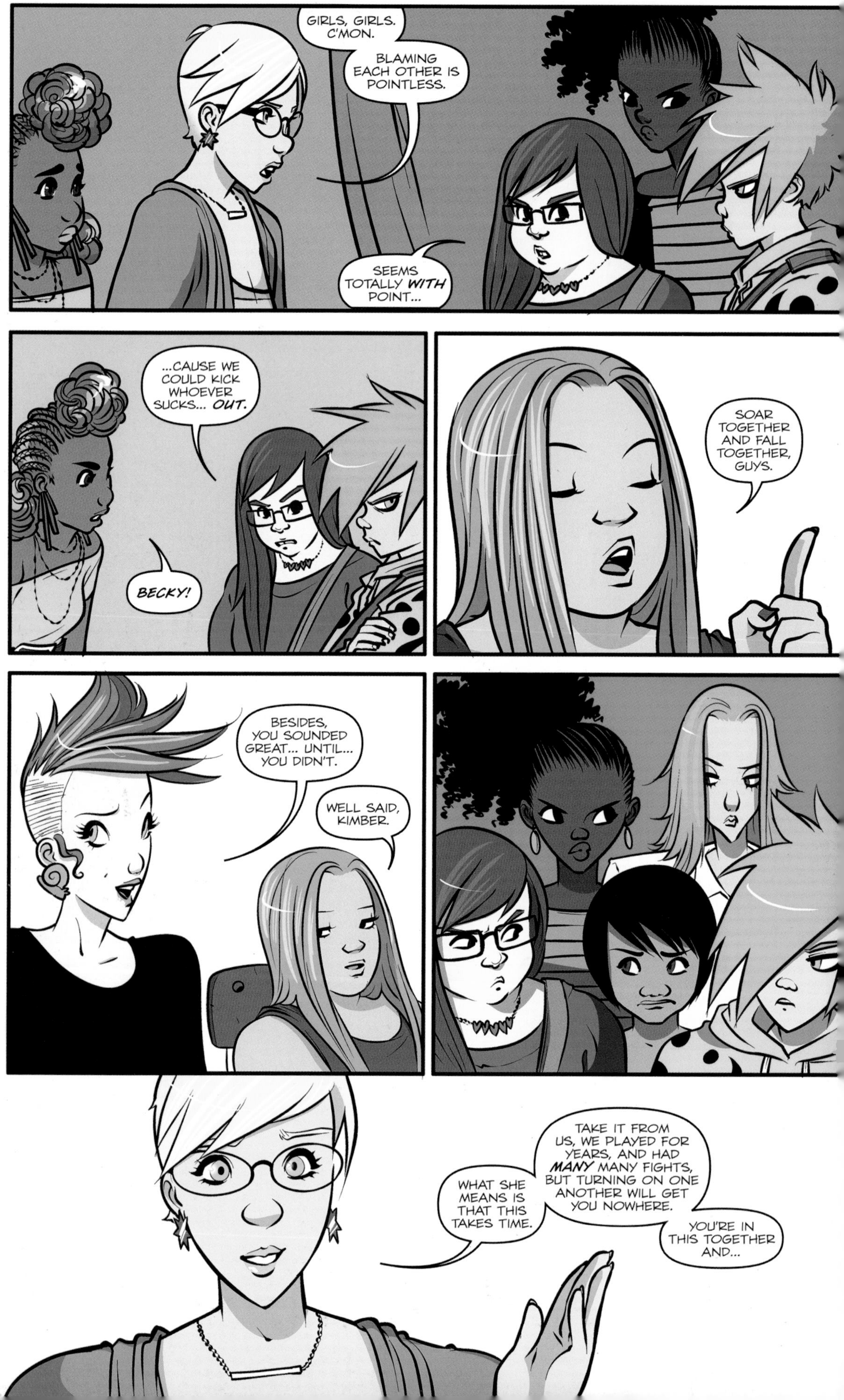
GIRLS, GIRLS. C'MON.
BLAMING EACH OTHER IS POINTLESS.
SEEMS TOTALLY *WITH* POINT...
...CAUSE WE COULD KICK WHOEVER SUCKS... *OUT.*
BECKY!
SOAR TOGETHER AND FALL TOGETHER, GUYS.
BESIDES, YOU SOUNDED GREAT... UNTIL... YOU DIDN'T.
WELL SAID, KIMBER.
WHAT SHE MEANS IS THAT THIS TAKES TIME.
TAKE IT FROM US, WE PLAYED FOR YEARS, AND HAD *MANY* MANY FIGHTS, BUT TURNING ON ONE ANOTHER WILL GET YOU NOWHERE.
YOU'RE IN THIS TOGETHER AND...

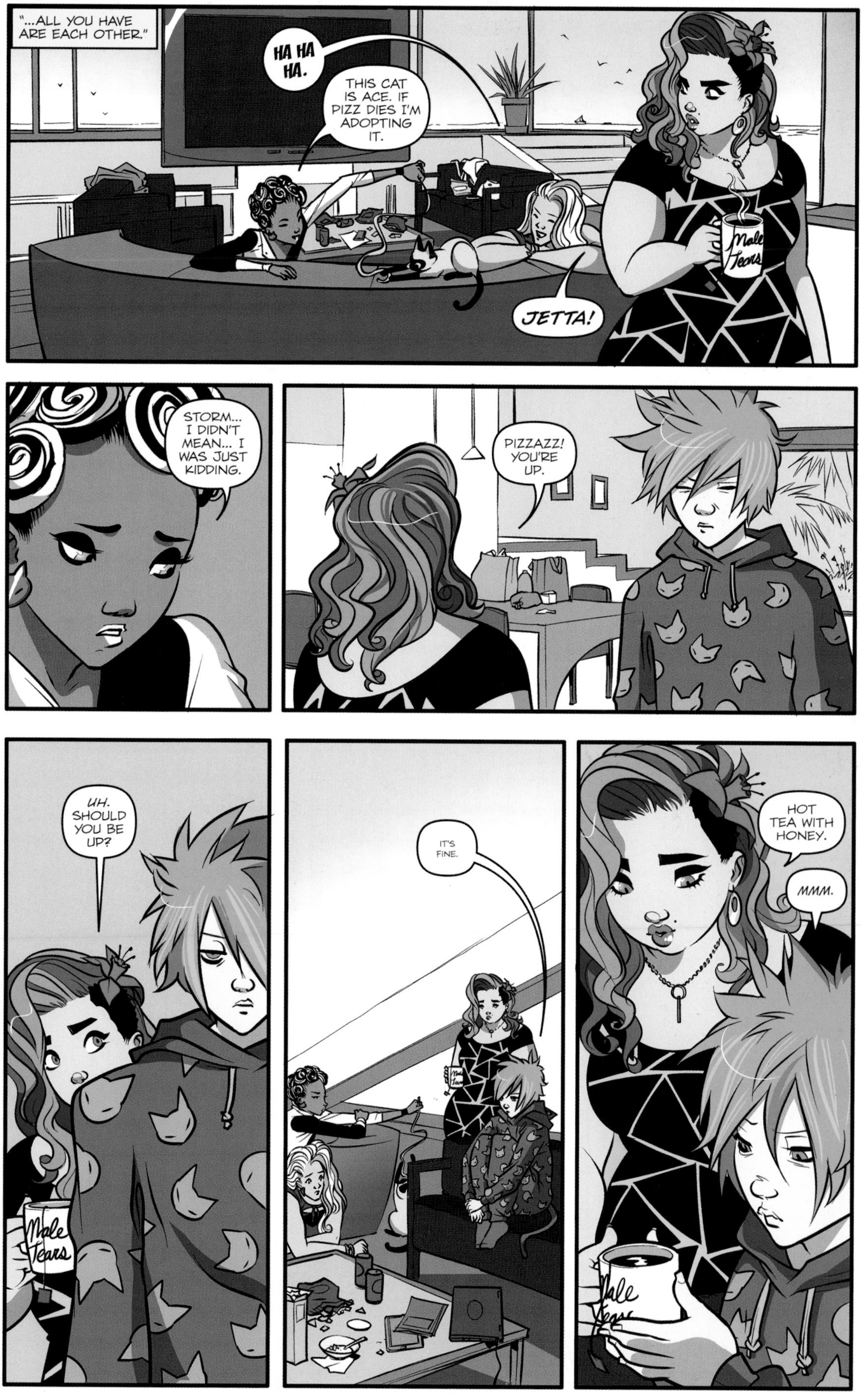
"...ALL YOU HAVE ARE EACH OTHER."
HA HA HA.
THIS CAT IS ACE. IF PIZZ DIES I'M ADOPTING IT.
JETTA!
Male Tears
STORM... I DIDN'T MEAN... I WAS JUST KIDDING.
PIZZAZZ! YOU'RE UP.
UH. SHOULD YOU BE UP?
Male Tears
IT'S FINE.
HOT TEA WITH HONEY.
MMM.

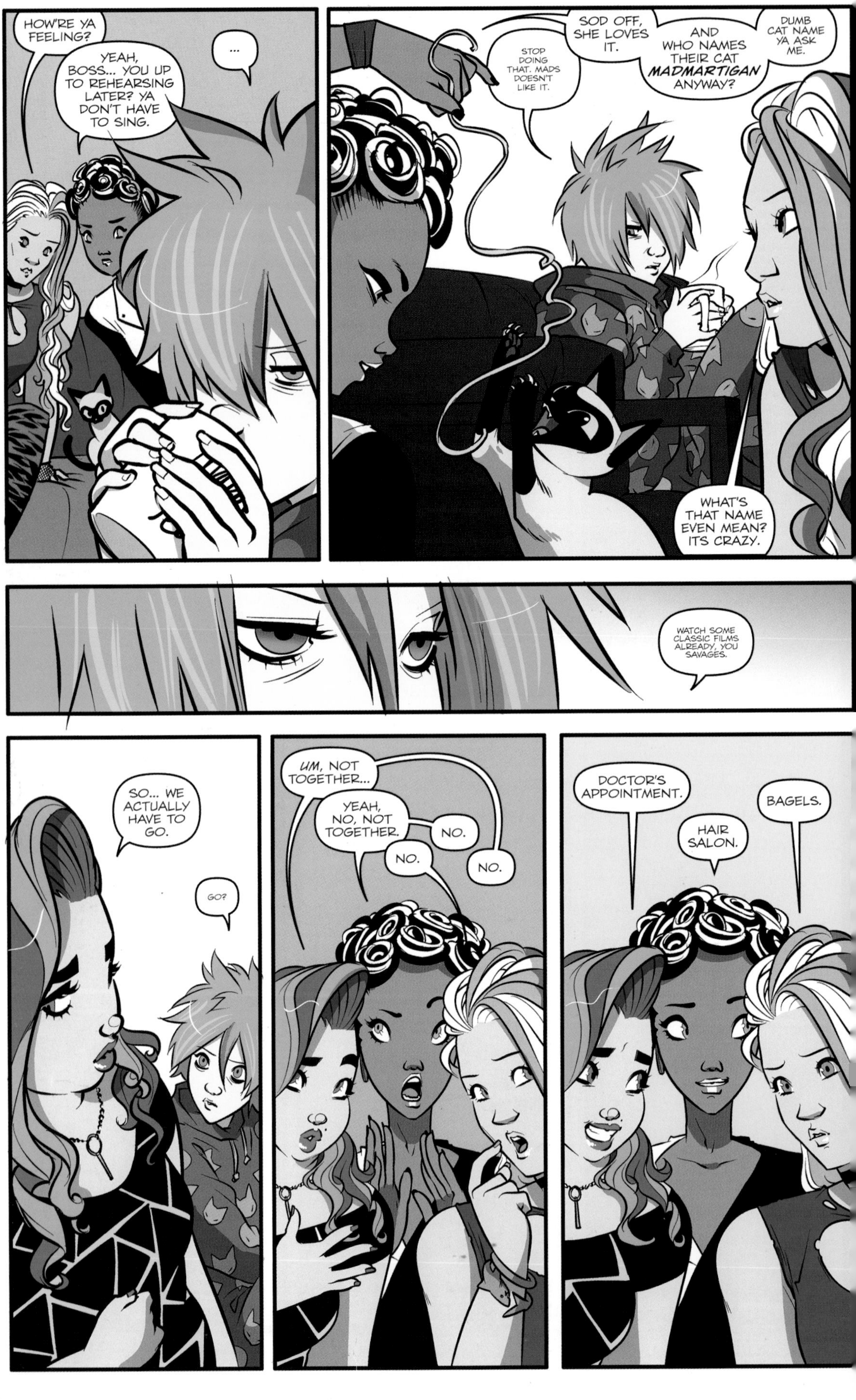
HOW'RE YA FEELING?
YEAH, BOSS... YOU UP TO REHEARSING LATER? YA DON'T HAVE TO SING.
...
STOP DOING THAT. MADS DOESN'T LIKE IT.
SOD OFF, SHE LOVES IT.
AND WHO NAMES THEIR CAT MADMARTIGAN ANYWAY?
DUMB CAT NAME YA ASK ME.
WHAT'S THAT NAME EVEN MEAN? ITS CRAZY.
WATCH SOME CLASSIC FILMS ALREADY, YOU SAVAGES.
SO... WE ACTUALLY HAVE TO GO.
GO?
UM, NOT TOGETHER...
YEAH, NO, NOT TOGETHER.
NO.
NO.
NO.
DOCTOR'S APPOINTMENT.
HAIR SALON.
BAGELS.

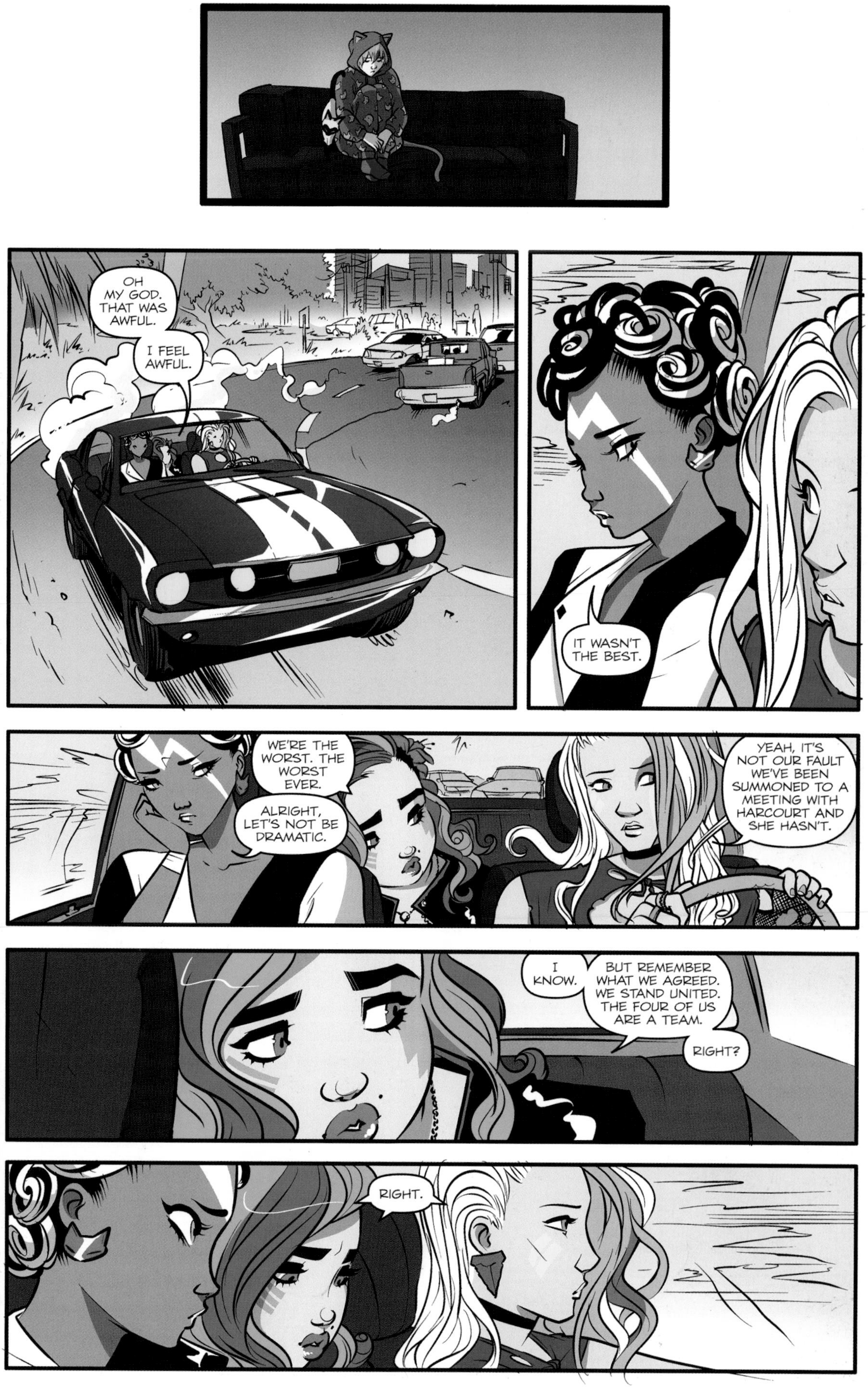
OH MY GOD. THAT WAS AWFUL.
I FEEL AWFUL.
IT WASN'T THE BEST.
WE'RE THE WORST. THE WORST EVER.
ALRIGHT, LET'S NOT BE DRAMATIC.
YEAH, IT'S NOT OUR FAULT WE'VE BEEN SUMMONED TO A MEETING WITH HARCOURT AND SHE HASN'T.
I KNOW.
BUT REMEMBER WHAT WE AGREED. WE STAND UNITED. THE FOUR OF US ARE A TEAM.
RIGHT?
RIGHT.

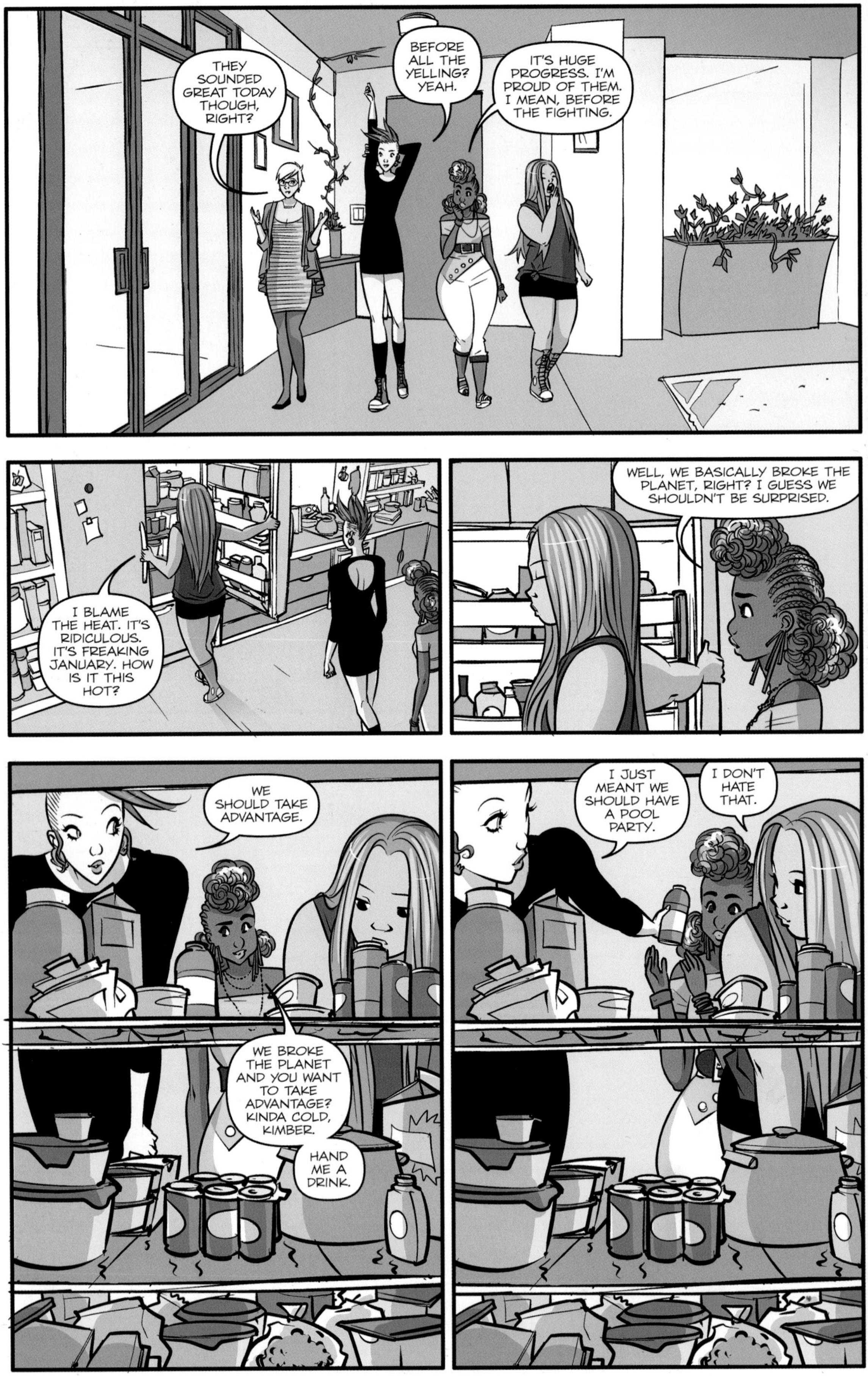
THEY SOUNDED GREAT TODAY THOUGH, RIGHT?
BEFORE ALL THE YELLING? YEAH.
IT'S HUGE PROGRESS. I'M PROUD OF THEM. I MEAN, BEFORE THE FIGHTING.
I BLAME THE HEAT. IT'S RIDICULOUS. IT'S FREAKING JANUARY. HOW IS IT THIS HOT?
WELL, WE BASICALLY BROKE THE PLANET, RIGHT? I GUESS WE SHOULDN'T BE SURPRISED.
WE SHOULD TAKE ADVANTAGE.
WE BROKE THE PLANET AND YOU WANT TO TAKE ADVANTAGE? KINDA COLD, KIMBER.
HAND ME A DRINK.
I JUST MEANT WE SHOULD HAVE A POOL PARTY.
I DON'T HATE THAT.

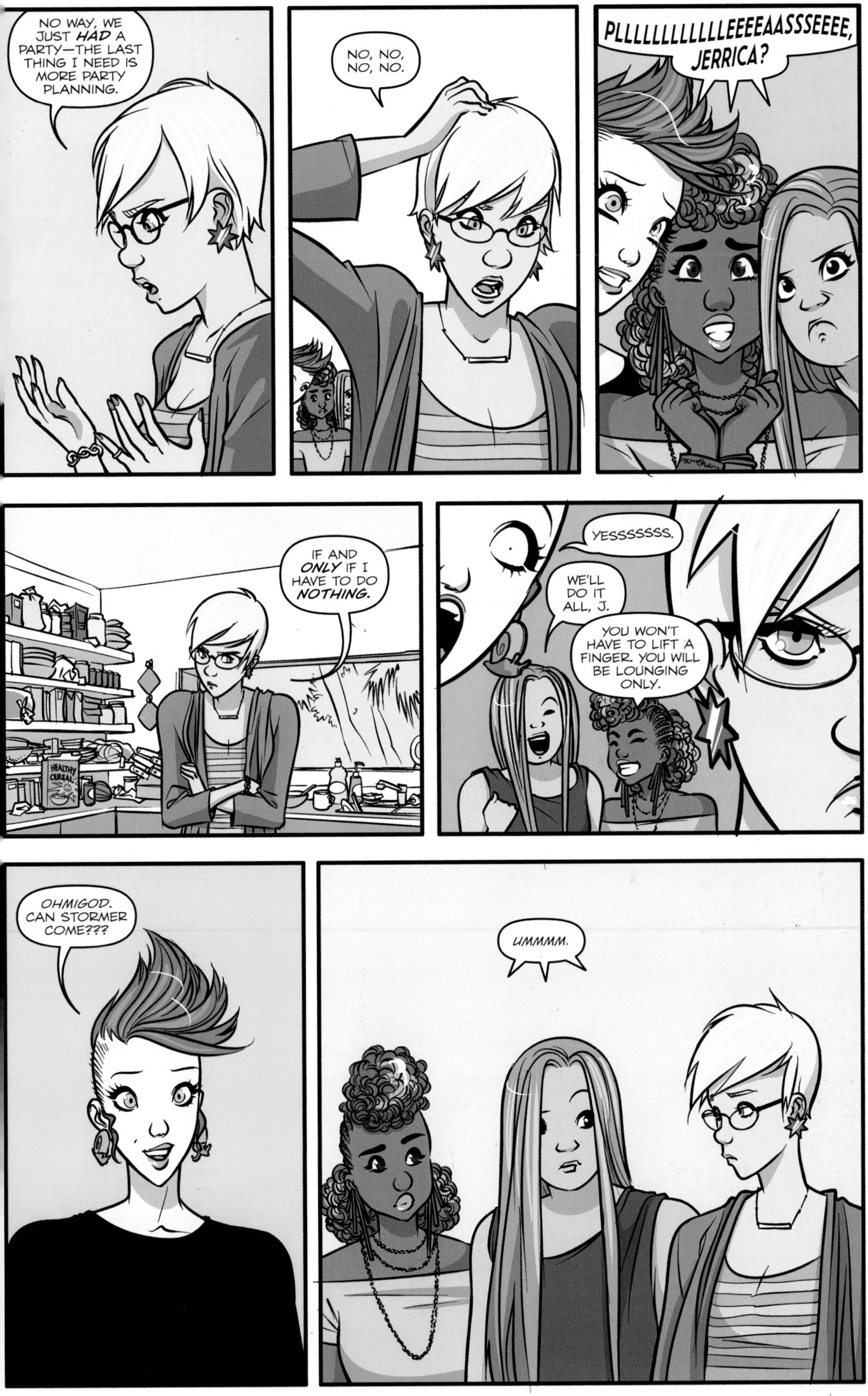
NO WAY, WE JUST HAD A PARTY—THE LAST THING I NEED IS MORE PARTY PLANNING.
NO, NO, NO, NO.
PLLLLLLLLLLLLEEEEAASSSEEEE, JERRICA?
IF AND ONLY IF I HAVE TO DO NOTHING.
HEALTHY CEREAL
YESSSSSSS.
WE'LL DO IT ALL, J.
YOU WON'T HAVE TO LIFT A FINGER. YOU WILL BE LOUNGING ONLY.
OHMIGOD. CAN STORMER COME???
UMMMM.

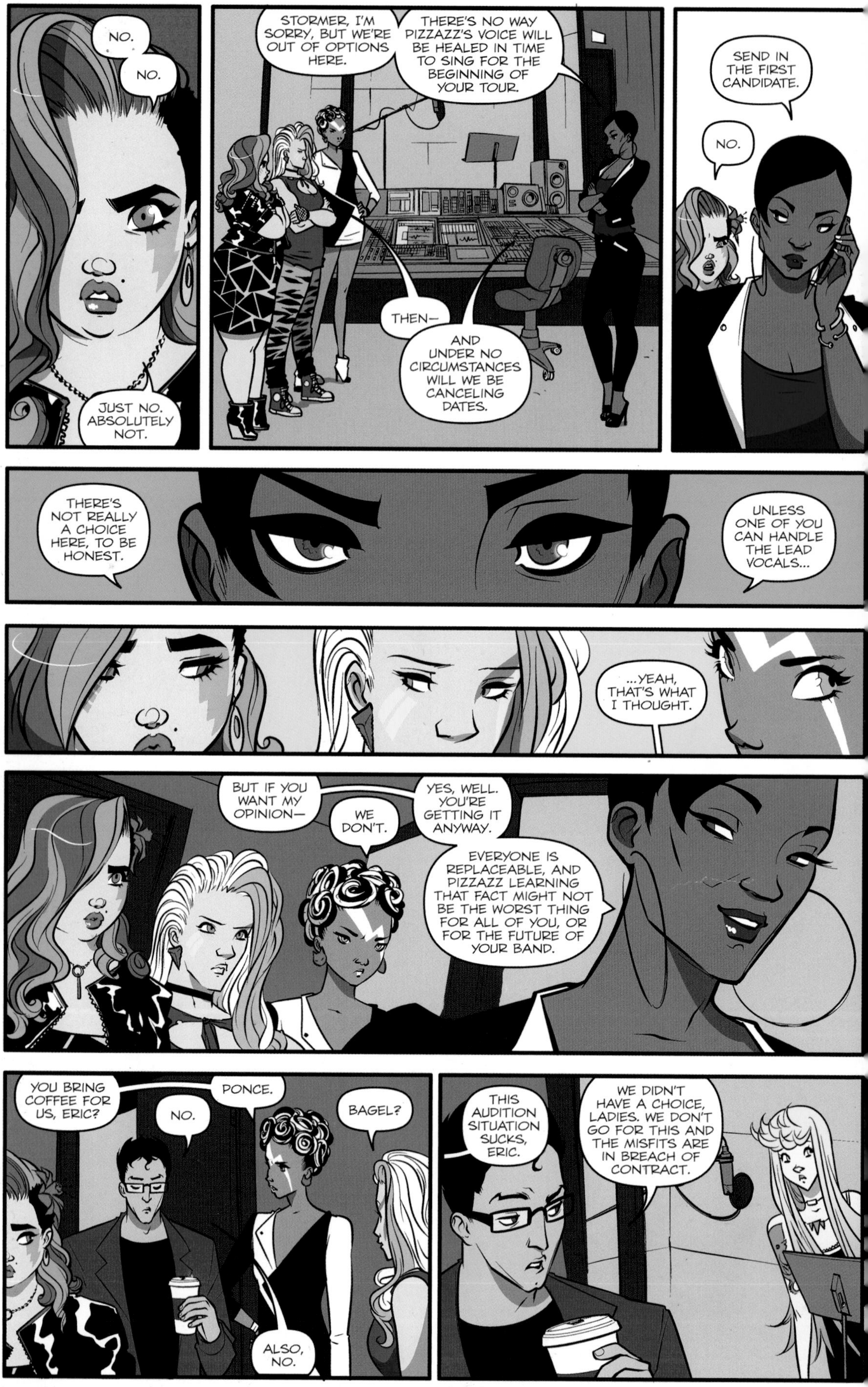

NO.
NO.
JUST NO. ABSOLUTELY NOT.
STORMER, I'M SORRY, BUT WE'RE OUT OF OPTIONS HERE.
THERE'S NO WAY PIZZAZZ'S VOICE WILL BE HEALED IN TIME TO SING FOR THE BEGINNING OF YOUR TOUR.
THEN—
AND UNDER NO CIRCUMSTANCES WILL WE BE CANCELING DATES.
SEND IN THE FIRST CANDIDATE.
NO.
THERE'S NOT REALLY A CHOICE HERE, TO BE HONEST.
UNLESS ONE OF YOU CAN HANDLE THE LEAD VOCALS...
...YEAH, THAT'S WHAT I THOUGHT.
BUT IF YOU WANT MY OPINION—
WE DON'T.
YES, WELL. YOU'RE GETTING IT ANYWAY.
EVERYONE IS REPLACEABLE, AND PIZZAZZ LEARNING THAT FACT MIGHT NOT BE THE WORST THING FOR ALL OF YOU, OR FOR THE FUTURE OF YOUR BAND.
YOU BRING COFFEE FOR US, ERIC?
NO.
PONCE.
BAGEL?
ALSO, NO.
THIS AUDITION SITUATION SUCKS, ERIC.
WE DIDN'T HAVE A CHOICE, LADIES. WE DON'T GO FOR THIS AND THE MISFITS ARE IN BREACH OF CONTRACT.

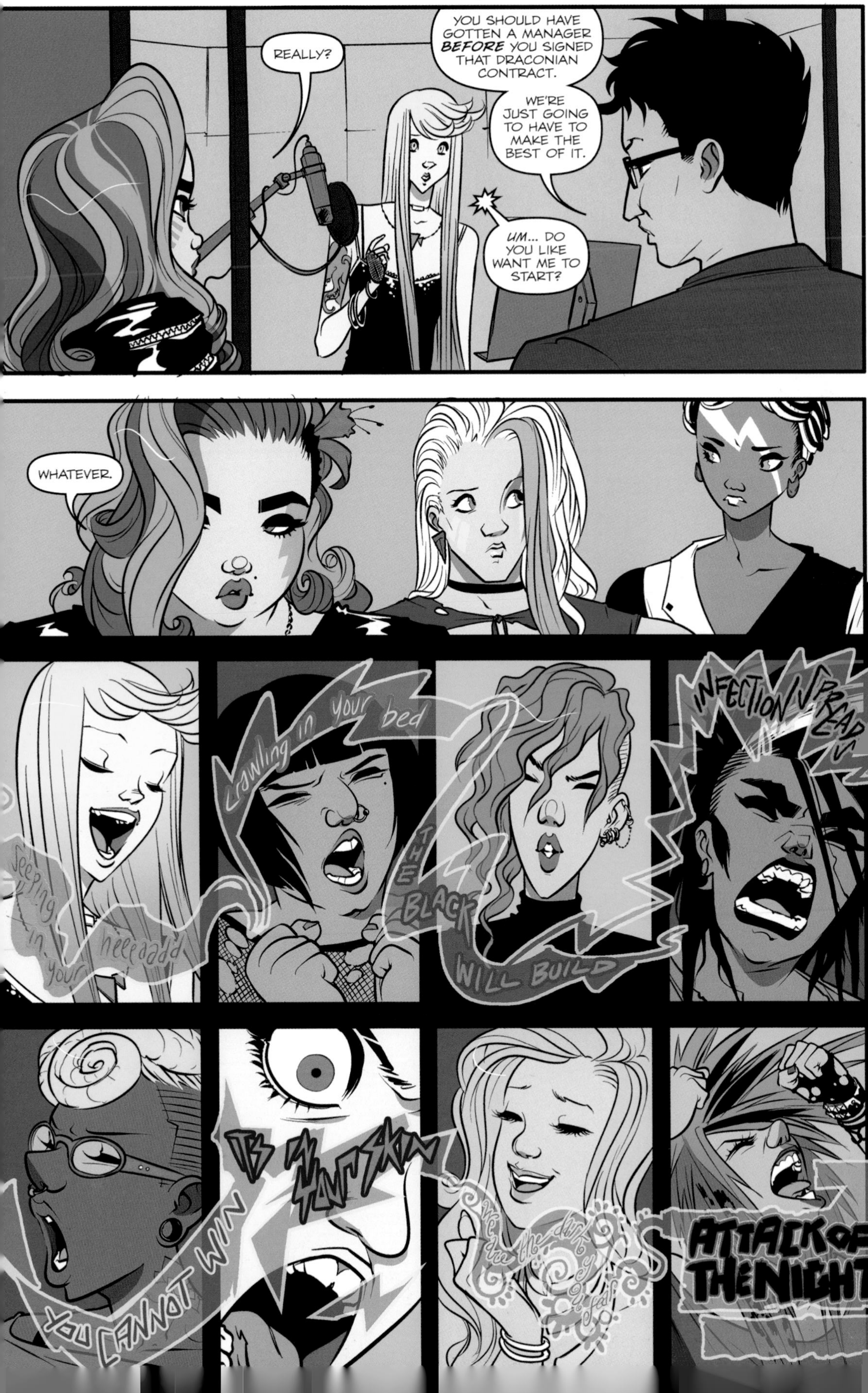
REALLY?
YOU SHOULD HAVE GOTTEN A MANAGER BEFORE YOU SIGNED THAT DRACONIAN CONTRACT.
WE'RE JUST GOING TO HAVE TO MAKE THE BEST OF IT.
UM... DO YOU LIKE WANT ME TO START?
WHATEVER.
seeping in your heeeaaadd
crawling in your bed
THE BLACK WILL BUILD
INFECTION SPREADS
YOU CANNOT WIN
ATTACK OF THE NIGHT

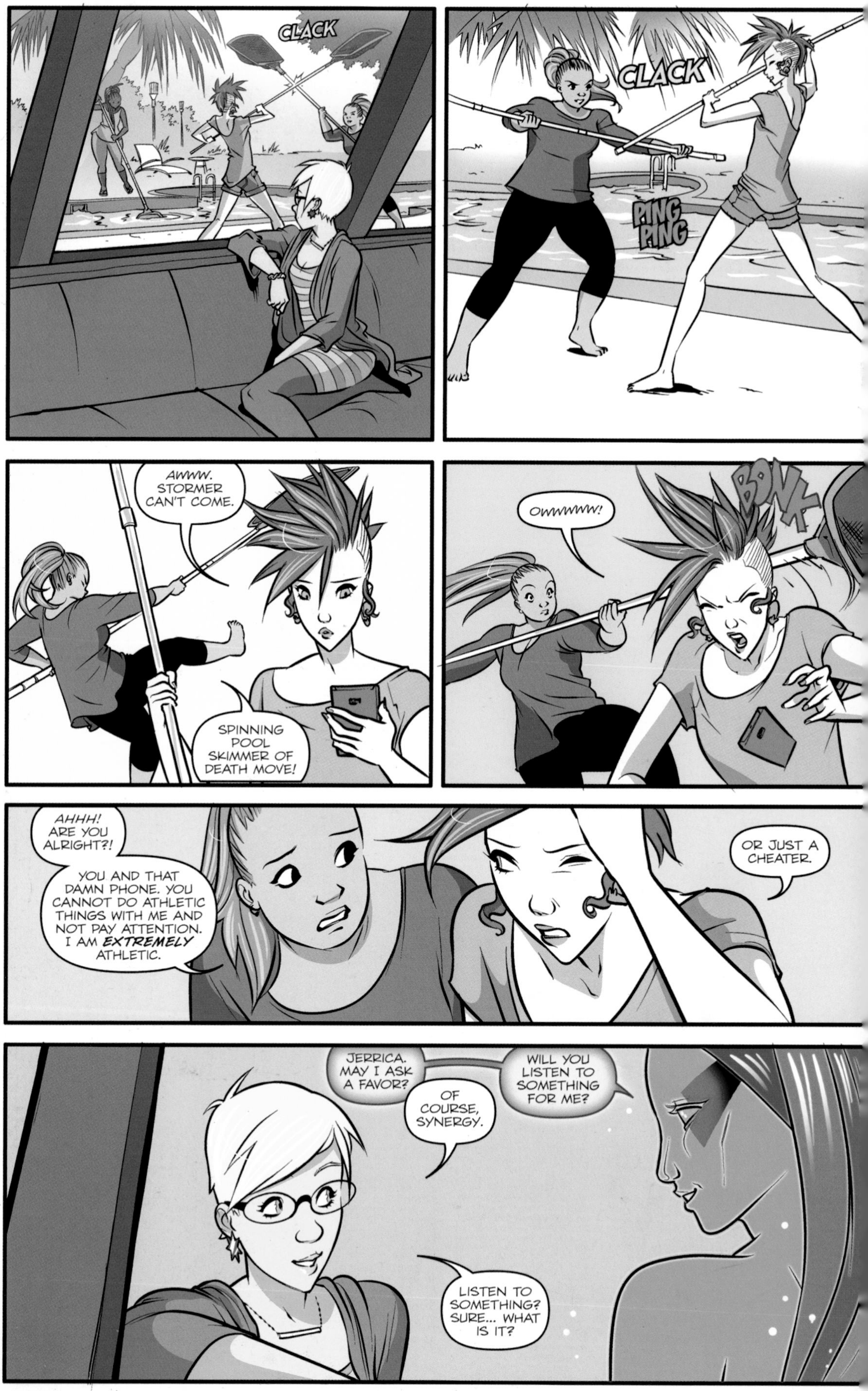
CLACK
CLACK
PING PING
AWWW. STORMER CAN'T COME.
SPINNING POOL SKIMMER OF DEATH MOVE!
OWWWWW!
BONK
AHHH! ARE YOU ALRIGHT?!
YOU AND THAT DAMN PHONE. YOU CANNOT DO ATHLETIC THINGS WITH ME AND NOT PAY ATTENTION. I AM EXTREMELY ATHLETIC.
OR JUST A CHEATER.
JERRICA. MAY I ASK A FAVOR?
OF COURSE, SYNERGY.
WILL YOU LISTEN TO SOMETHING FOR ME?
LISTEN TO SOMETHING? SURE... WHAT IS IT?

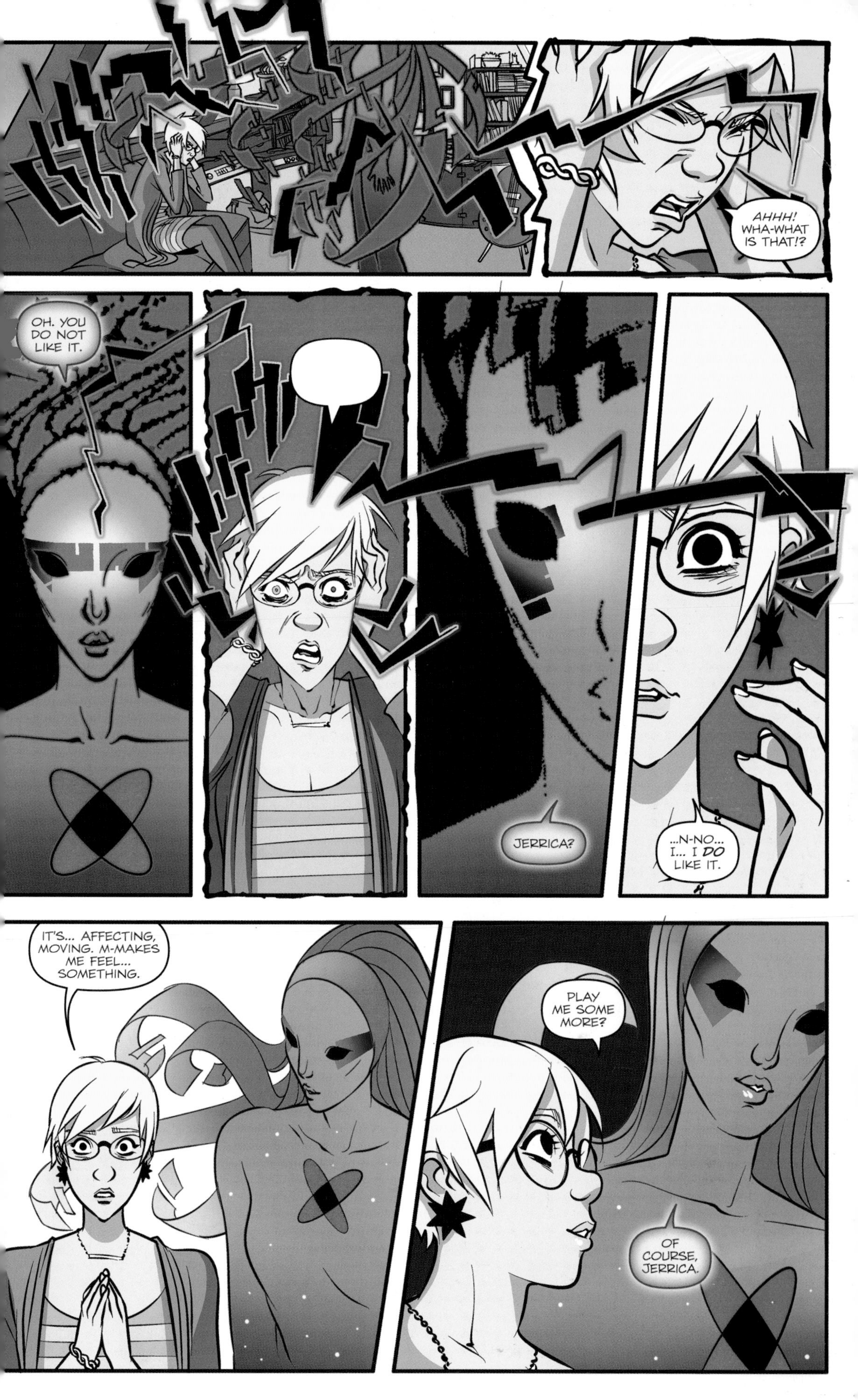
AHHH! WHA-WHAT IS THAT!?
OH. YOU DO NOT LIKE IT.
JERRICA?
...N-NO... I... I *DO* LIKE IT.
IT'S... AFFECTING, MOVING. M-MAKES ME FEEL... SOMETHING.
PLAY ME SOME MORE?
OF COURSE, JERRICA.

THIS IS AGONY!!!

AGREED.

THESE PEOPLE SUCK, ERIC.

THEY'RE NOT GREAT.

THIS IS THE BEST ELISE CAN DO? WE MIGHT BE BETTER IN BREACH OF BLOODY CONTRACT.

OH. THANK. GOD.

I WAS DYING.

ROXY! YOU TEXTED CLASH!?!?!

WE ALWAYS TEXT CLASH WHEN WE NEED COFFEE.

CANDY COATED ZIPS

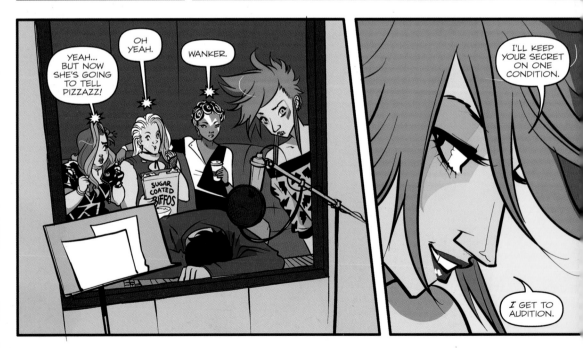

YEAH... BUT NOW SHE'S GOING TO TELL PIZZAZZ!

OH YEAH.

WANKER.

SUGAR COATED BIFFOS

I'LL KEEP YOUR SECRET ON ONE CONDITION.

I GET TO AUDITION.

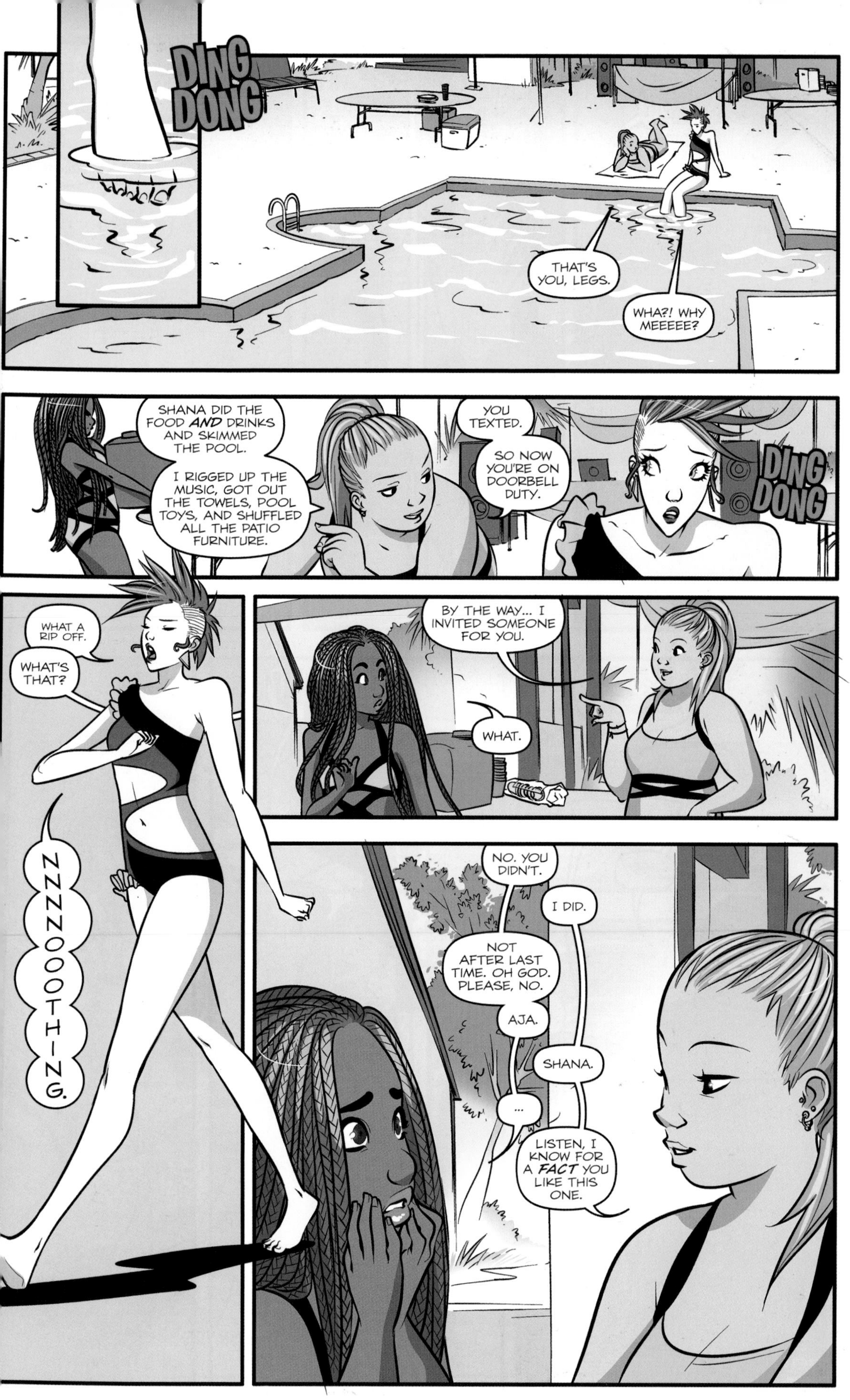
DING DONG
THAT'S YOU, LEGS.
WHA?! WHY MEEEEE?
SHANA DID THE FOOD AND DRINKS AND SKIMMED THE POOL.
I RIGGED UP THE MUSIC, GOT OUT THE TOWELS, POOL TOYS, AND SHUFFLED ALL THE PATIO FURNITURE.
YOU TEXTED.
SO NOW YOU'RE ON DOORBELL DUTY.
DING DONG
WHAT A RIP OFF.
WHAT'S THAT?
NNNNOOOOTHING.
BY THE WAY... I INVITED SOMEONE FOR YOU.
WHAT.
NO. YOU DIDN'T.
I DID.
NOT AFTER LAST TIME. OH GOD. PLEASE, NO.
AJA.
SHANA.
...
LISTEN, I KNOW FOR A FACT YOU LIKE THIS ONE.

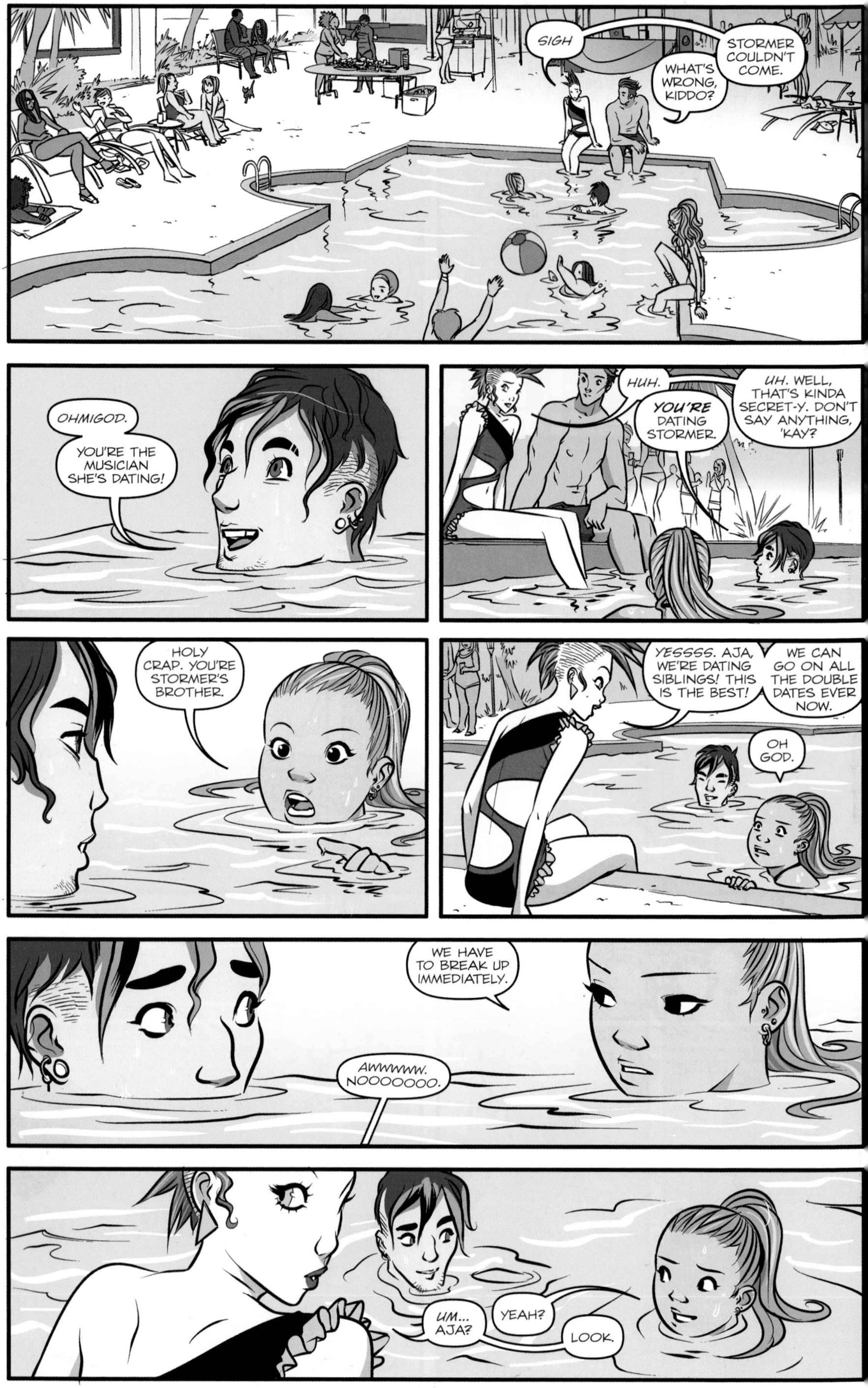
SIGH
WHAT'S WRONG, KIDDO?
STORMER COULDN'T COME.
OHMIGOD.
YOU'RE THE MUSICIAN SHE'S DATING!
HUH.
YOU'RE DATING STORMER.
UH. WELL, THAT'S KINDA SECRET-Y. DON'T SAY ANYTHING, 'KAY?
HOLY CRAP. YOU'RE STORMER'S BROTHER.
YESSSS. AJA, WE'RE DATING SIBLINGS! THIS IS THE BEST!
WE CAN GO ON ALL THE DOUBLE DATES EVER NOW.
OH GOD.
WE HAVE TO BREAK UP IMMEDIATELY.
AWWWWW. NOOOOOOO.
UM... AJA?
YEAH?
LOOK.

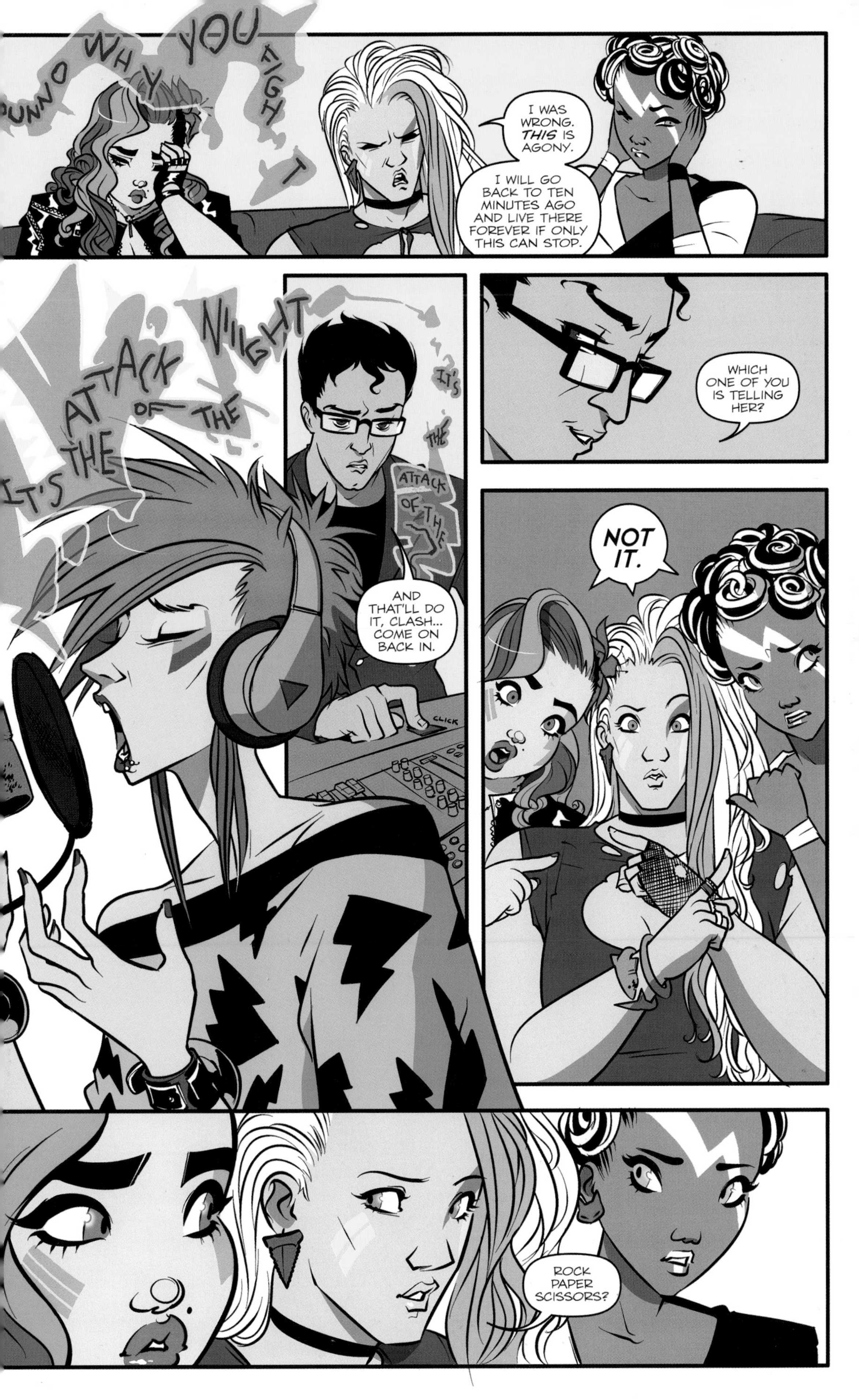
DUNNO WHY YOU FIGHT IT
I WAS WRONG. THIS IS AGONY.
I WILL GO BACK TO TEN MINUTES AGO AND LIVE THERE FOREVER IF ONLY THIS CAN STOP.
IT'S THE ATTACK OF THE NIGHT
IT'S THE ATTACK OF THE
AND THAT'LL DO IT, CLASH... COME ON BACK IN.
CLICK
WHICH ONE OF YOU IS TELLING HER?
NOT IT.
ROCK PAPER SCISSORS?

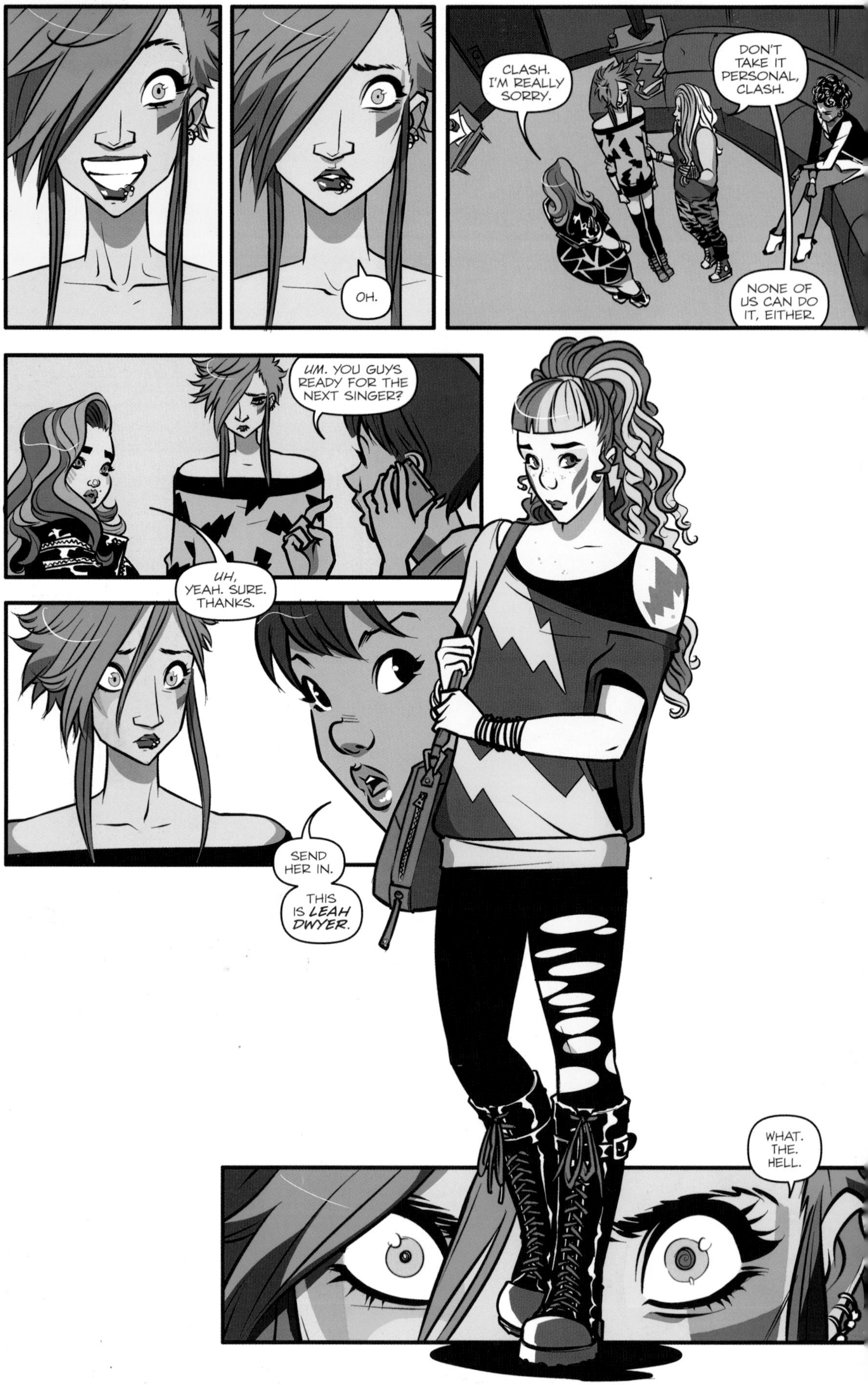
OH.
CLASH. I'M REALLY SORRY.
DON'T TAKE IT PERSONAL, CLASH.
NONE OF US CAN DO IT, EITHER.
UM. YOU GUYS READY FOR THE NEXT SINGER?
UH, YEAH. SURE. THANKS.
SEND HER IN.
THIS IS LEAH DWYER.
WHAT. THE. HELL.

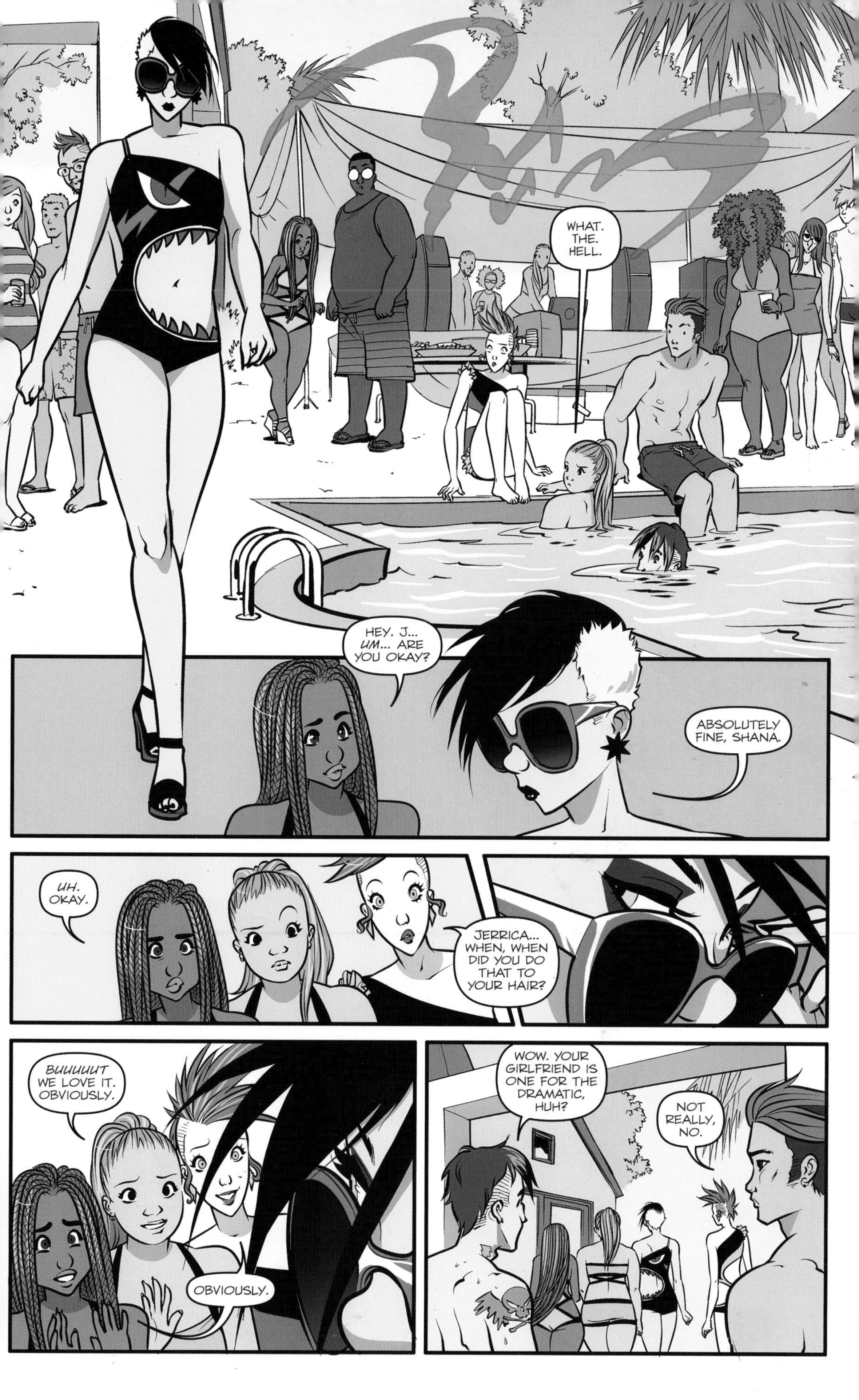
WHAT. THE. HELL.
HEY. J... UM... ARE YOU OKAY?
ABSOLUTELY FINE, SHANA.
UH. OKAY.
JERRICA... WHEN, WHEN DID YOU DO THAT TO YOUR HAIR?
BUUUUUT WE LOVE IT. OBVIOUSLY.
OBVIOUSLY.
WOW. YOUR GIRLFRIEND IS ONE FOR THE DRAMATIC, HUH?
NOT REALLY, NO.

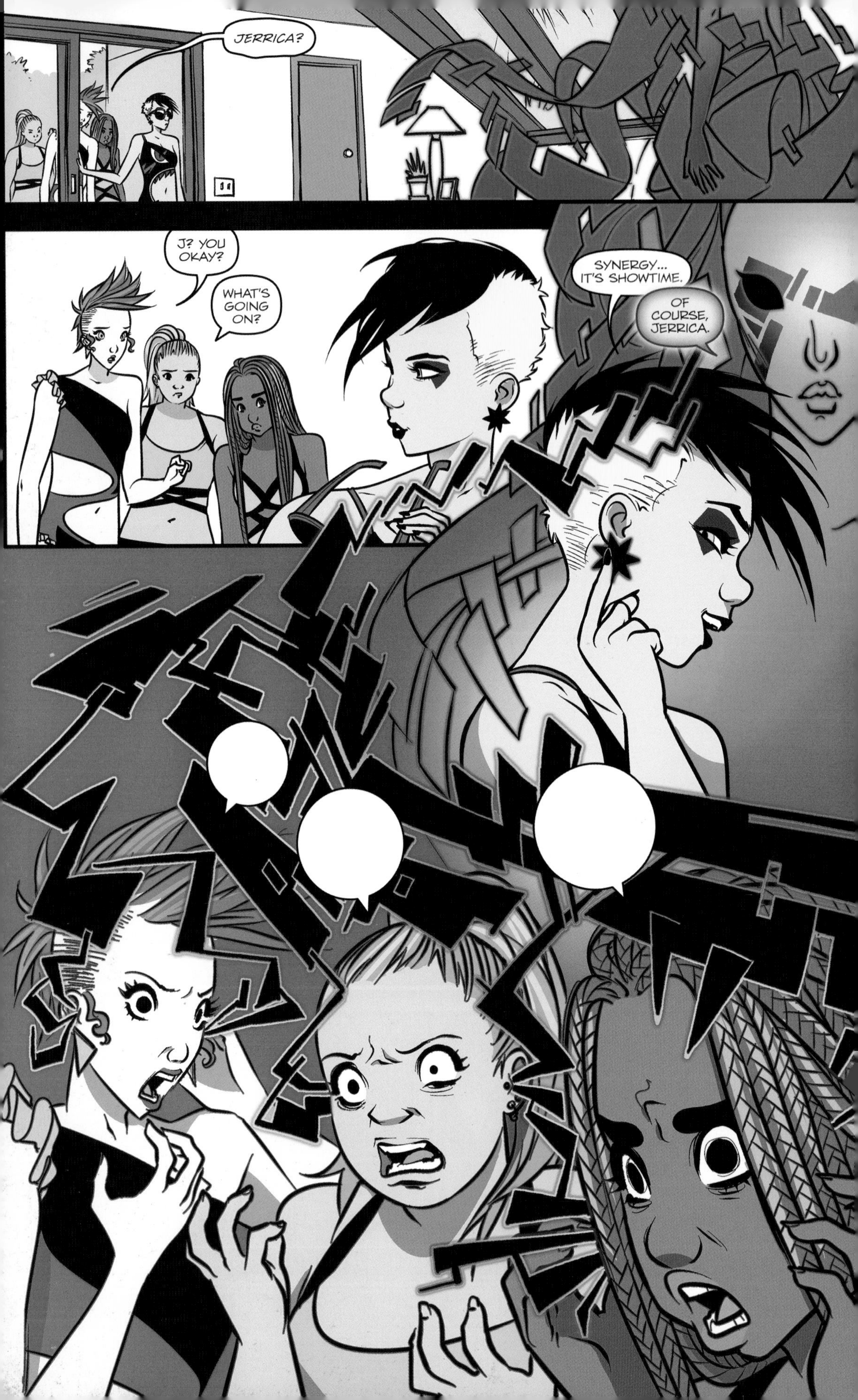
JERRICA?
J? YOU OKAY?
WHAT'S GOING ON?
SYNERGY... IT'S SHOWTIME.
OF COURSE, JERRICA.

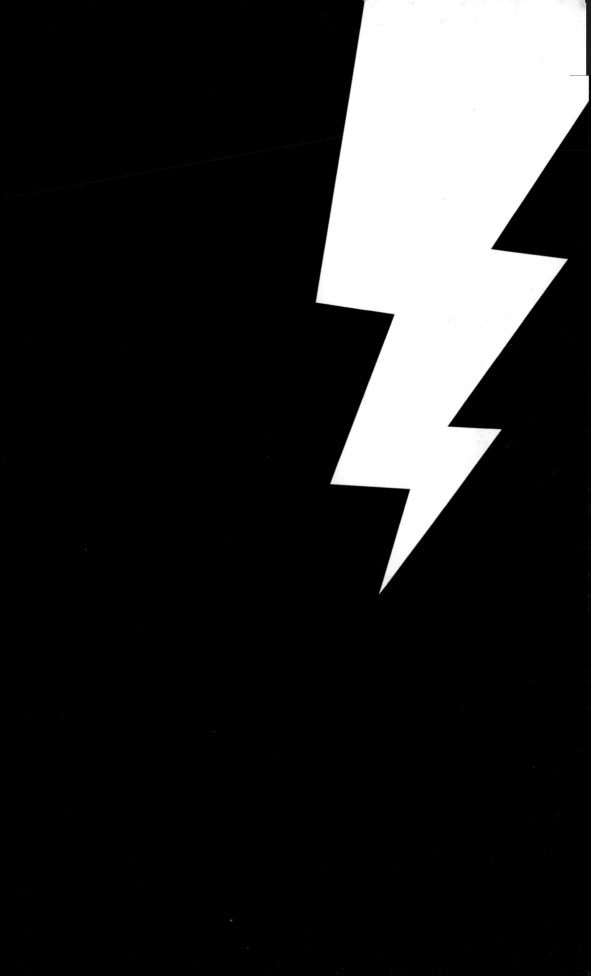

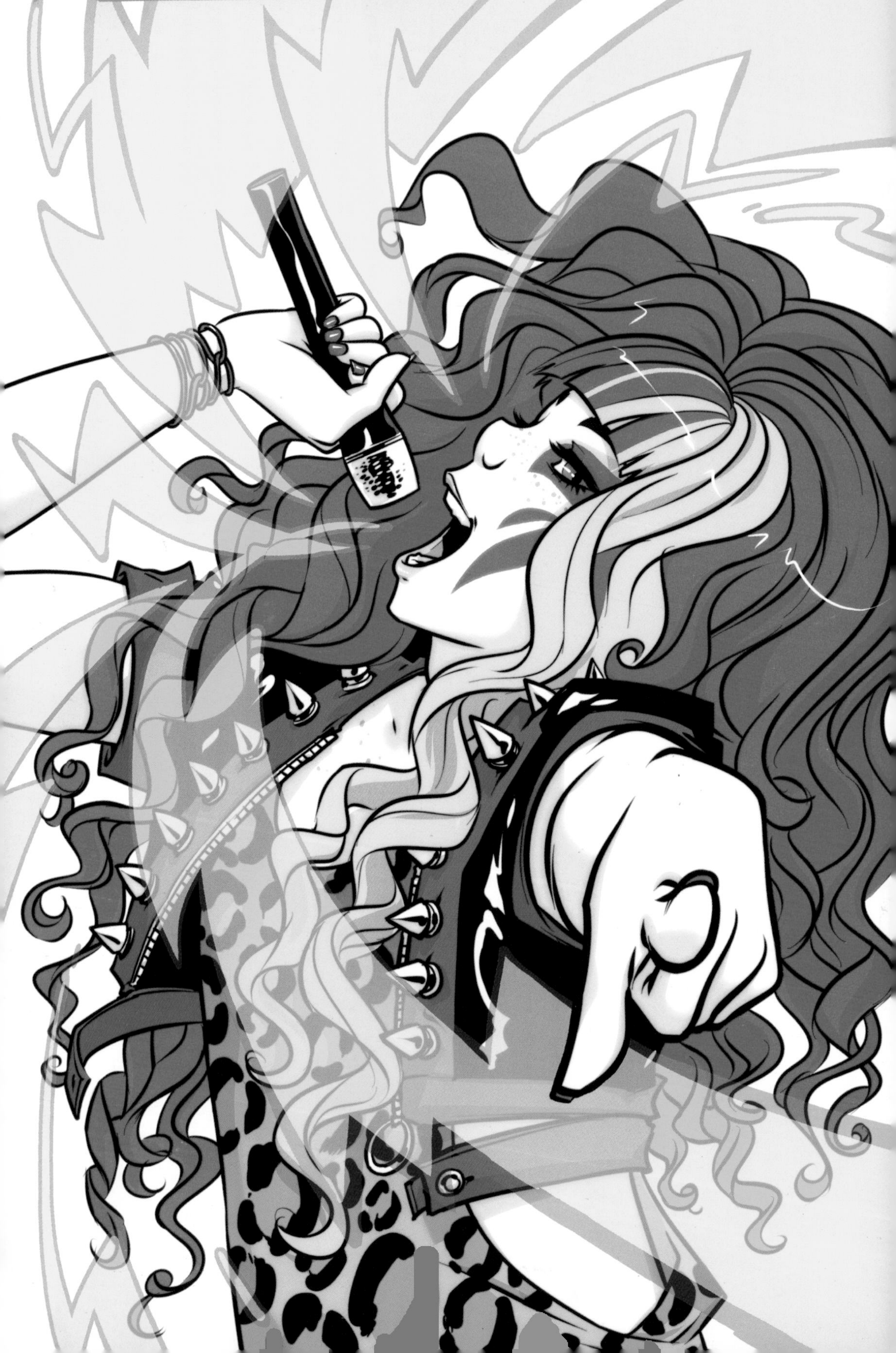

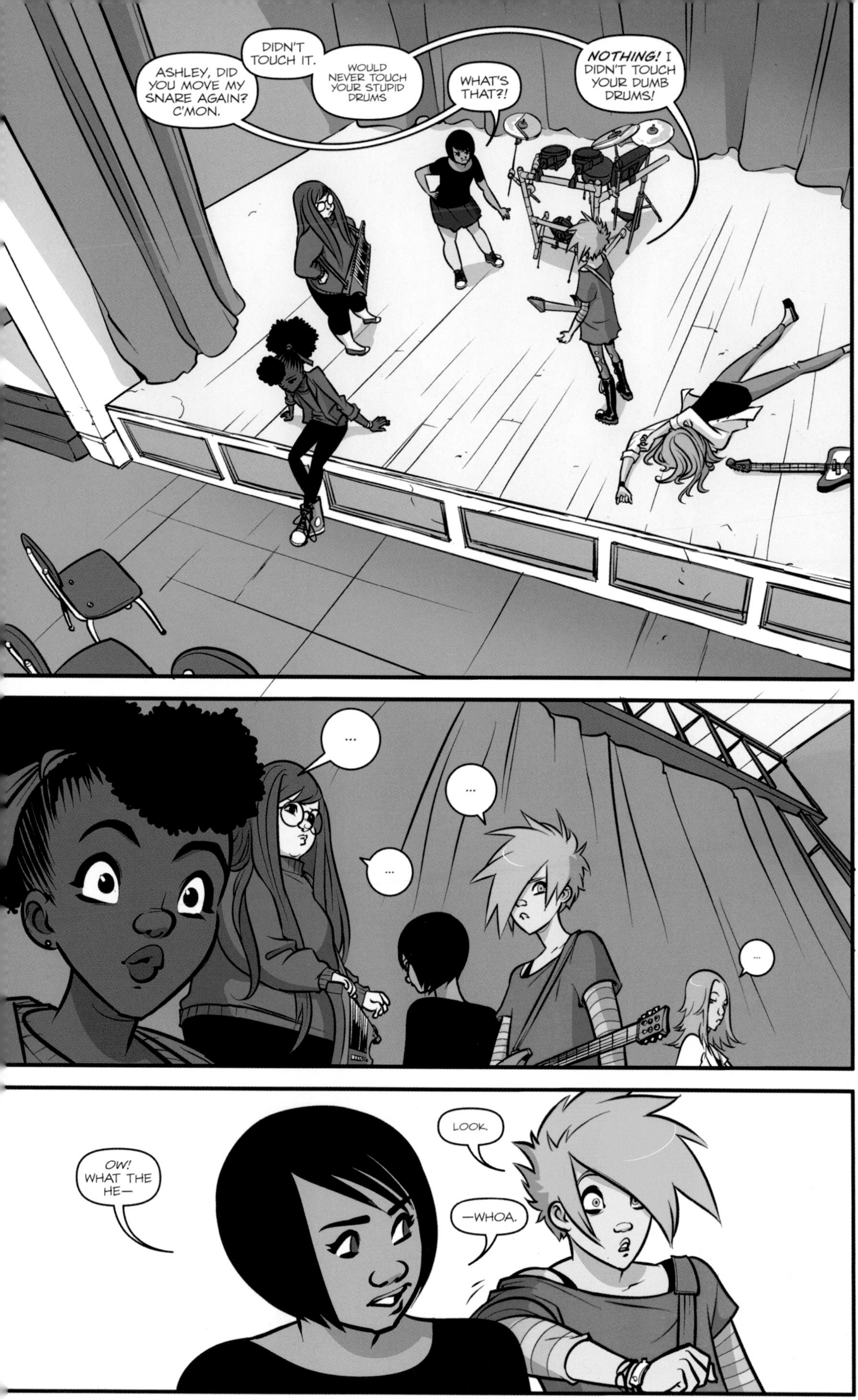
ASHLEY, DID YOU MOVE MY SNARE AGAIN? C'MON.
DIDN'T TOUCH IT.
WOULD NEVER TOUCH YOUR STUPID DRUMS
WHAT'S THAT?!
NOTHING! I DIDN'T TOUCH YOUR DUMB DRUMS!
...
...
...
...
OW! WHAT THE HE—
LOOK.
—WHOA.

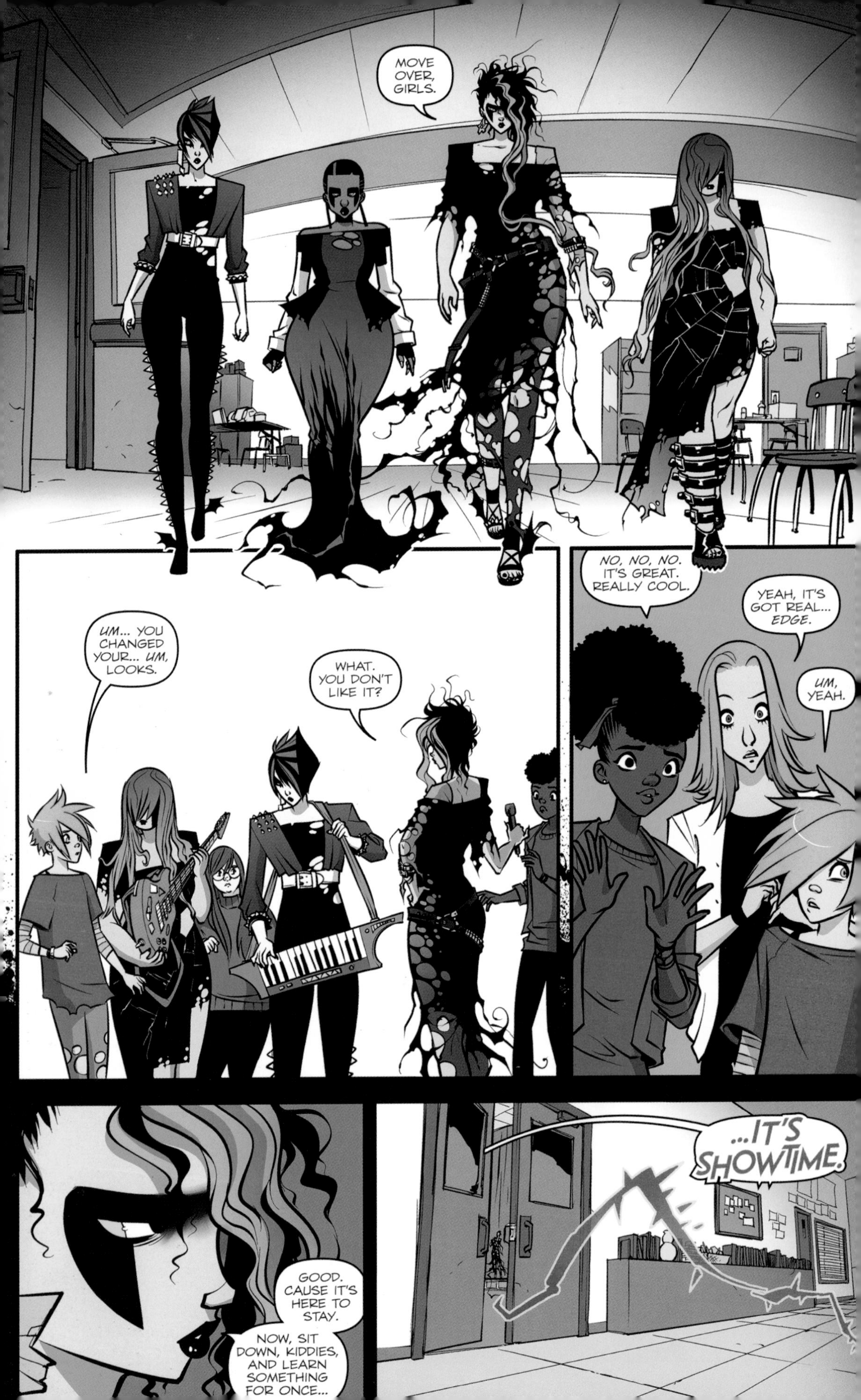
MOVE OVER, GIRLS.
UM... YOU CHANGED YOUR... UM, LOOKS.
WHAT. YOU DON'T LIKE IT?
NO, NO, NO. IT'S GREAT. REALLY COOL.
YEAH, IT'S GOT REAL... EDGE.
UM, YEAH.
GOOD. CAUSE IT'S HERE TO STAY.
NOW, SIT DOWN, KIDDIES, AND LEARN SOMETHING FOR ONCE...
...IT'S SHOWTIME.

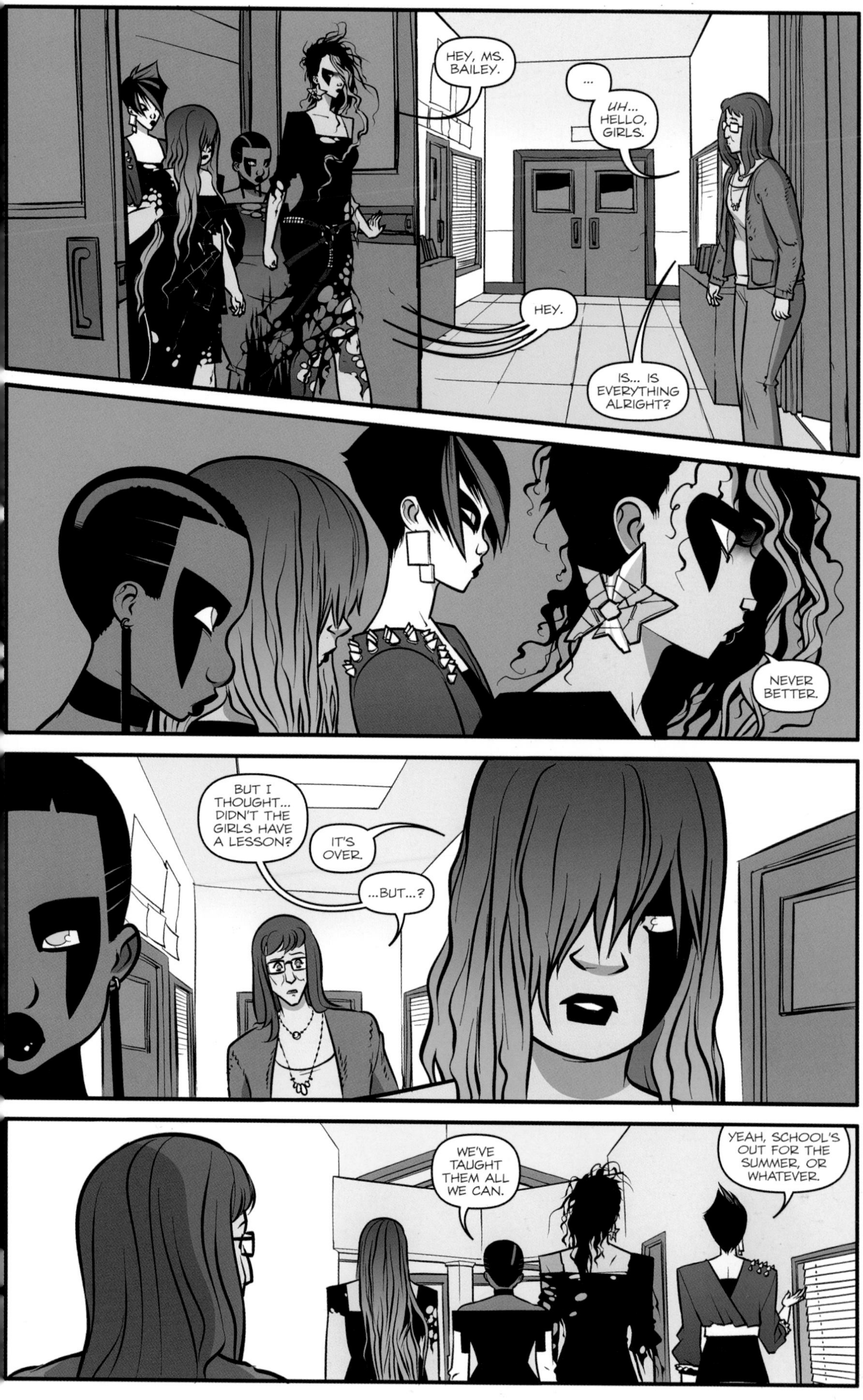
HEY, MS. BAILEY.
...
UH... HELLO, GIRLS.
HEY.
IS... IS EVERYTHING ALRIGHT?
NEVER BETTER.
BUT I THOUGHT... DIDN'T THE GIRLS HAVE A LESSON?
IT'S OVER.
...BUT...?
WE'VE TAUGHT THEM ALL WE CAN.
YEAH, SCHOOL'S OUT FOR THE SUMMER, OR WHATEVER.

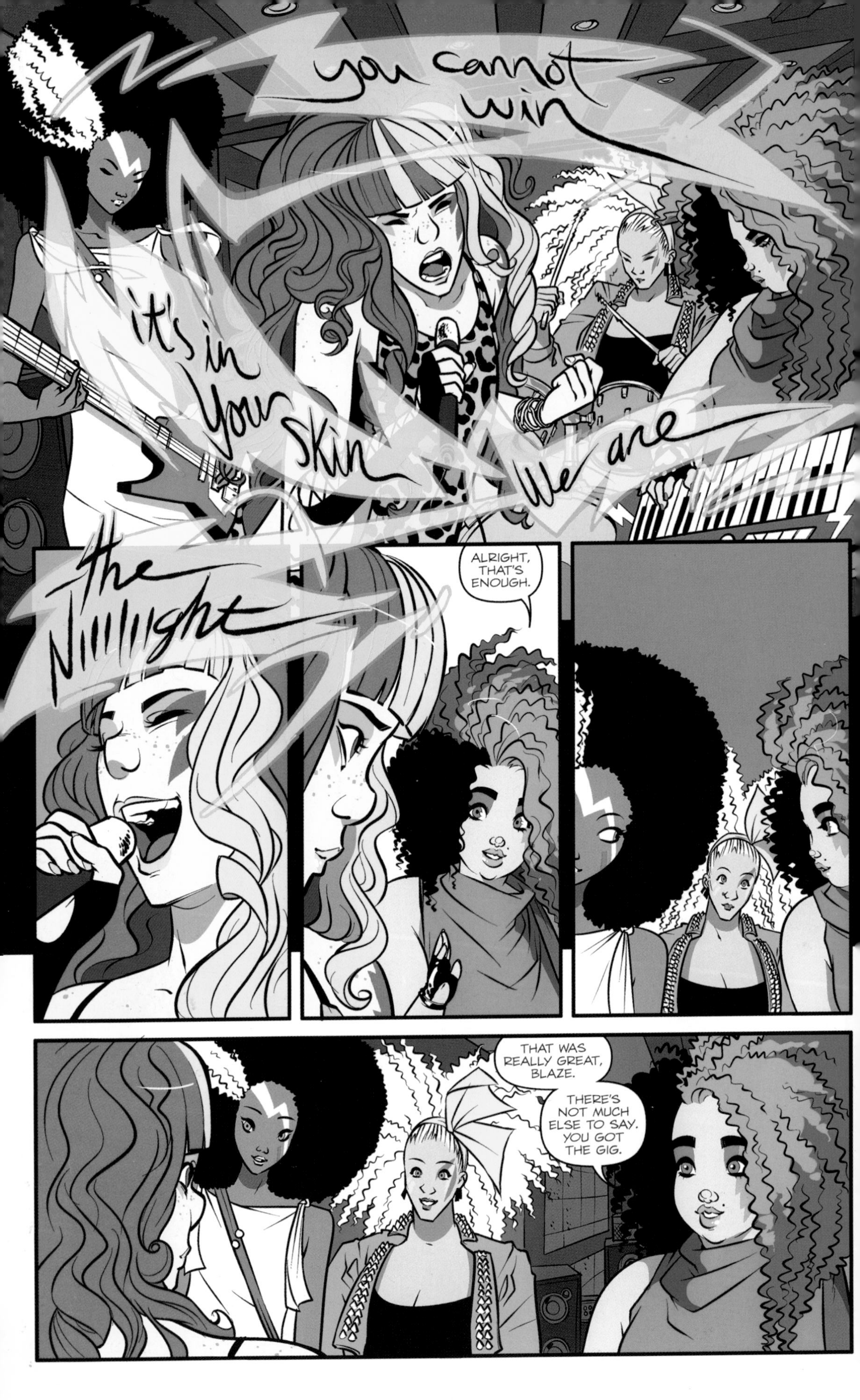
you cannot win
it's in your skin
We are
the Niiiiight
ALRIGHT, THAT'S ENOUGH.
THAT WAS REALLY GREAT, BLAZE.
THERE'S NOT MUCH ELSE TO SAY. YOU GOT THE GIG.

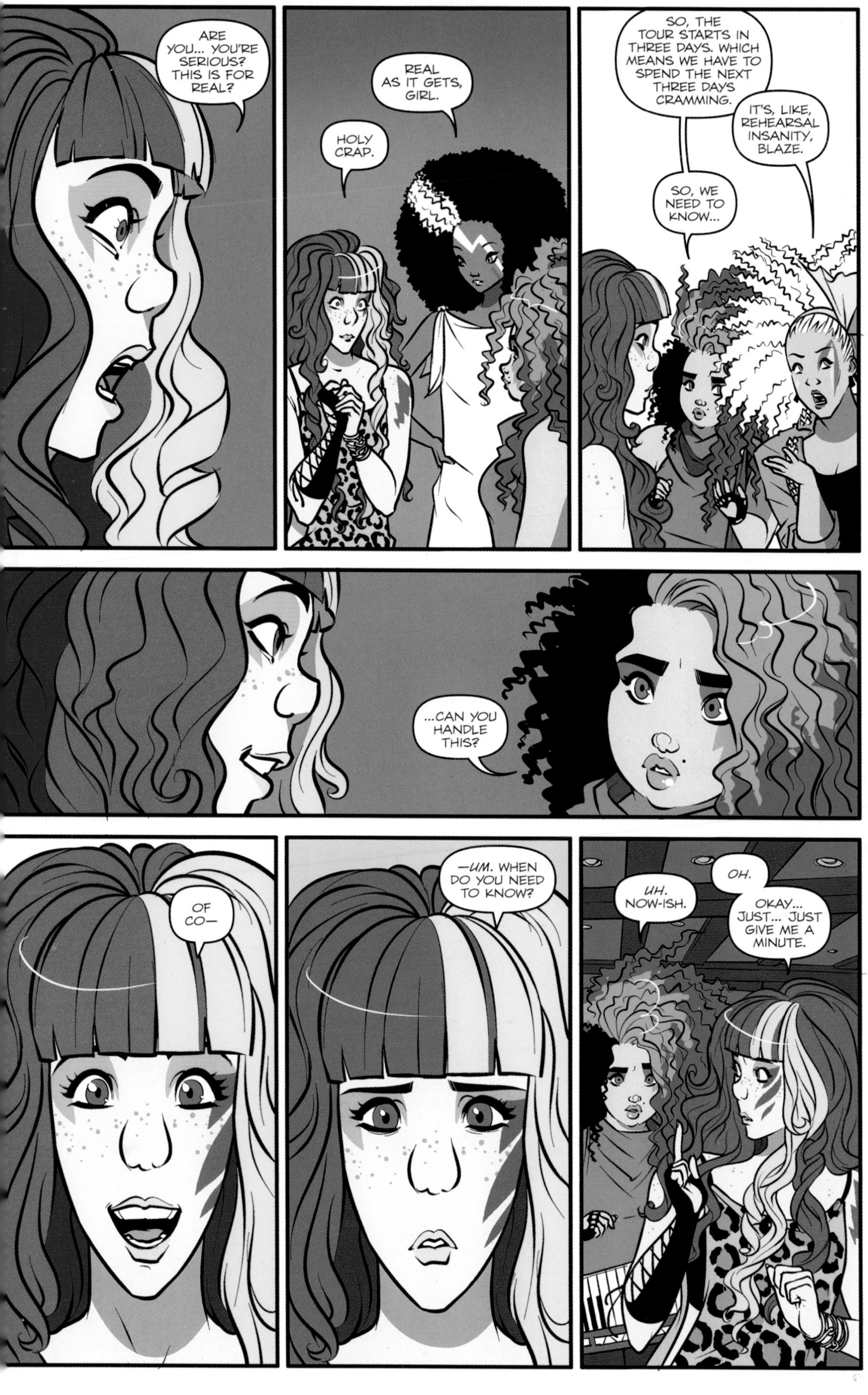
ARE YOU... YOU'RE SERIOUS? THIS IS FOR REAL?
HOLY CRAP.
REAL AS IT GETS, GIRL.
SO, THE TOUR STARTS IN THREE DAYS. WHICH MEANS WE HAVE TO SPEND THE NEXT THREE DAYS CRAMMING.
IT'S, LIKE, REHEARSAL INSANITY, BLAZE.
SO, WE NEED TO KNOW...
...CAN YOU HANDLE THIS?
OF CO—
—UM. WHEN DO YOU NEED TO KNOW?
UH. NOW-ISH.
OH.
OKAY... JUST... JUST GIVE ME A MINUTE.

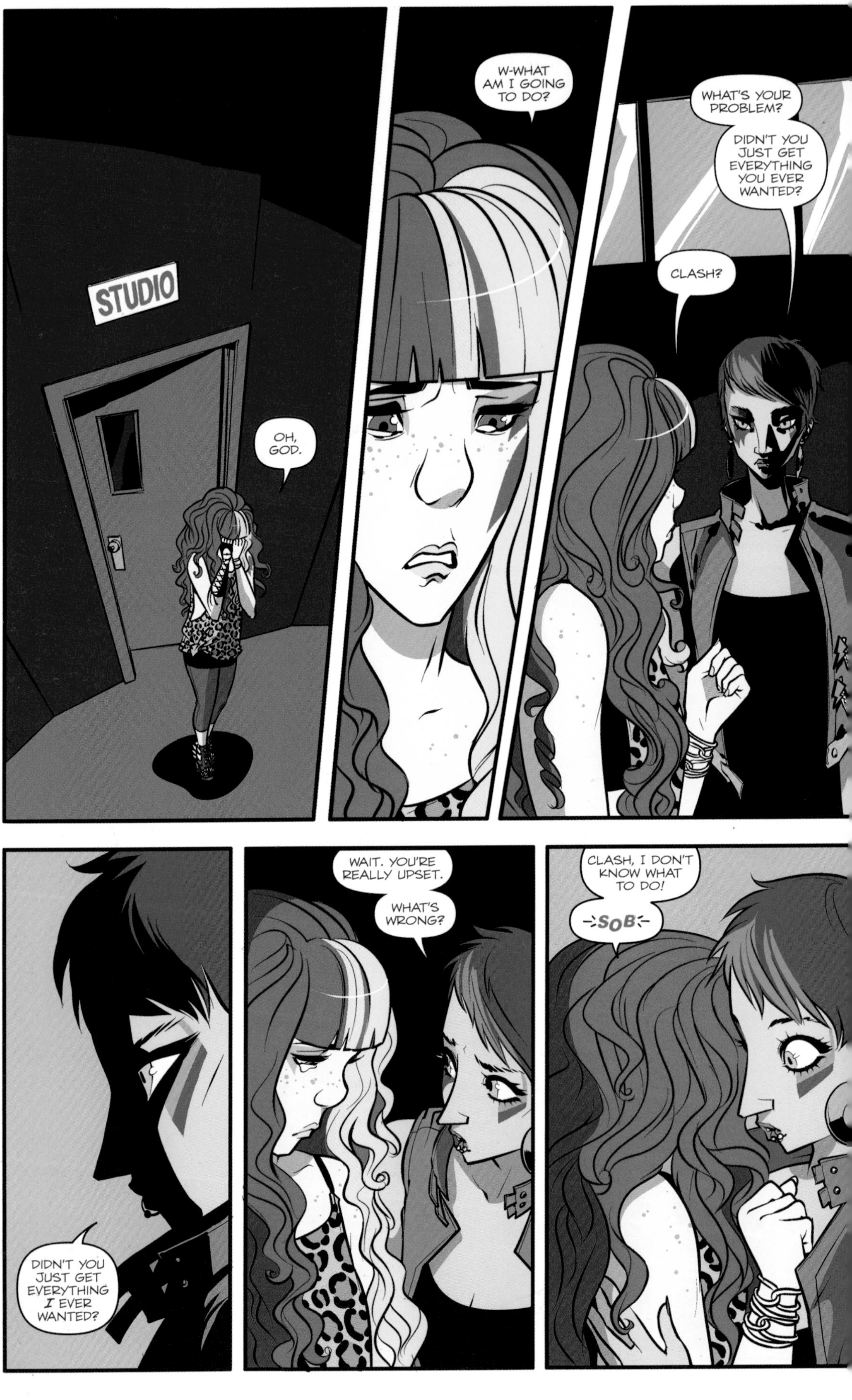
STUDIO
OH, GOD.
W-WHAT AM I GOING TO DO?
WHAT'S YOUR PROBLEM?
DIDN'T YOU JUST GET EVERYTHING YOU EVER WANTED?
CLASH?
DIDN'T YOU JUST GET EVERYTHING *I* EVER WANTED?
WAIT. YOU'RE REALLY UPSET.
WHAT'S WRONG?
CLASH, I DON'T KNOW WHAT TO DO!
SOB

TALK TO ME. WHAT'S GOING ON?

THIS IS... I MEAN THIS IS CRAZY DREAM COME TRUE STUFF. EVERYTHING I ALWAYS WANTED.

BUUUUT?

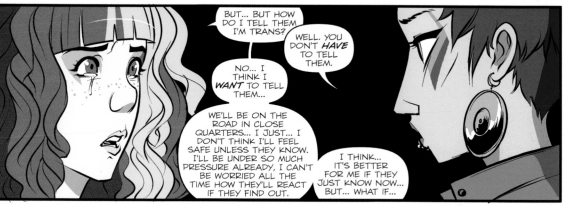

BUT... BUT HOW DO I TELL THEM I'M TRANS?

WELL. YOU DON'T *HAVE* TO TELL THEM.

NO... I THINK I *WANT* TO TELL THEM...

WE'LL BE ON THE ROAD IN CLOSE QUARTERS... I JUST... I DON'T THINK I'LL FEEL SAFE UNLESS THEY KNOW. I'LL BE UNDER SO MUCH PRESSURE ALREADY, I CAN'T BE WORRIED ALL THE TIME HOW THEY'LL REACT IF THEY FIND OUT.

I THINK... IT'S BETTER FOR ME IF THEY JUST KNOW NOW... BUT... WHAT IF...

BUT WHAT IF THEY'RE NOT OKAY WITH IT?

WHAT IF THEY SAY I CAN'T HAVE THIS, THAT I CAN'T *DO* THIS?

WHAT IF THEY HATE ME?

THEN THEY'RE NOT EVEN WORTH IT.

BUT THAT'S NOT GOING TO HAPPEN.

THEY'RE GONNA BE FINE WITH IT. I PROMISE YOU.

AND WE'RE GONNA TELL THEM. *RIGHT NOW.*

OH, NO. NOT NOW. NO, I CAN'T.

WE HAVE TO. THEY NEED AN ANSWER NOW, AND IF THEY'RE WANKERS THAT ARE GOING TO HAVE A PROBLEM WITH IT, THEN WE SHOULD KNOW NOW.

AND THEN WE GO HOME AND BURN ALL OUR MISFITS GEAR.

REALLY?

HELL, YEAH.

SINCE WHEN DO YOU SAY WANKERS?

TOO MUCH TIME WITH JETTA.

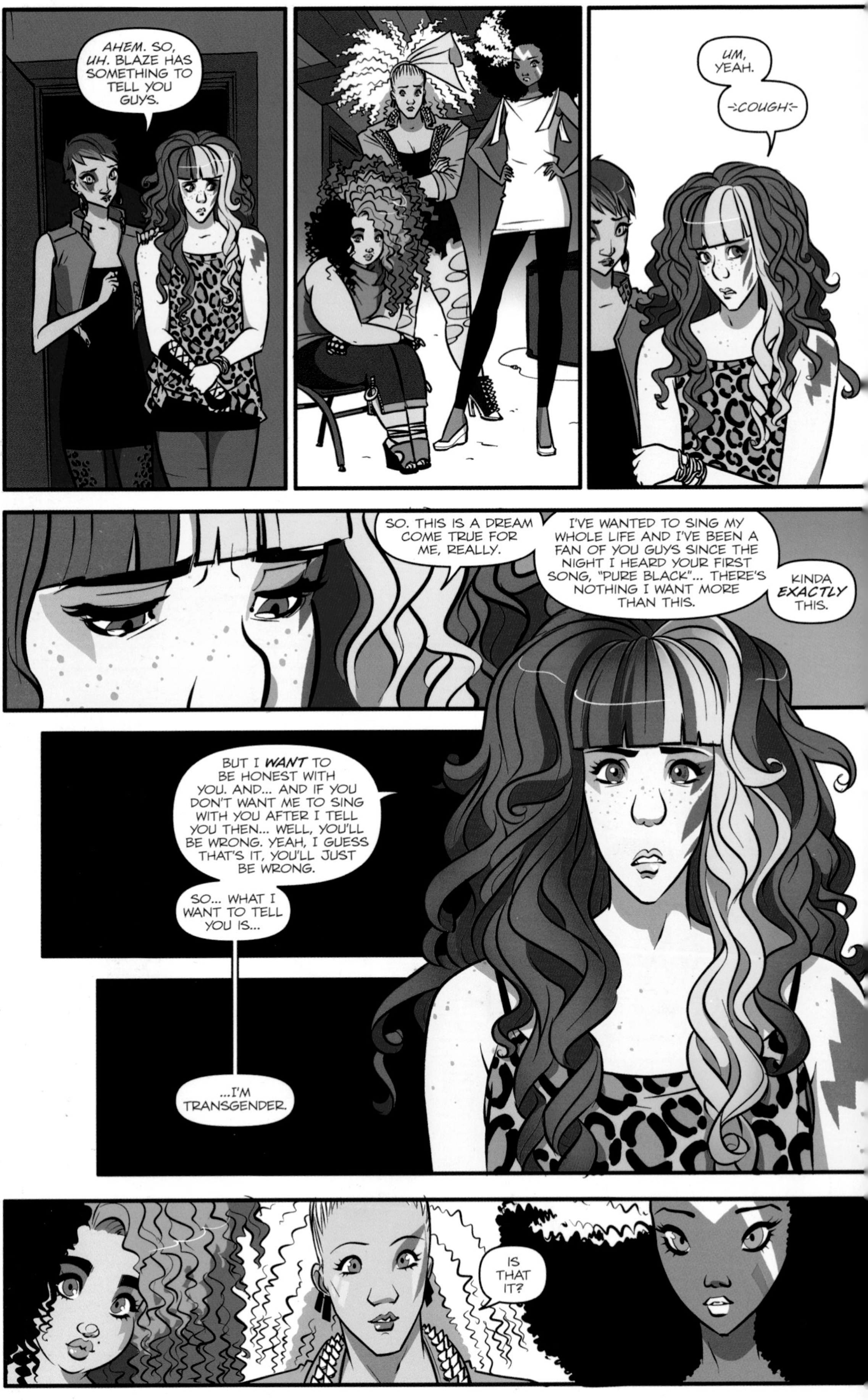
AHEM. SO, UH. BLAZE HAS SOMETHING TO TELL YOU GUYS.
UM, YEAH.
~COUGH~
SO. THIS IS A DREAM COME TRUE FOR ME, REALLY.
I'VE WANTED TO SING MY WHOLE LIFE AND I'VE BEEN A FAN OF YOU GUYS SINCE THE NIGHT I HEARD YOUR FIRST SONG, "PURE BLACK"... THERE'S NOTHING I WANT MORE THAN THIS.
KINDA EXACTLY THIS.
BUT I WANT TO BE HONEST WITH YOU. AND... AND IF YOU DON'T WANT ME TO SING WITH YOU AFTER I TELL YOU THEN... WELL, YOU'LL BE WRONG. YEAH, I GUESS THAT'S IT, YOU'LL JUST BE WRONG.
SO... WHAT I WANT TO TELL YOU IS...
...I'M TRANSGENDER.
IS THAT IT?

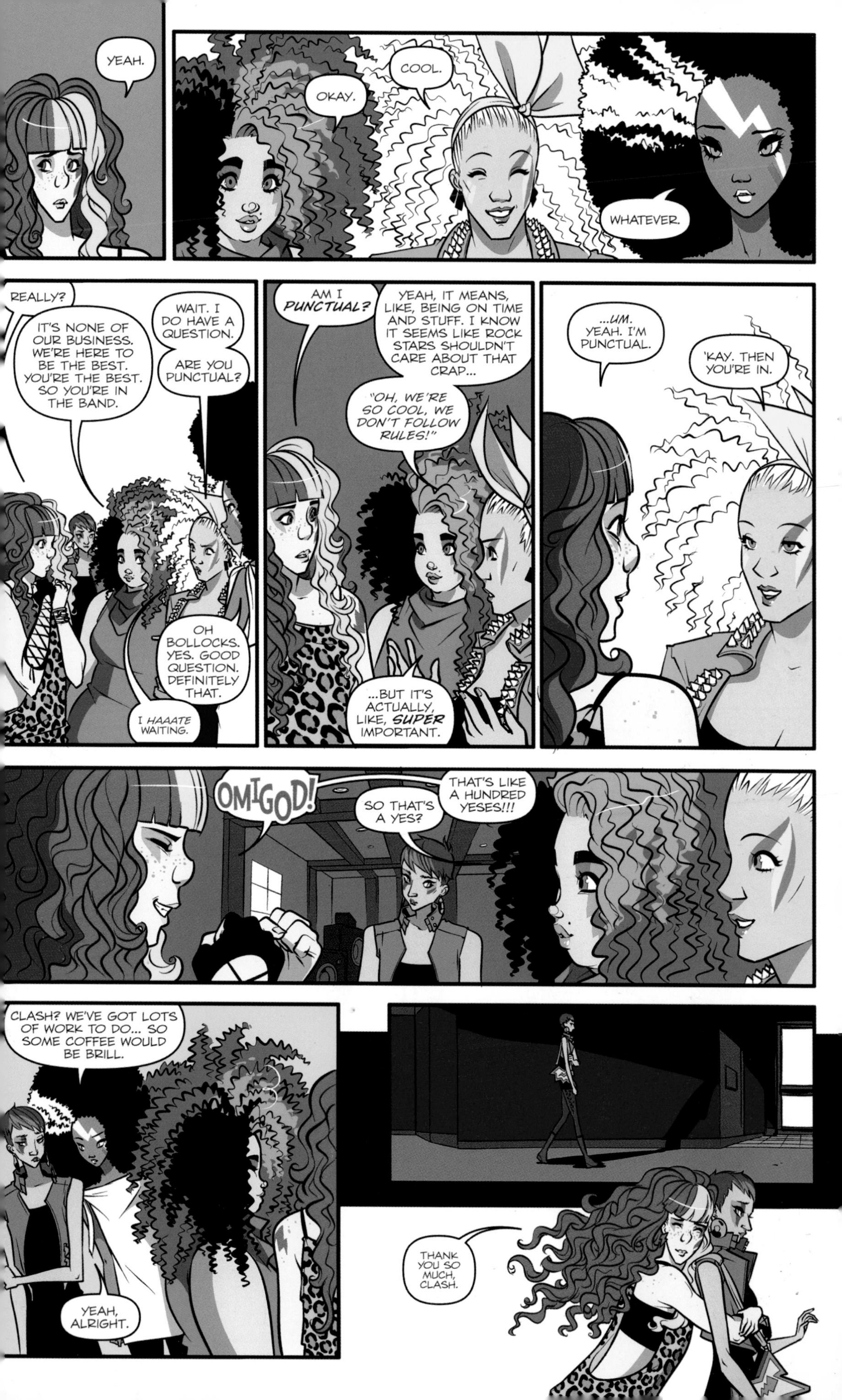
YEAH.
OKAY.
COOL.
WHATEVER.
REALLY?
IT'S NONE OF OUR BUSINESS. WE'RE HERE TO BE THE BEST. YOU'RE THE BEST. SO YOU'RE IN THE BAND.
WAIT. I DO HAVE A QUESTION.
ARE YOU PUNCTUAL?
OH BOLLOCKS. YES. GOOD QUESTION. DEFINITELY THAT.
I HAAATE WAITING.
AM I PUNCTUAL?
YEAH, IT MEANS, LIKE, BEING ON TIME AND STUFF. I KNOW IT SEEMS LIKE ROCK STARS SHOULDN'T CARE ABOUT THAT CRAP...
"OH, WE'RE SO COOL, WE DON'T FOLLOW RULES!"
...BUT IT'S ACTUALLY, LIKE, SUPER IMPORTANT.
...UM. YEAH. I'M PUNCTUAL.
'KAY. THEN YOU'RE IN.
OMIGOD!
SO THAT'S A YES?
THAT'S LIKE A HUNDRED YESES!!!
CLASH? WE'VE GOT LOTS OF WORK TO DO... SO SOME COFFEE WOULD BE BRILL.
YEAH, ALRIGHT.
THANK YOU SO MUCH, CLASH.

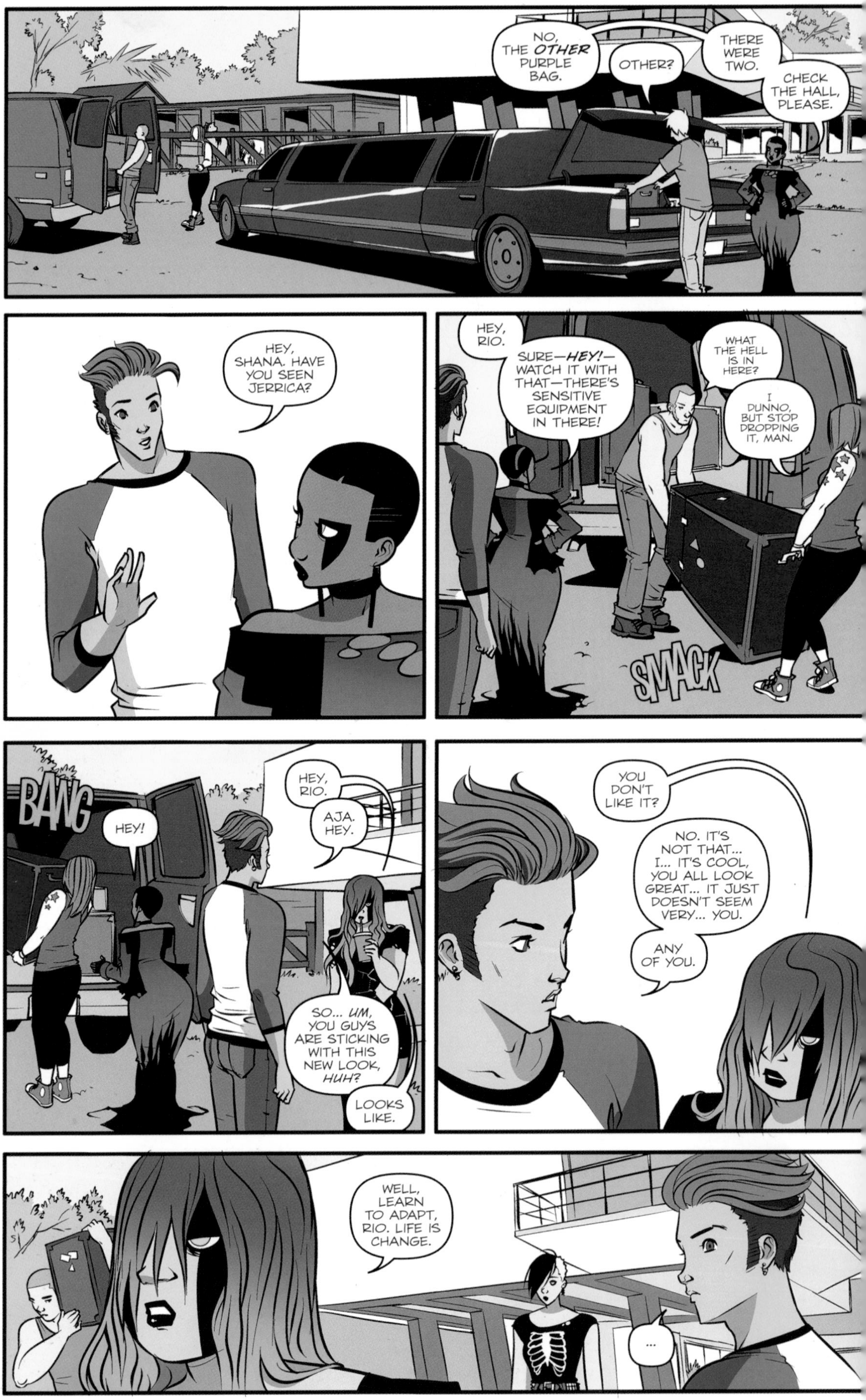

NO, THE OTHER PURPLE BAG.
OTHER?
THERE WERE TWO.
CHECK THE HALL, PLEASE.
HEY, SHANA. HAVE YOU SEEN JERRICA?
HEY, RIO.
SURE—HEY!—WATCH IT WITH THAT—THERE'S SENSITIVE EQUIPMENT IN THERE!
WHAT THE HELL IS IN HERE?
I DUNNO, BUT STOP DROPPING IT, MAN.
SMACK
BANG
HEY!
HEY, RIO.
AJA. HEY.
SO... UM, YOU GUYS ARE STICKING WITH THIS NEW LOOK, HUH?
LOOKS LIKE.
YOU DON'T LIKE IT?
NO. IT'S NOT THAT... I... IT'S COOL, YOU ALL LOOK GREAT... IT JUST DOESN'T SEEM VERY... YOU.
ANY OF YOU.
WELL, LEARN TO ADAPT, RIO. LIFE IS CHANGE.
...

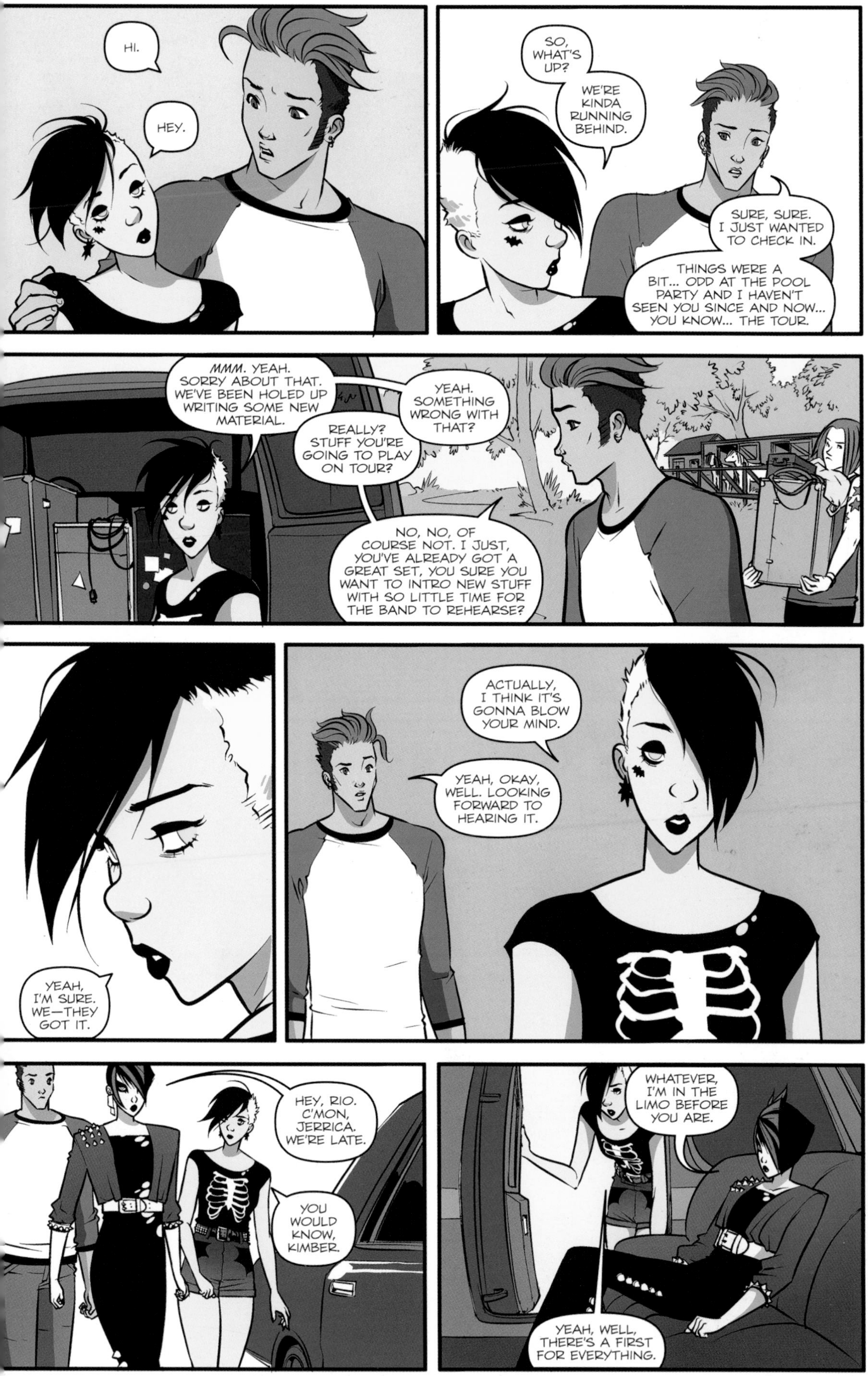
HI.
HEY.
SO, WHAT'S UP?
WE'RE KINDA RUNNING BEHIND.
SURE, SURE. I JUST WANTED TO CHECK IN.
THINGS WERE A BIT... ODD AT THE POOL PARTY AND I HAVEN'T SEEN YOU SINCE AND NOW... YOU KNOW... THE TOUR.
MMM. YEAH. SORRY ABOUT THAT. WE'VE BEEN HOLED UP WRITING SOME NEW MATERIAL.
REALLY? STUFF YOU'RE GOING TO PLAY ON TOUR?
YEAH. SOMETHING WRONG WITH THAT?
NO, NO, OF COURSE NOT. I JUST, YOU'VE ALREADY GOT A GREAT SET, YOU SURE YOU WANT TO INTRO NEW STUFF WITH SO LITTLE TIME FOR THE BAND TO REHEARSE?
YEAH, I'M SURE. WE—THEY GOT IT.
ACTUALLY, I THINK IT'S GONNA BLOW YOUR MIND.
YEAH, OKAY, WELL. LOOKING FORWARD TO HEARING IT.
HEY, RIO. C'MON, JERRICA. WE'RE LATE.
YOU WOULD KNOW, KIMBER.
WHATEVER, I'M IN THE LIMO BEFORE YOU ARE.
YEAH, WELL, THERE'S A FIRST FOR EVERYTHING.

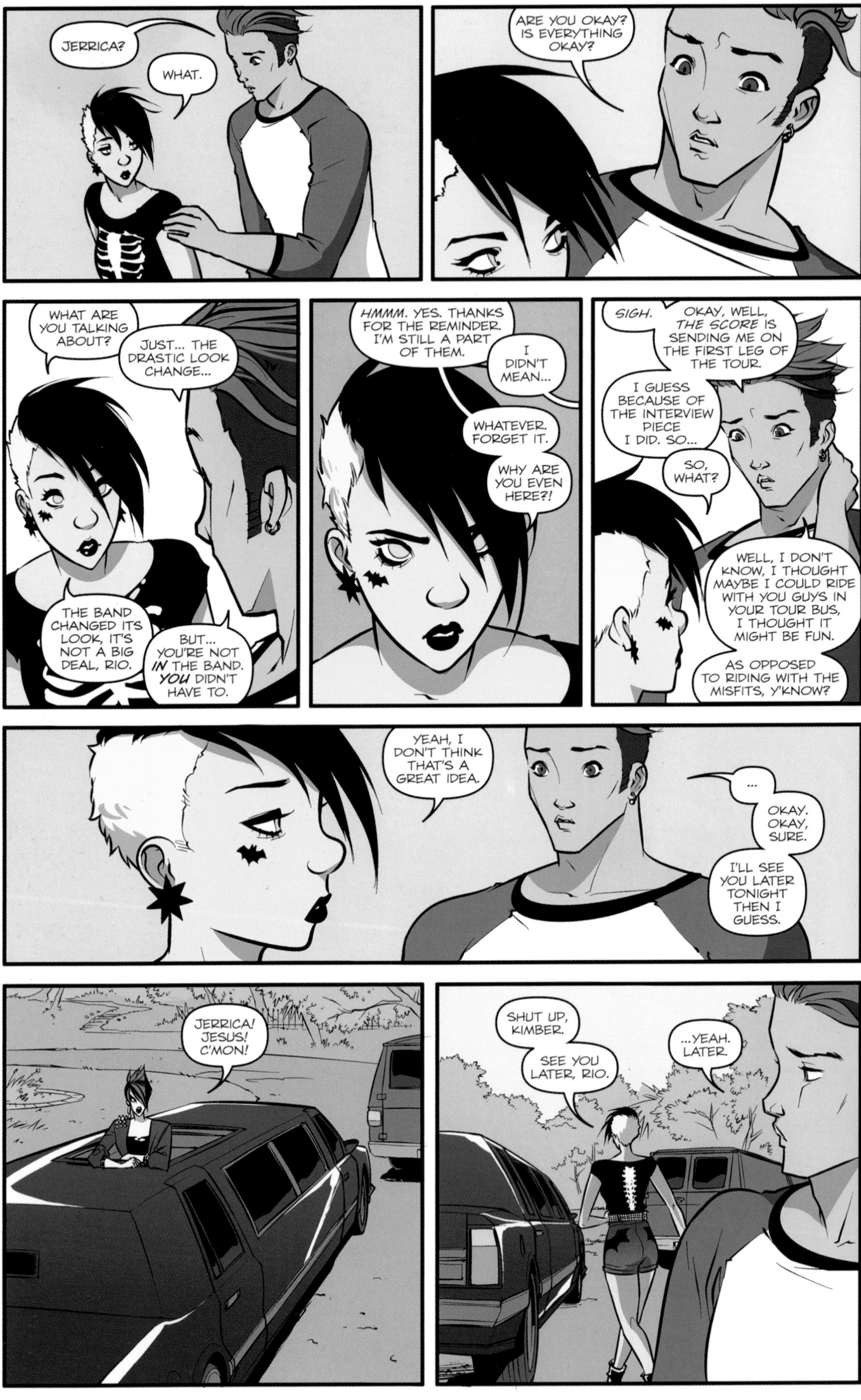

JERRICA?
WHAT.
ARE YOU OKAY? IS EVERYTHING OKAY?
WHAT ARE YOU TALKING ABOUT?
JUST... THE DRASTIC LOOK CHANGE...
THE BAND CHANGED ITS LOOK, IT'S NOT A BIG DEAL, RIO.
BUT... YOU'RE NOT *IN* THE BAND. *YOU* DIDN'T HAVE TO.
HMMM. YES. THANKS FOR THE REMINDER. I'M STILL A PART OF THEM.
I DIDN'T MEAN...
WHATEVER. FORGET IT.
WHY ARE YOU EVEN HERE?!
SIGH.
OKAY, WELL, *THE SCORE* IS SENDING ME ON THE FIRST LEG OF THE TOUR.
I GUESS BECAUSE OF THE INTERVIEW PIECE I DID. SO...
SO, WHAT?
WELL, I DON'T KNOW, I THOUGHT MAYBE I COULD RIDE WITH YOU GUYS IN YOUR TOUR BUS, I THOUGHT IT MIGHT BE FUN.
AS OPPOSED TO RIDING WITH THE MISFITS, Y'KNOW?
YEAH, I DON'T THINK THAT'S A GREAT IDEA.
...
OKAY. OKAY, SURE.
I'LL SEE YOU LATER TONIGHT THEN I GUESS.
JERRICA! JESUS! C'MON!
SHUT UP, KIMBER.
SEE YOU LATER, RIO.
...YEAH. LATER.

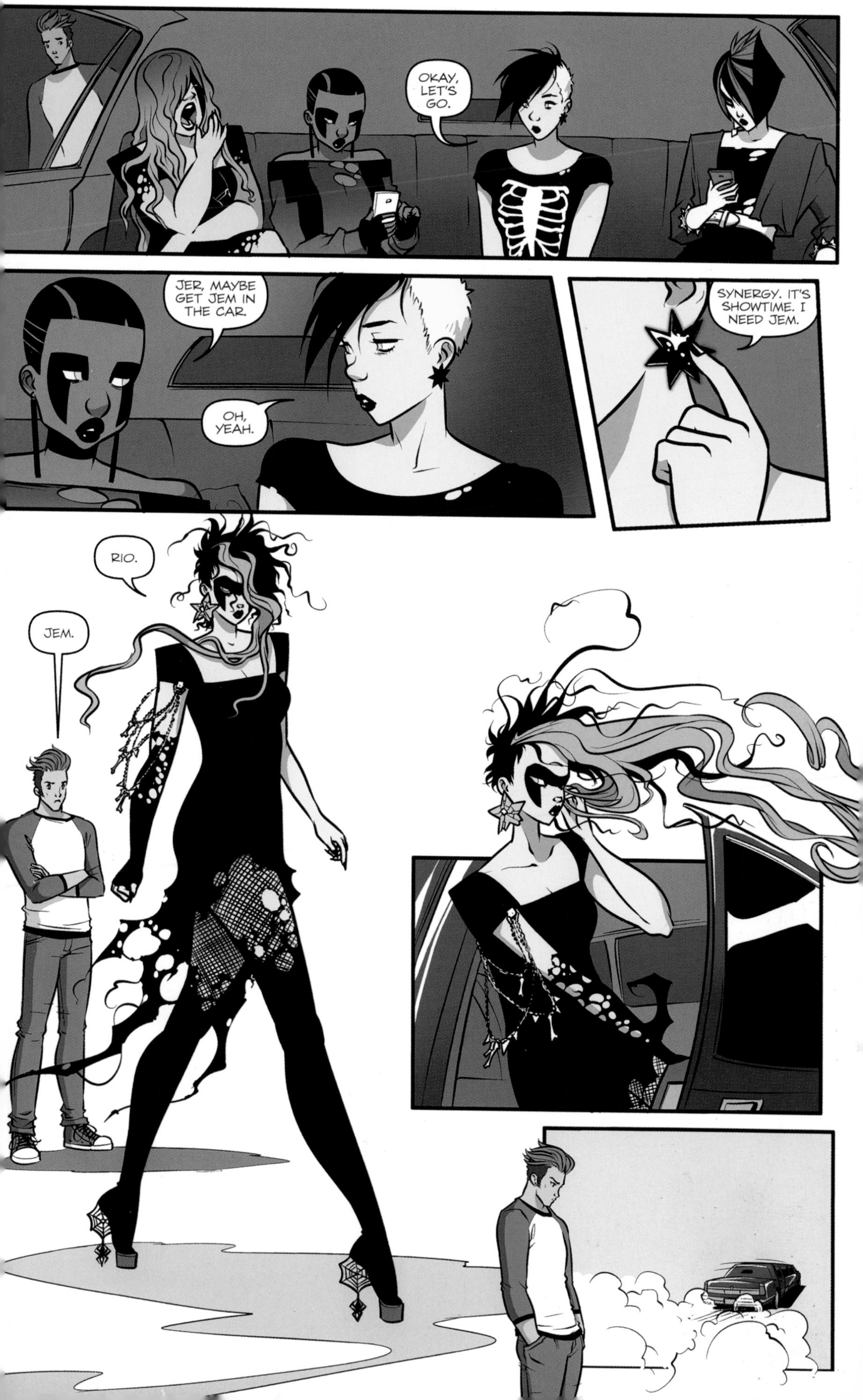
OKAY, LET'S GO.
JER, MAYBE GET JEM IN THE CAR.
OH, YEAH.
SYNERGY. IT'S SHOWTIME. I NEED JEM.
RIO.
JEM.

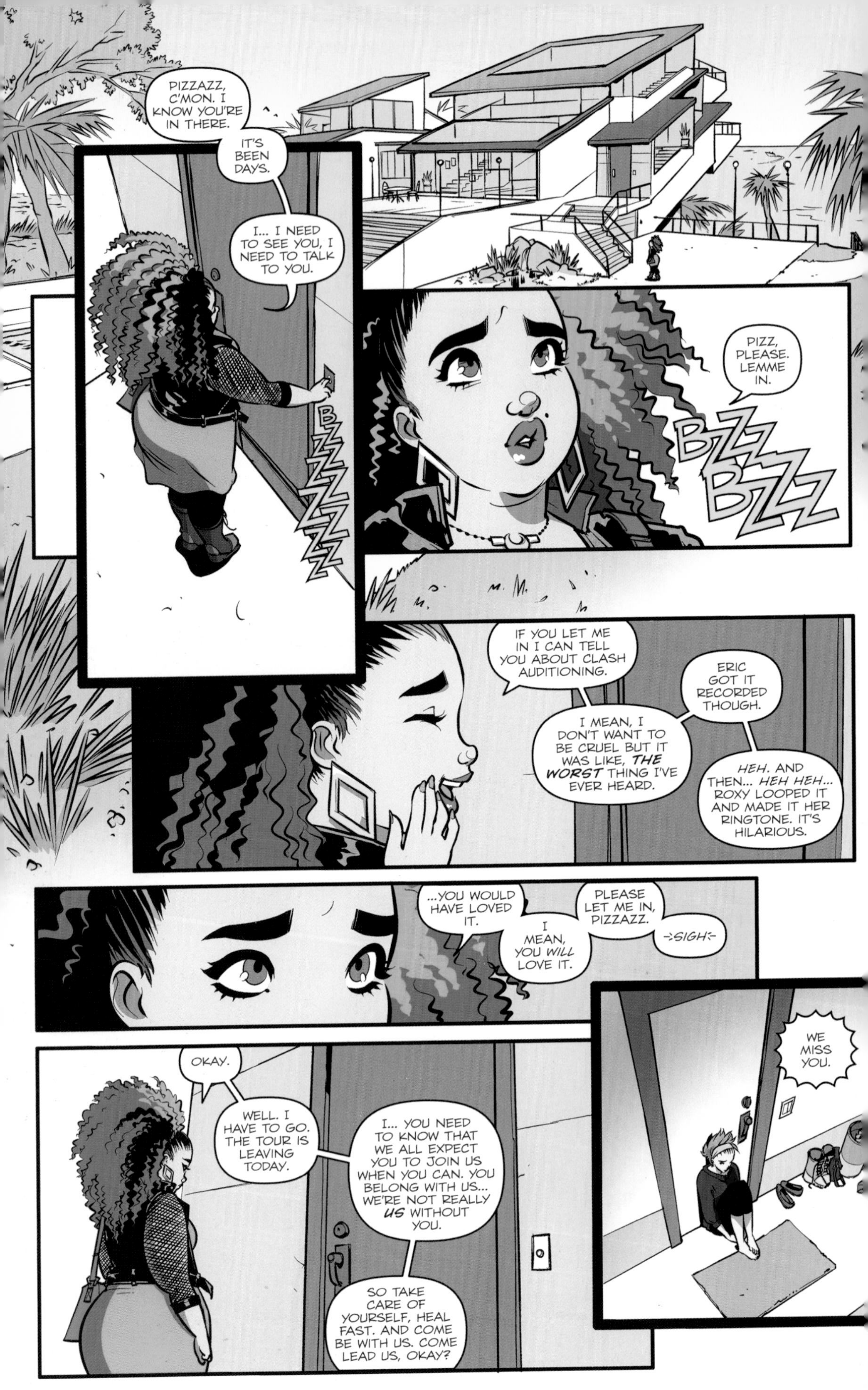
PIZZAZZ, C'MON. I KNOW YOU'RE IN THERE.
IT'S BEEN DAYS.
I... I NEED TO SEE YOU, I NEED TO TALK TO YOU.
BZZZZZZZ
PIZZ, PLEASE. LEMME IN.
BZZZ BZZZ
IF YOU LET ME IN I CAN TELL YOU ABOUT CLASH AUDITIONING.
ERIC GOT IT RECORDED THOUGH.
I MEAN, I DON'T WANT TO BE CRUEL BUT IT WAS LIKE, THE WORST THING I'VE EVER HEARD.
HEH. AND THEN... HEH HEH... ROXY LOOPED IT AND MADE IT HER RINGTONE. IT'S HILARIOUS.
...YOU WOULD HAVE LOVED IT.
I MEAN, YOU WILL LOVE IT.
PLEASE LET ME IN, PIZZAZZ.
SIGH
OKAY.
WELL. I HAVE TO GO. THE TOUR IS LEAVING TODAY.
I... YOU NEED TO KNOW THAT WE ALL EXPECT YOU TO JOIN US WHEN YOU CAN. YOU BELONG WITH US... WE'RE NOT REALLY US WITHOUT YOU.
SO TAKE CARE OF YOURSELF, HEAL FAST. AND COME BE WITH US. COME LEAD US, OKAY?
WE MISS YOU.

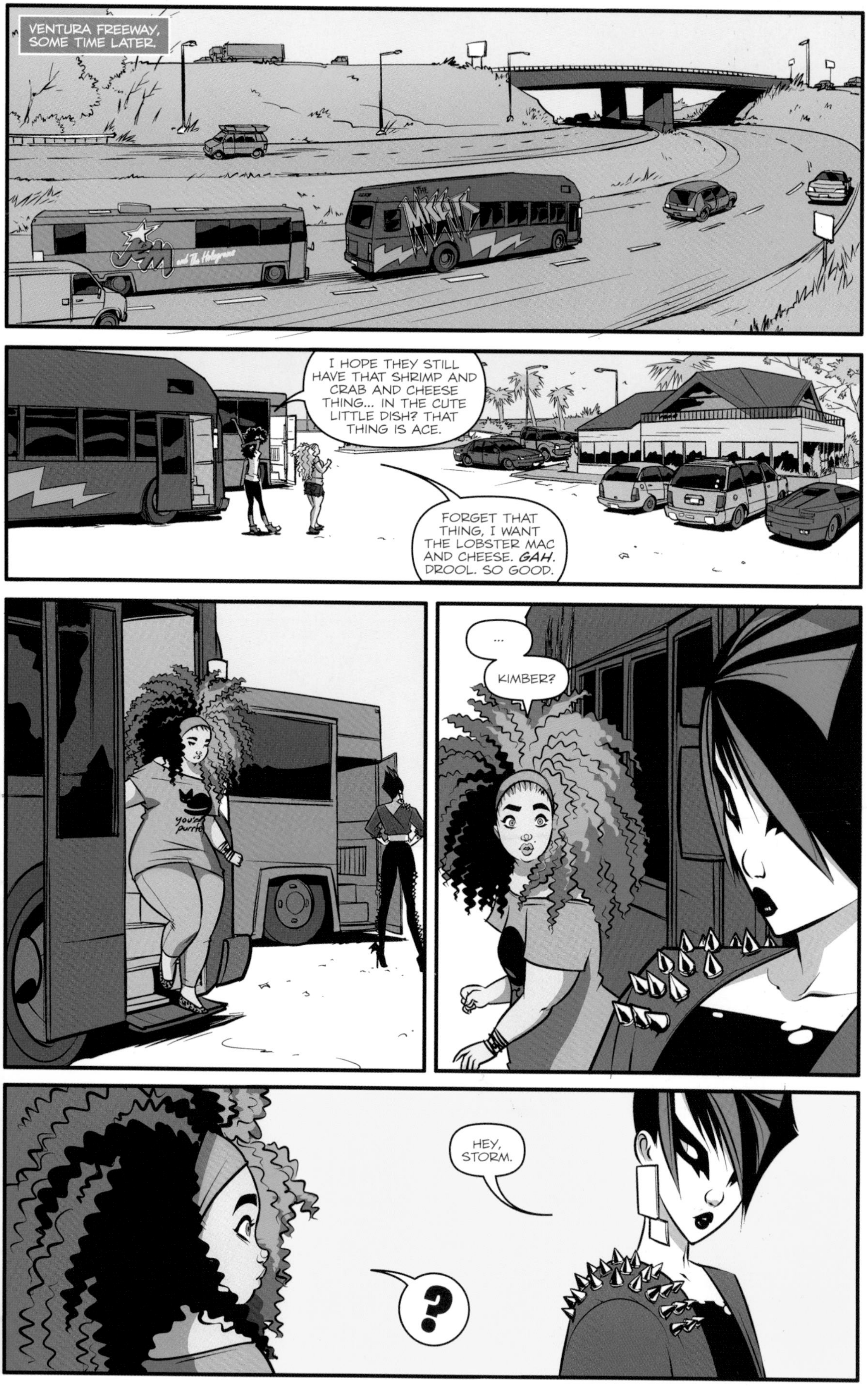
VENTURA FREEWAY, SOME TIME LATER.
I HOPE THEY STILL HAVE THAT SHRIMP AND CRAB AND CHEESE THING... IN THE CUTE LITTLE DISH? THAT THING IS ACE.
FORGET THAT THING, I WANT THE LOBSTER MAC AND CHEESE. GAH. DROOL. SO GOOD.
...
KIMBER?
HEY, STORM.
?

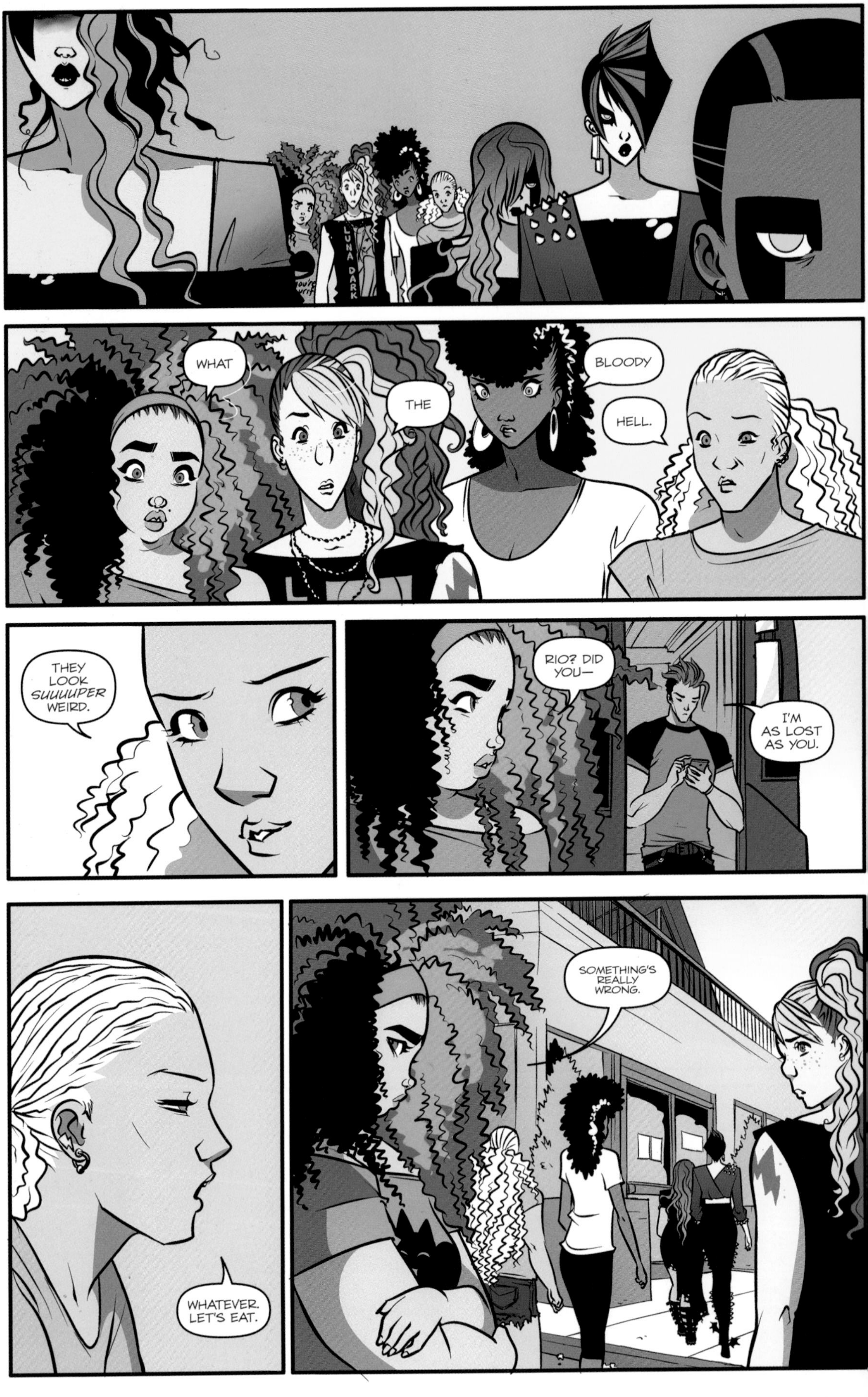

LUNA DARK
WHAT
THE
BLOODY
HELL.
THEY LOOK SUUUUPER WEIRD.
RIO? DID YOU—
I'M AS LOST AS YOU.
WHATEVER. LET'S EAT.
SOMETHING'S REALLY WRONG.

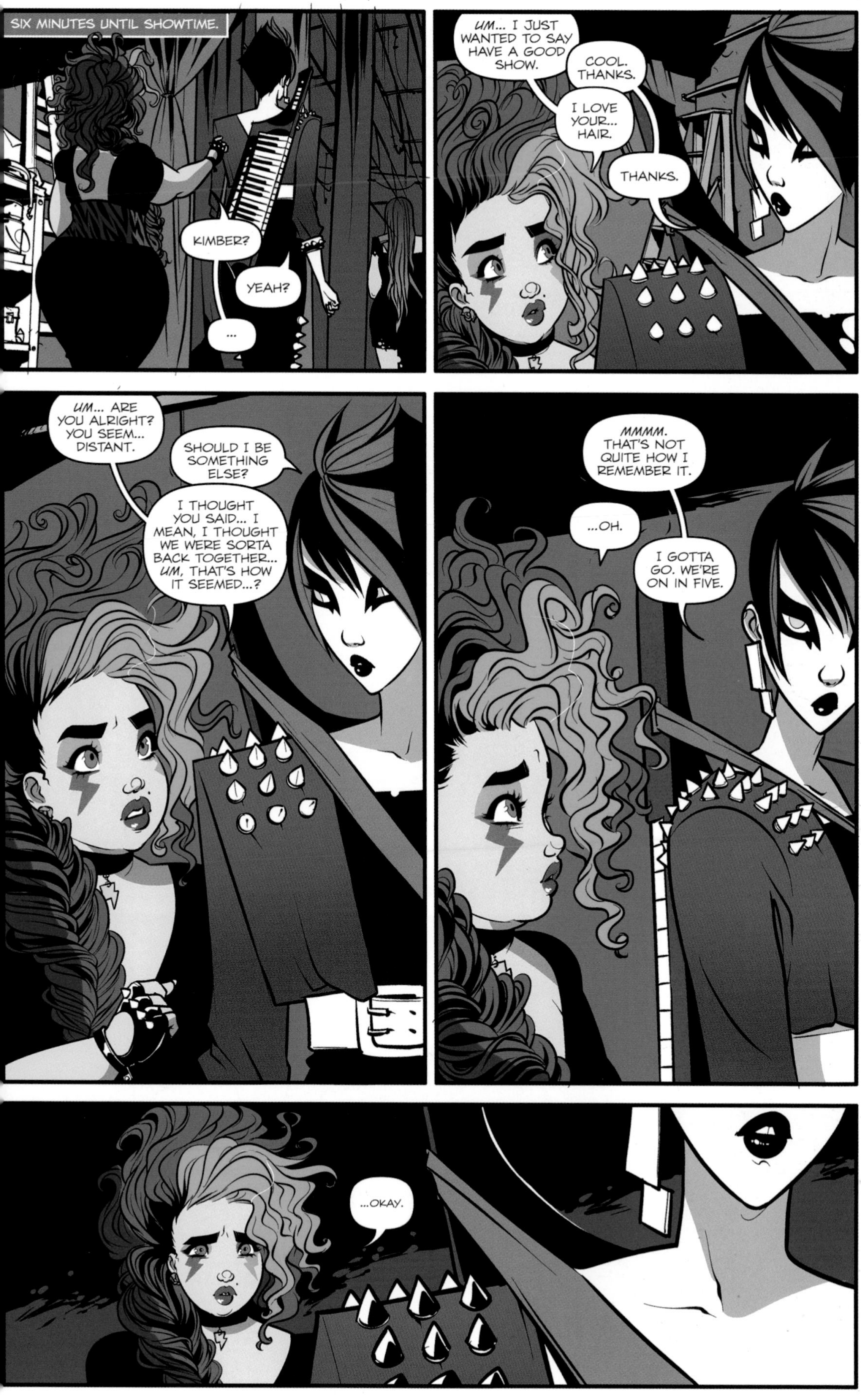
SIX MINUTES UNTIL SHOWTIME.
KIMBER?
YEAH?
...
UM... I JUST WANTED TO SAY HAVE A GOOD SHOW.
COOL. THANKS.
I LOVE YOUR... HAIR.
THANKS.
UM... ARE YOU ALRIGHT? YOU SEEM... DISTANT.
SHOULD I BE SOMETHING ELSE?
I THOUGHT YOU SAID... I MEAN, I THOUGHT WE WERE SORTA BACK TOGETHER... *UM*, THAT'S HOW IT SEEMED...?
MMMM. THAT'S NOT QUITE HOW I REMEMBER IT.
...OH.
I GOTTA GO. WE'RE ON IN FIVE.
...OKAY.

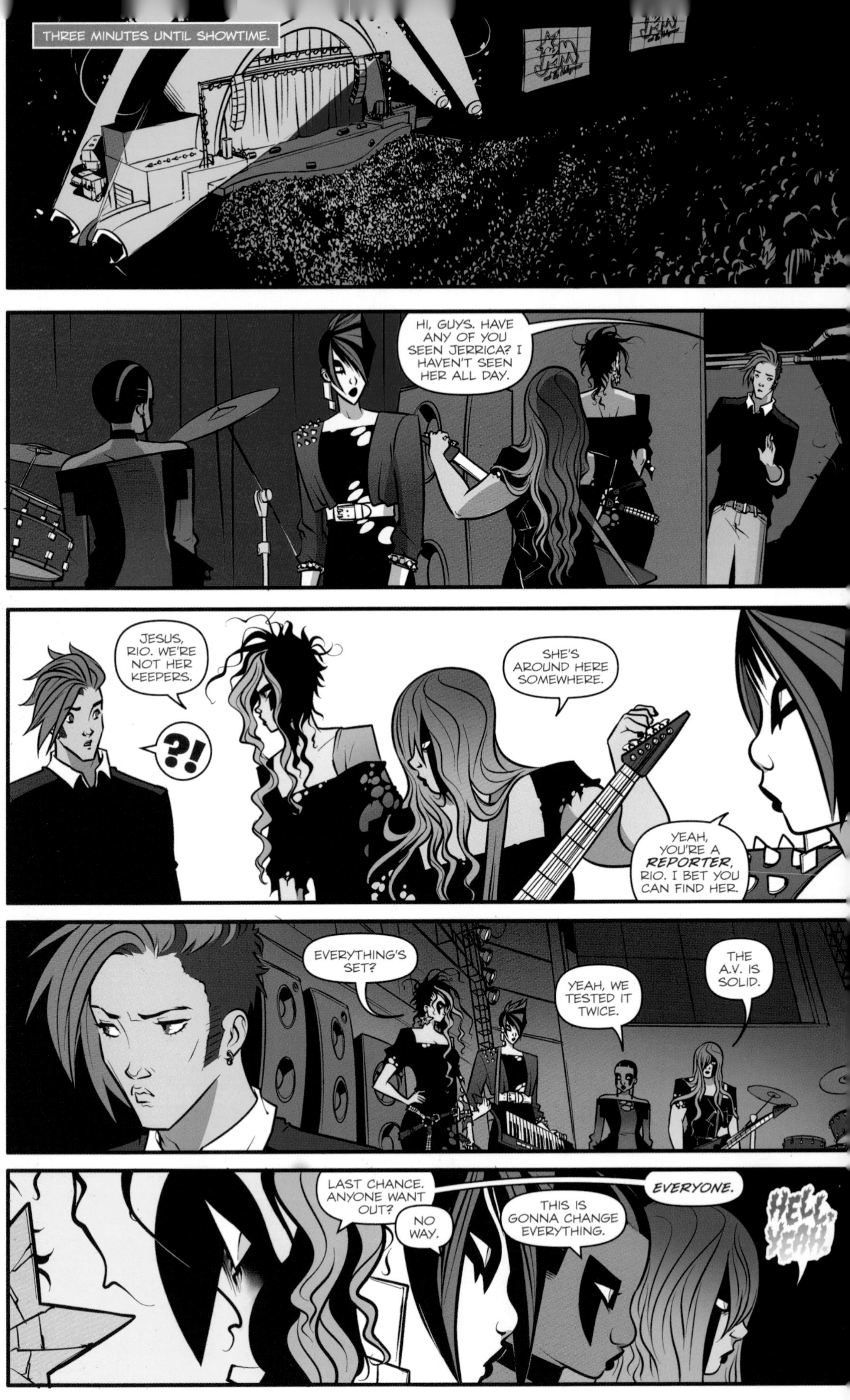
THREE MINUTES UNTIL SHOWTIME.
HI, GUYS. HAVE ANY OF YOU SEEN JERRICA? I HAVEN'T SEEN HER ALL DAY.
JESUS, RIO. WE'RE NOT HER KEEPERS.
?!
SHE'S AROUND HERE SOMEWHERE.
YEAH, YOU'RE A REPORTER, RIO. I BET YOU CAN FIND HER.
EVERYTHING'S SET?
YEAH, WE TESTED IT TWICE.
THE A.V. IS SOLID.
LAST CHANCE. ANYONE WANT OUT?
NO WAY.
THIS IS GONNA CHANGE EVERYTHING.
EVERYONE.
HELL, YEAH

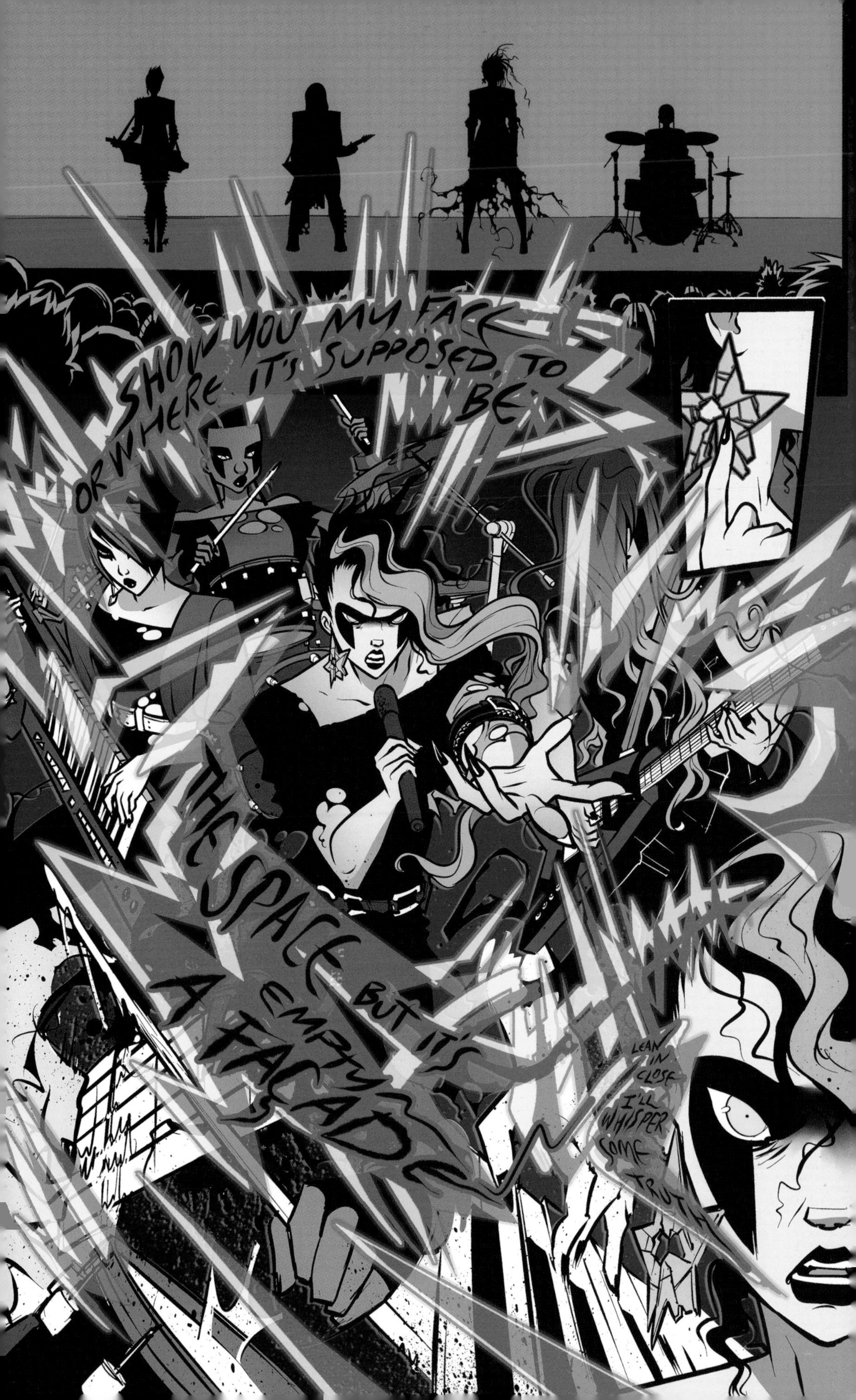
SHOW YOU MY FACE
OR WHERE IT'S SUPPOSED TO BE
THE SPACE BUT IT'S EMPTY
A FACADE
LEAN IN CLOSE
I'LL WHISPER SOME TRUTH

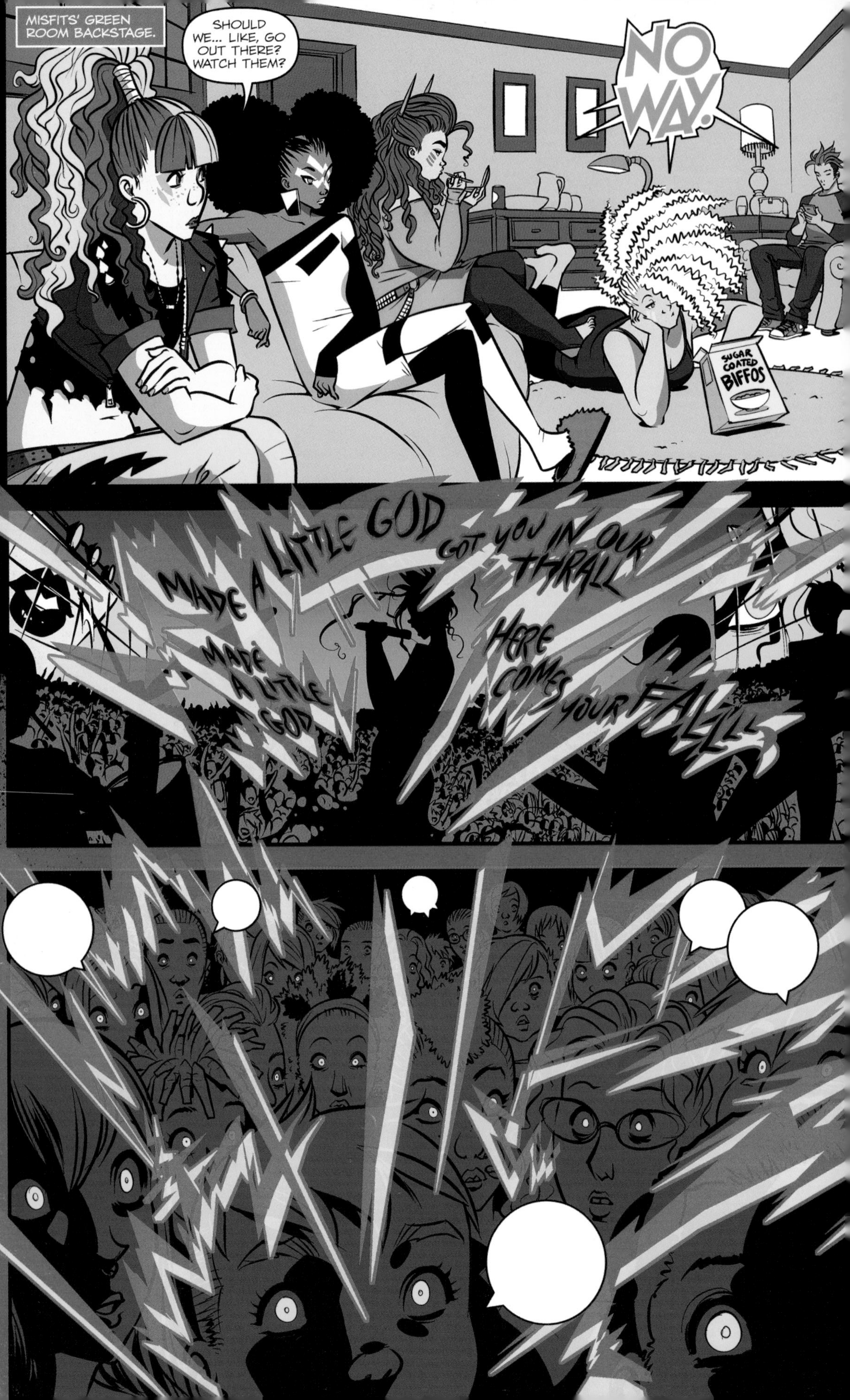
MISFITS' GREEN ROOM BACKSTAGE.
SHOULD WE... LIKE, GO OUT THERE? WATCH THEM?
NO WAY.
SUGAR COATED BIFFOS
MADE A LITTLE GOD
GOT YOU IN OUR THRALL
MADE A LITTLE GOD
HERE COMES YOUR FALL

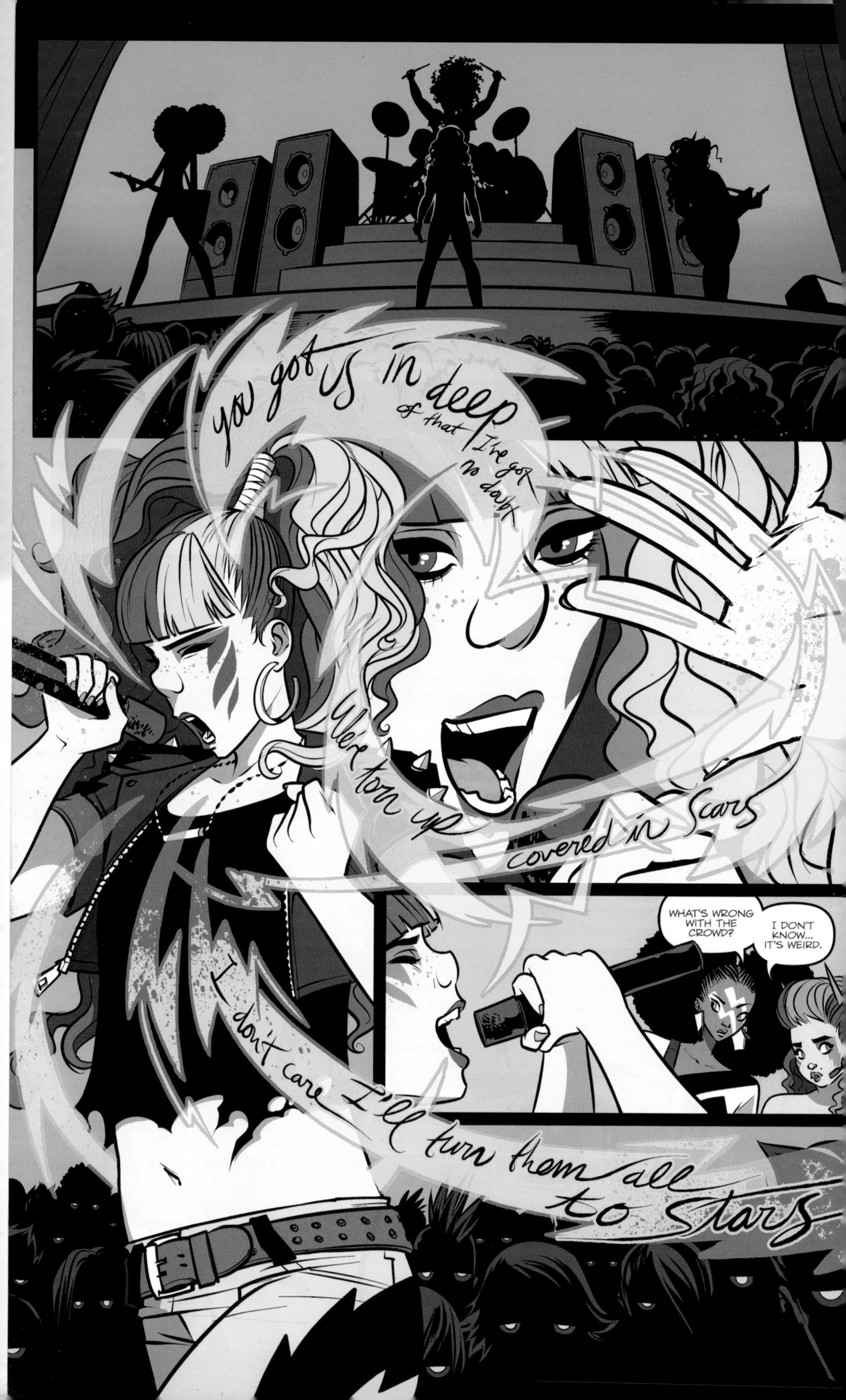
you got us in deep
of that I've got no doubt
We're torn up
covered in Scars
WHAT'S WRONG WITH THE CROWD?
I DON'T KNOW... IT'S WEIRD.
I don't care I'll turn them all to Stars

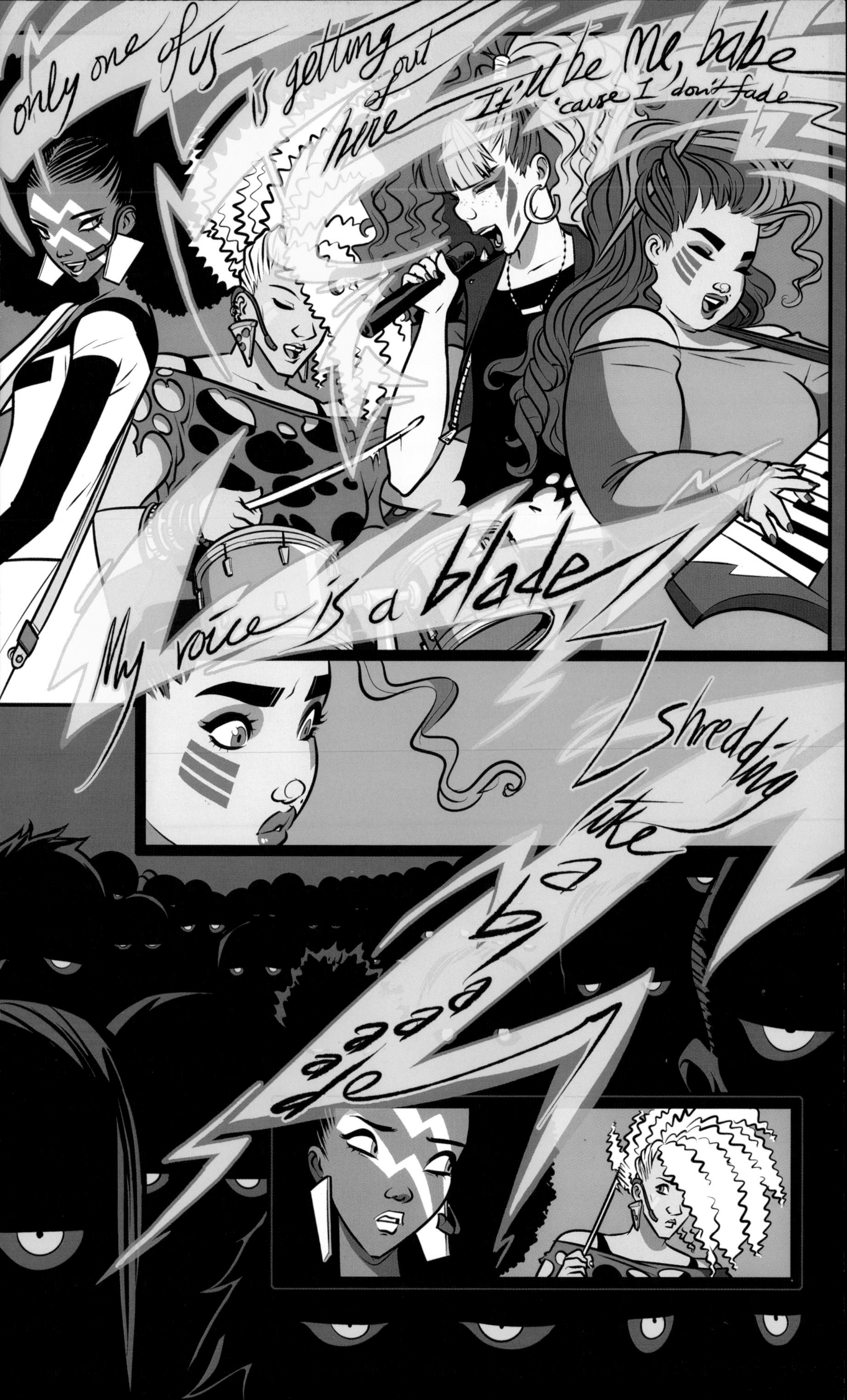

only one of us—
is getting out of here
It'll be me, babe
'cause I don't fade
My voice is a blade
shredding like a b
aaaade

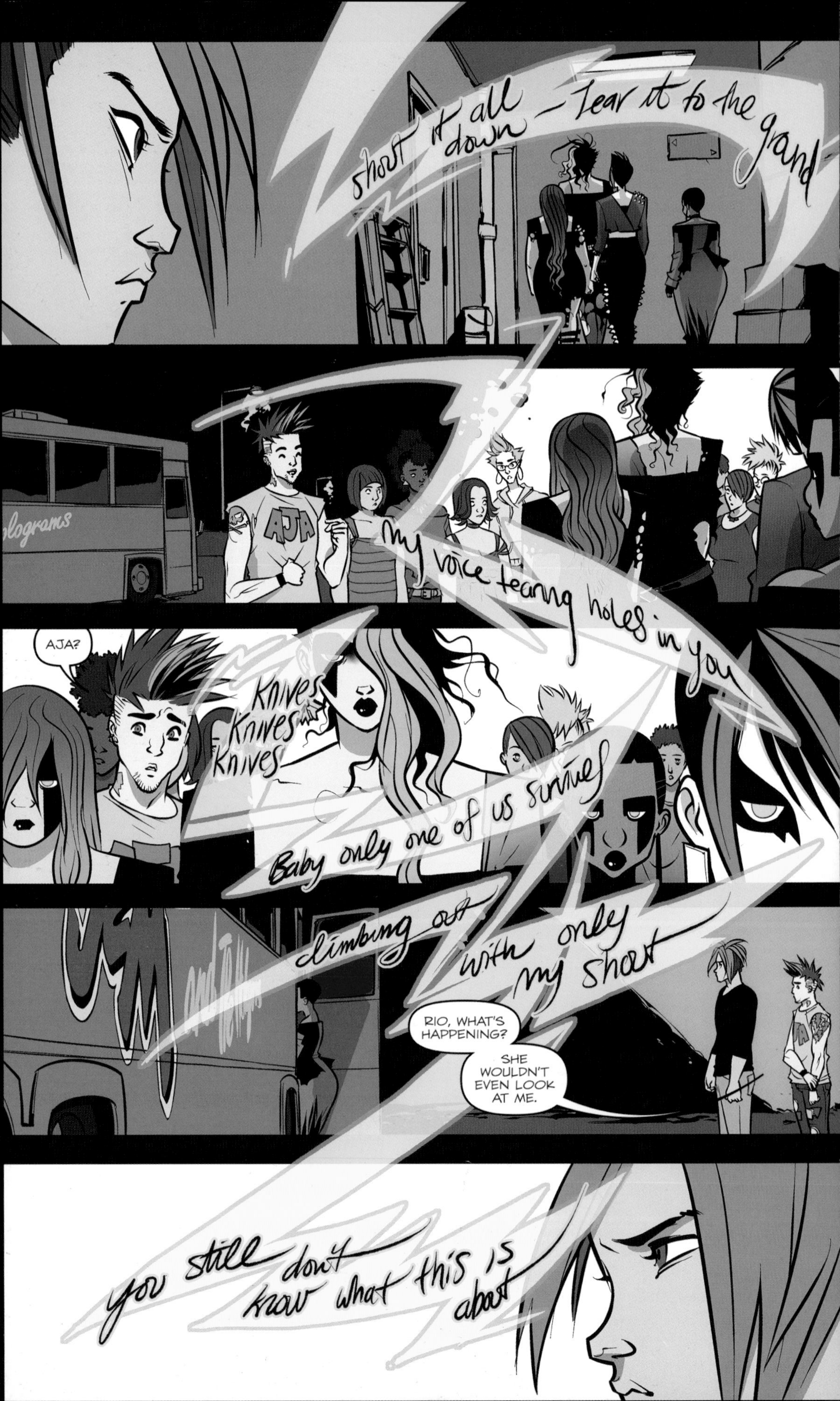

shout it all down — tear it to the grand
My voice tearing holes in you
AJA?
Knives Knives Knives
Baby only one of us survives
climbing out with only my shout
RIO, WHAT'S HAPPENING?
SHE WOULDN'T EVEN LOOK AT ME.
you still don't know what this is about

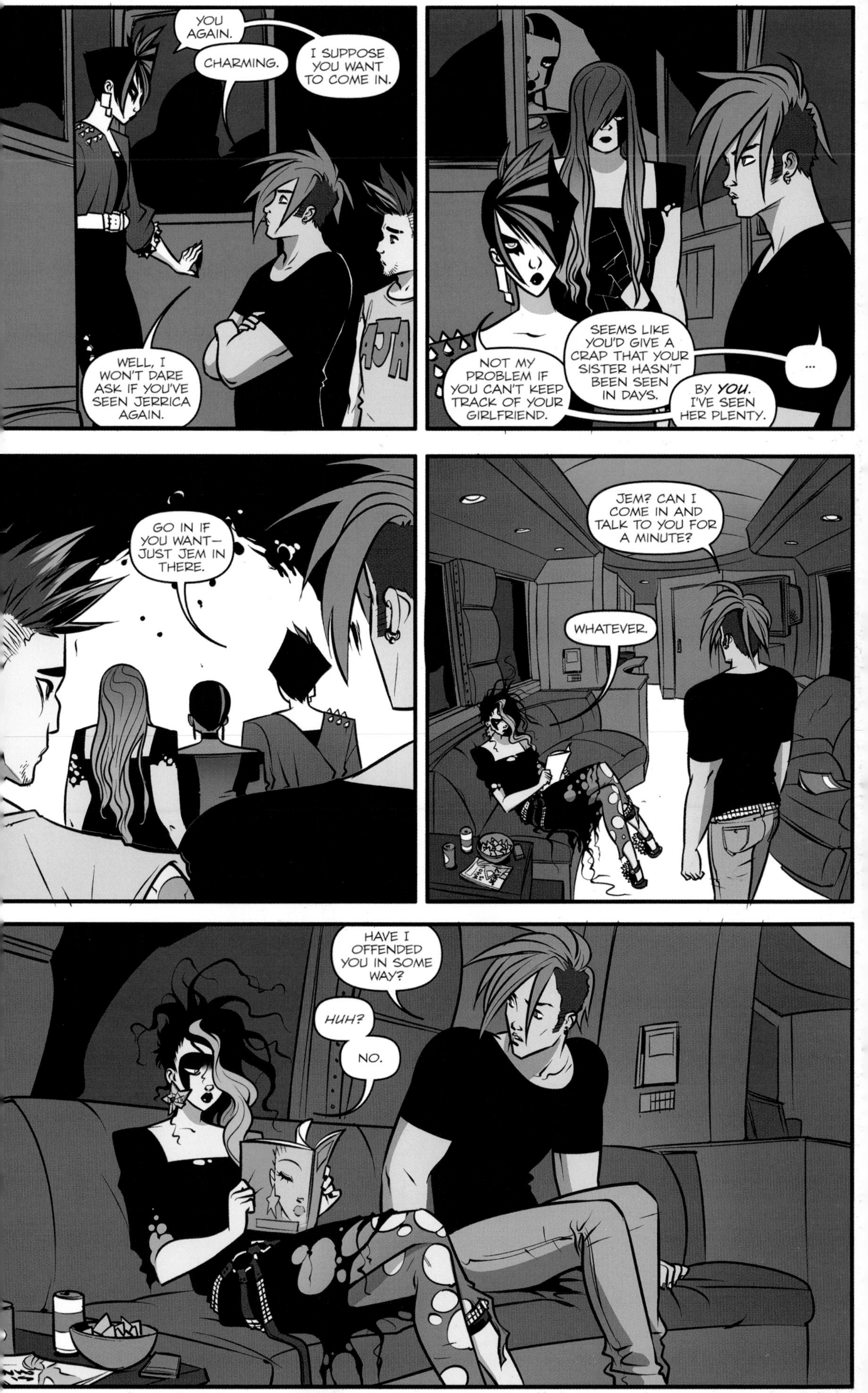
YOU AGAIN.
CHARMING.
I SUPPOSE YOU WANT TO COME IN.
WELL, I WON'T DARE ASK IF YOU'VE SEEN JERRICA AGAIN.
NOT MY PROBLEM IF YOU CAN'T KEEP TRACK OF YOUR GIRLFRIEND.
SEEMS LIKE YOU'D GIVE A CRAP THAT YOUR SISTER HASN'T BEEN SEEN IN DAYS.
BY *YOU*. I'VE SEEN HER PLENTY.
...
GO IN IF YOU WANT— JUST JEM IN THERE.
JEM? CAN I COME IN AND TALK TO YOU FOR A MINUTE?
WHATEVER.
HAVE I OFFENDED YOU IN SOME WAY?
HUH?
NO.

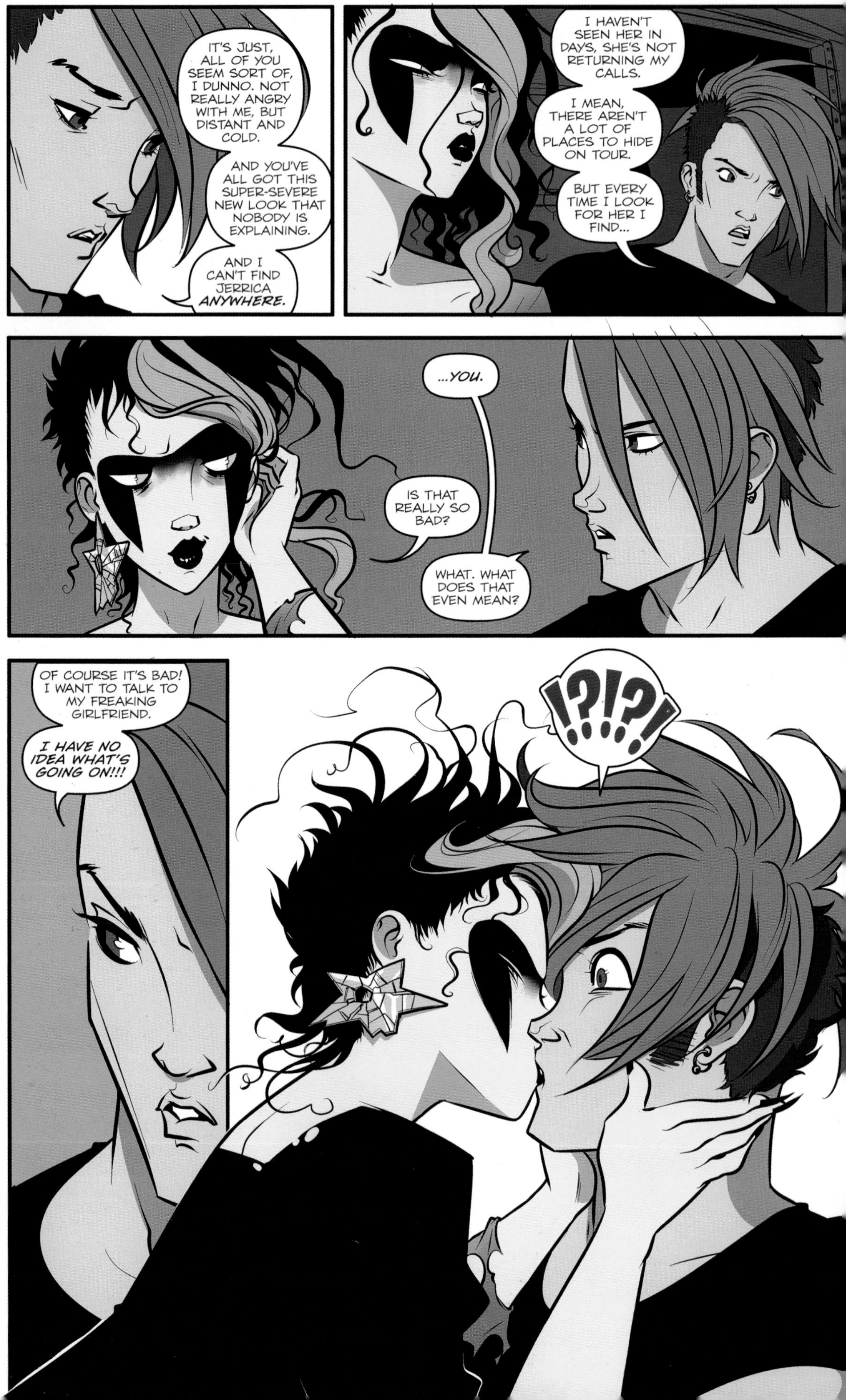
IT'S JUST, ALL OF YOU SEEM SORT OF, I DUNNO. NOT REALLY ANGRY WITH ME, BUT DISTANT AND COLD.
AND YOU'VE ALL GOT THIS SUPER-SEVERE NEW LOOK THAT NOBODY IS EXPLAINING.
AND I CAN'T FIND JERRICA *ANYWHERE.*
I HAVEN'T SEEN HER IN DAYS, SHE'S NOT RETURNING MY CALLS.
I MEAN, THERE AREN'T A LOT OF PLACES TO HIDE ON TOUR.
BUT EVERY TIME I LOOK FOR HER I FIND...
...*YOU.*
IS THAT REALLY SO BAD?
WHAT. WHAT DOES THAT EVEN MEAN?
OF COURSE IT'S BAD! I WANT TO TALK TO MY FREAKING GIRLFRIEND.
I HAVE NO IDEA WHAT'S GOING ON!!!
!?!?!

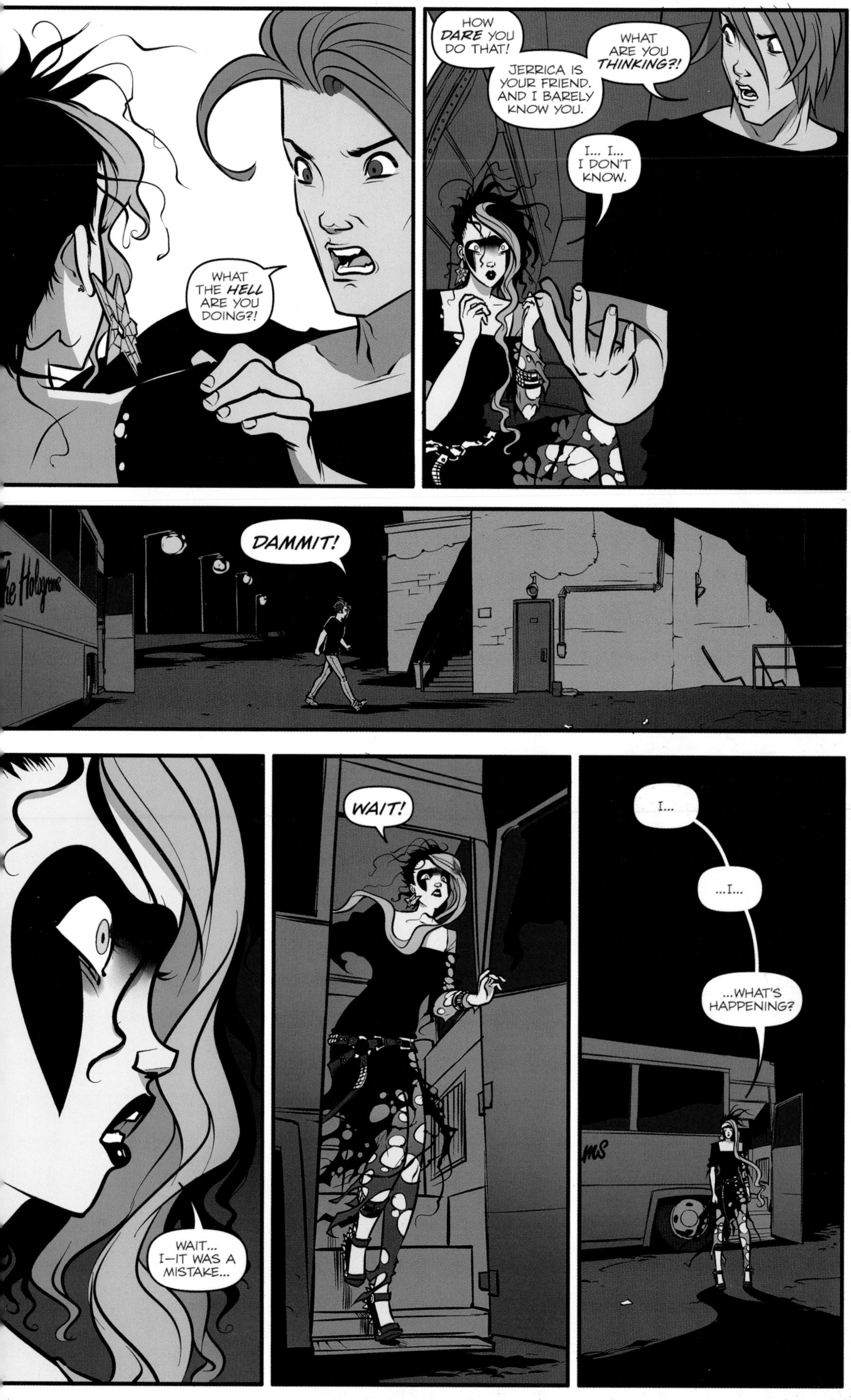
WHAT THE HELL ARE YOU DOING?!
HOW DARE YOU DO THAT!
WHAT ARE YOU THINKING?!
JERRICA IS YOUR FRIEND. AND I BARELY KNOW YOU.
I... I... I DON'T KNOW.
The Holograms
DAMMIT!
WAIT... I—IT WAS A MISTAKE...
WAIT!
I...
...I...
...WHAT'S HAPPENING?

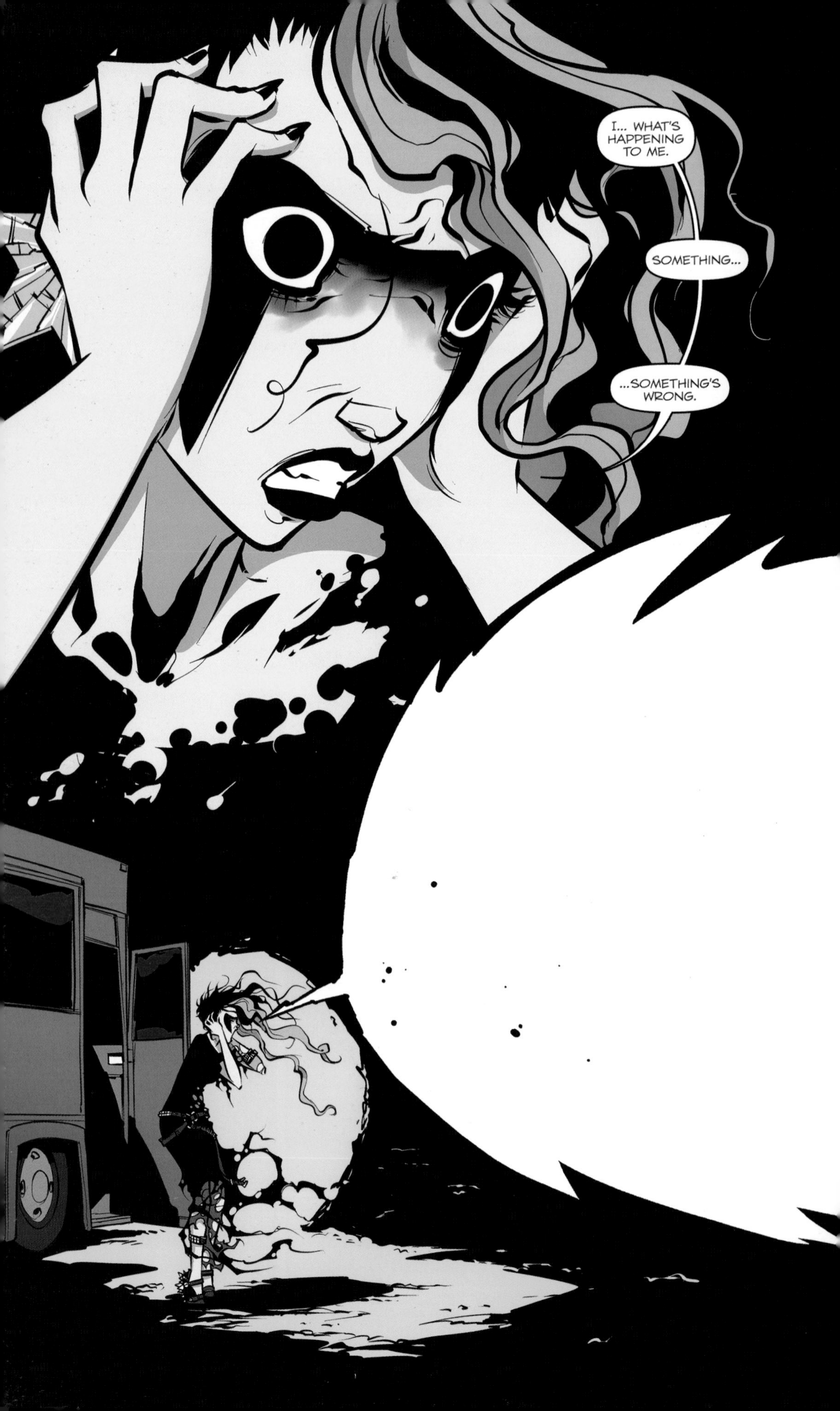
I... WHAT'S HAPPENING TO ME.
SOMETHING...
...SOMETHING'S WRONG.

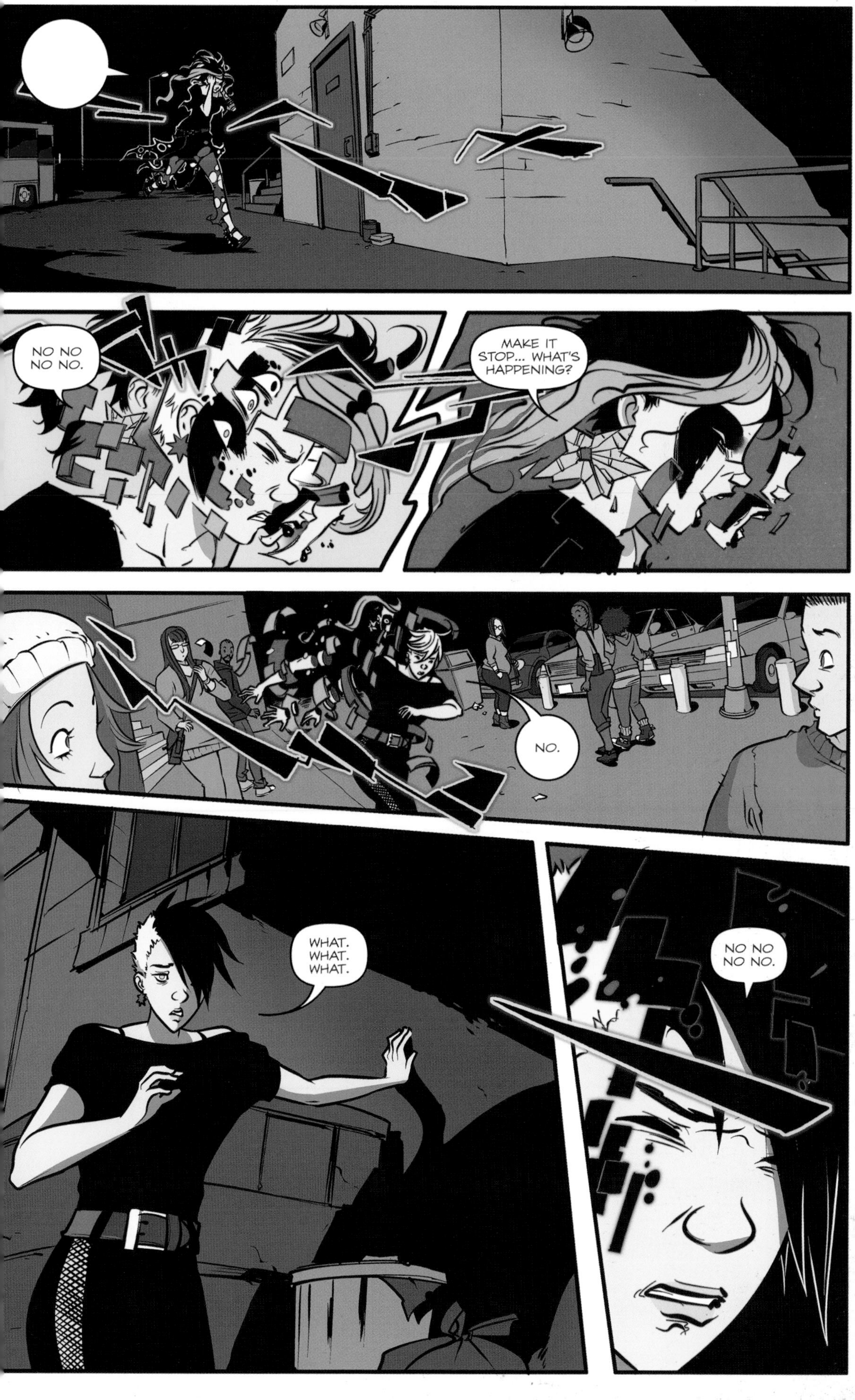
NO NO
NO NO.
MAKE IT
STOP... WHAT'S
HAPPENING?
NO.
WHAT.
WHAT.
WHAT.
NO NO
NO NO.

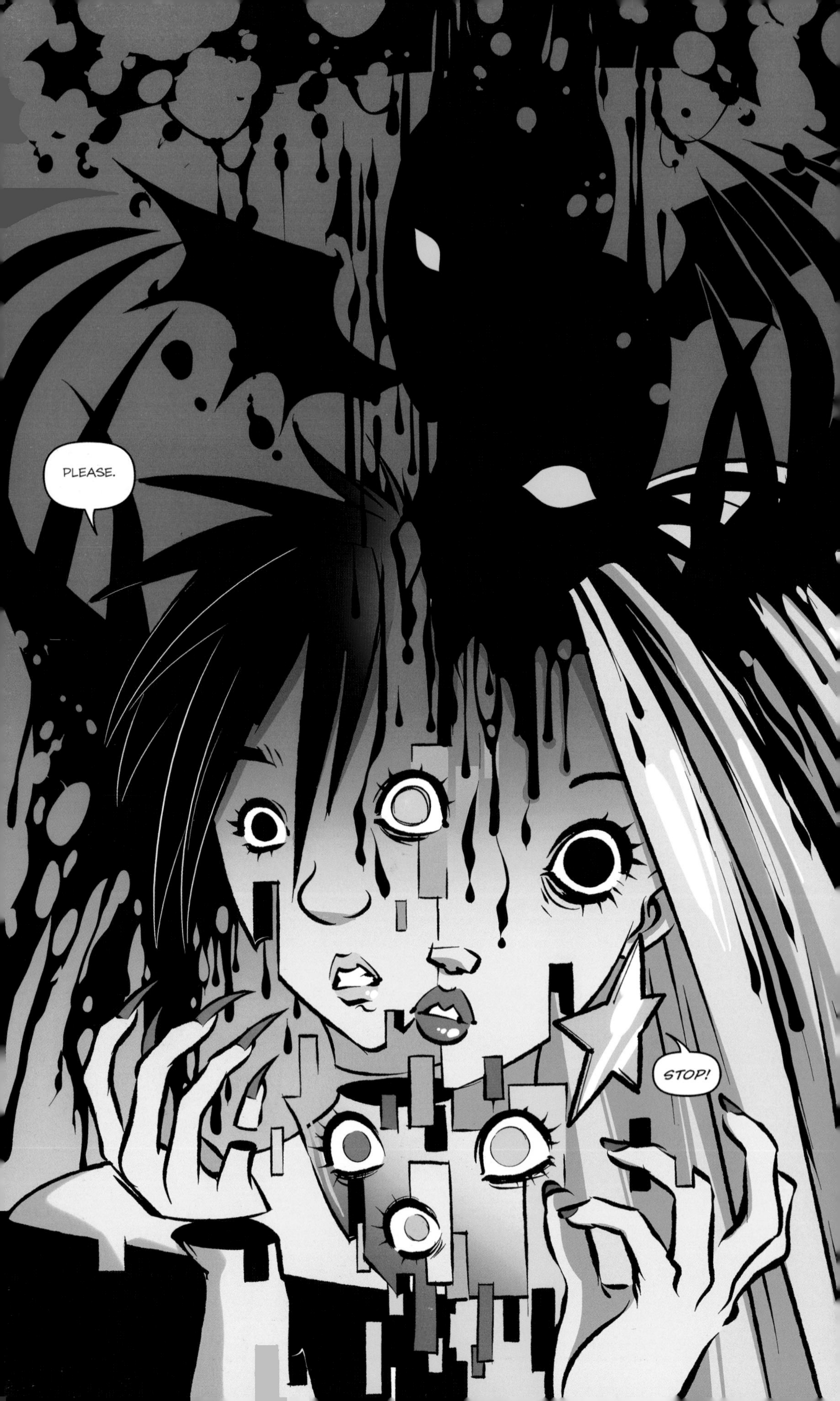
PLEASE.
STOP!

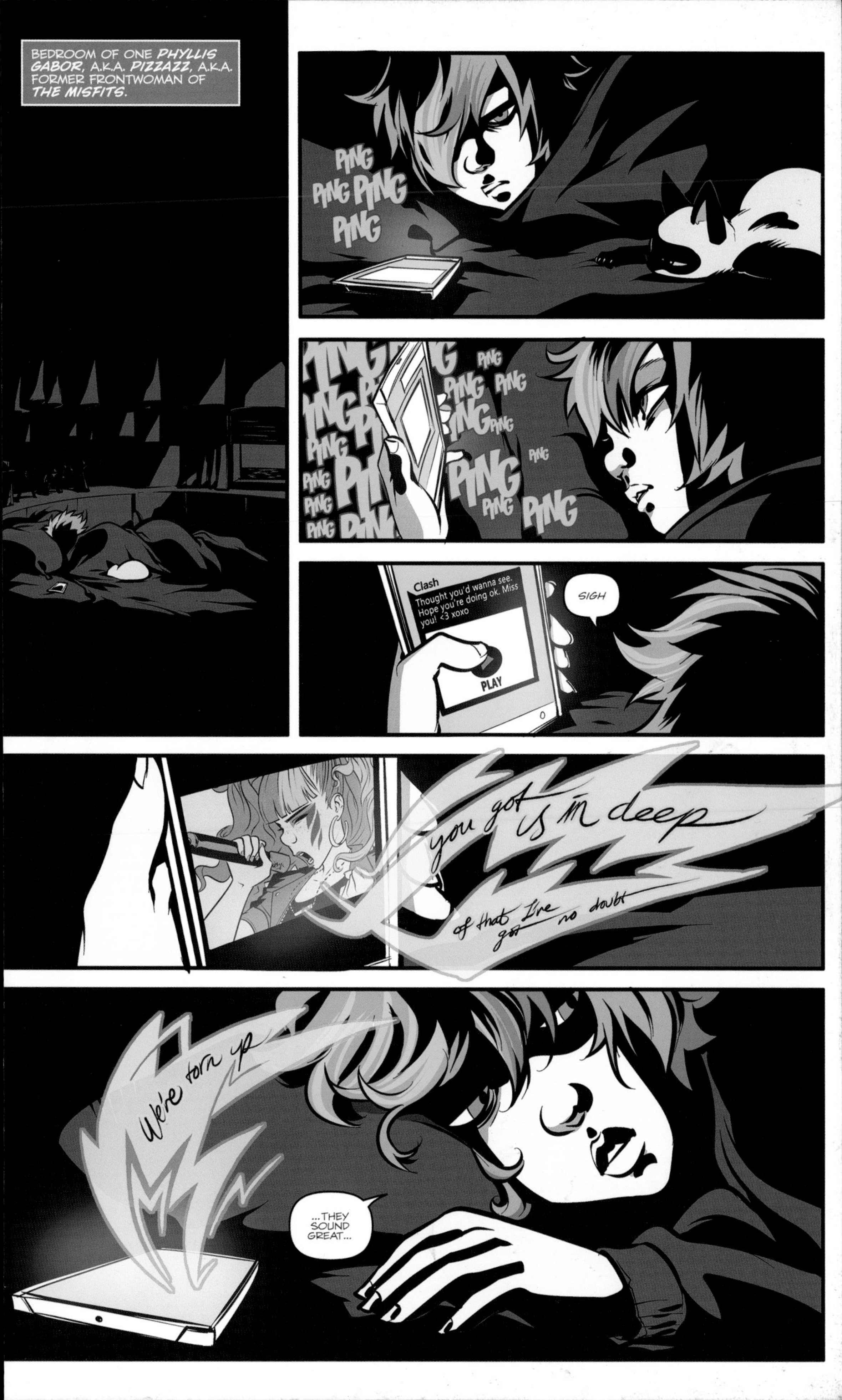

BEDROOM OF ONE PHYLLIS GABOR, A.K.A. PIZZAZZ, A.K.A. FORMER FRONTWOMAN OF THE MISFITS.
PING PING PING PING
PING PING PING PING PING PING PING PING PING
Clash
Thought you'd wanna see. Hope you're doing ok. Miss you! <3 xoxo
PLAY
SIGH
you got us in deep
of that I've got no doubt
We're torn up
...THEY SOUND GREAT...

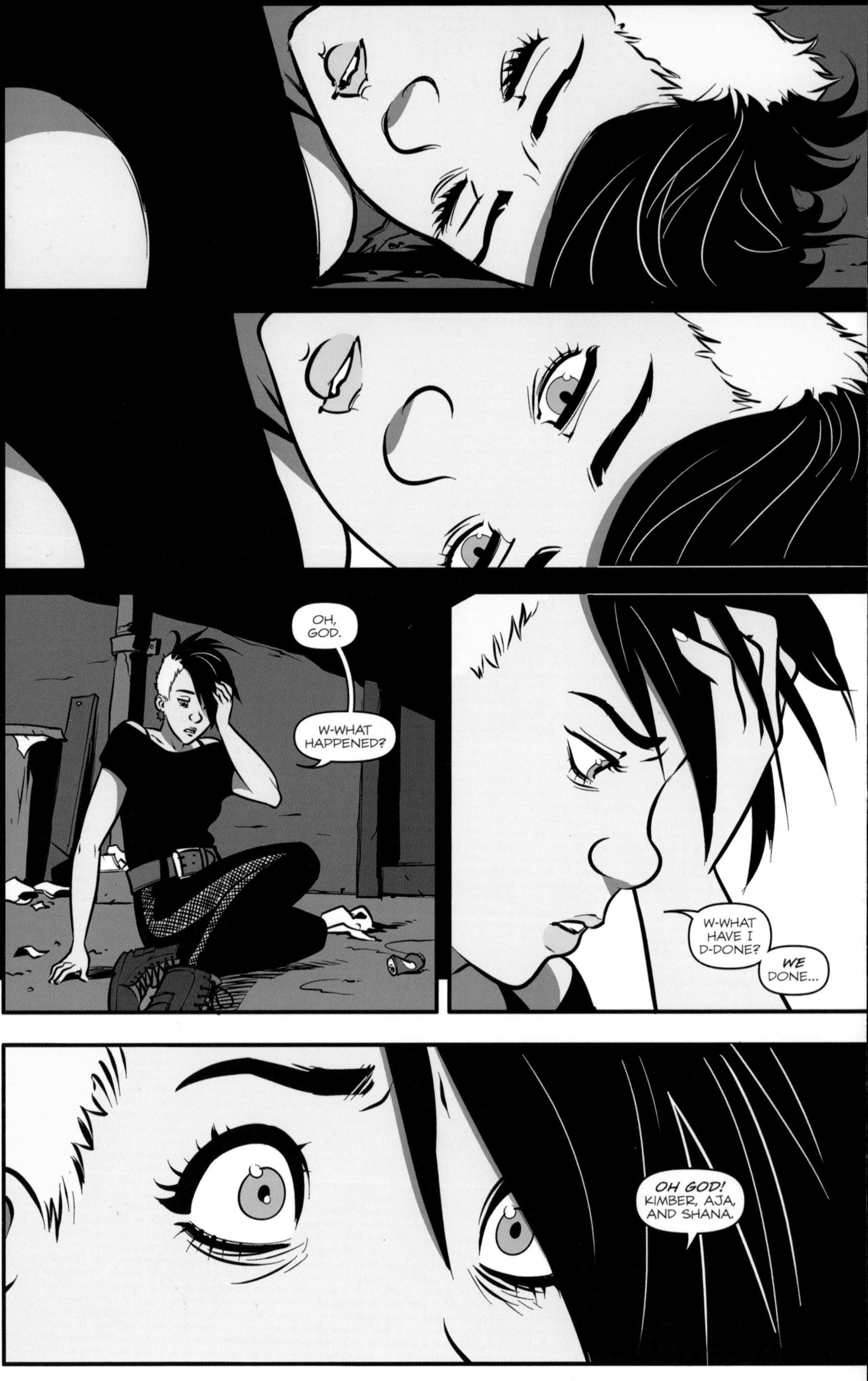

OH, GOD.
W-WHAT HAPPENED?
W-WHAT HAVE I D-DONE?
WE DONE...
OH GOD! KIMBER, AJA, AND SHANA.

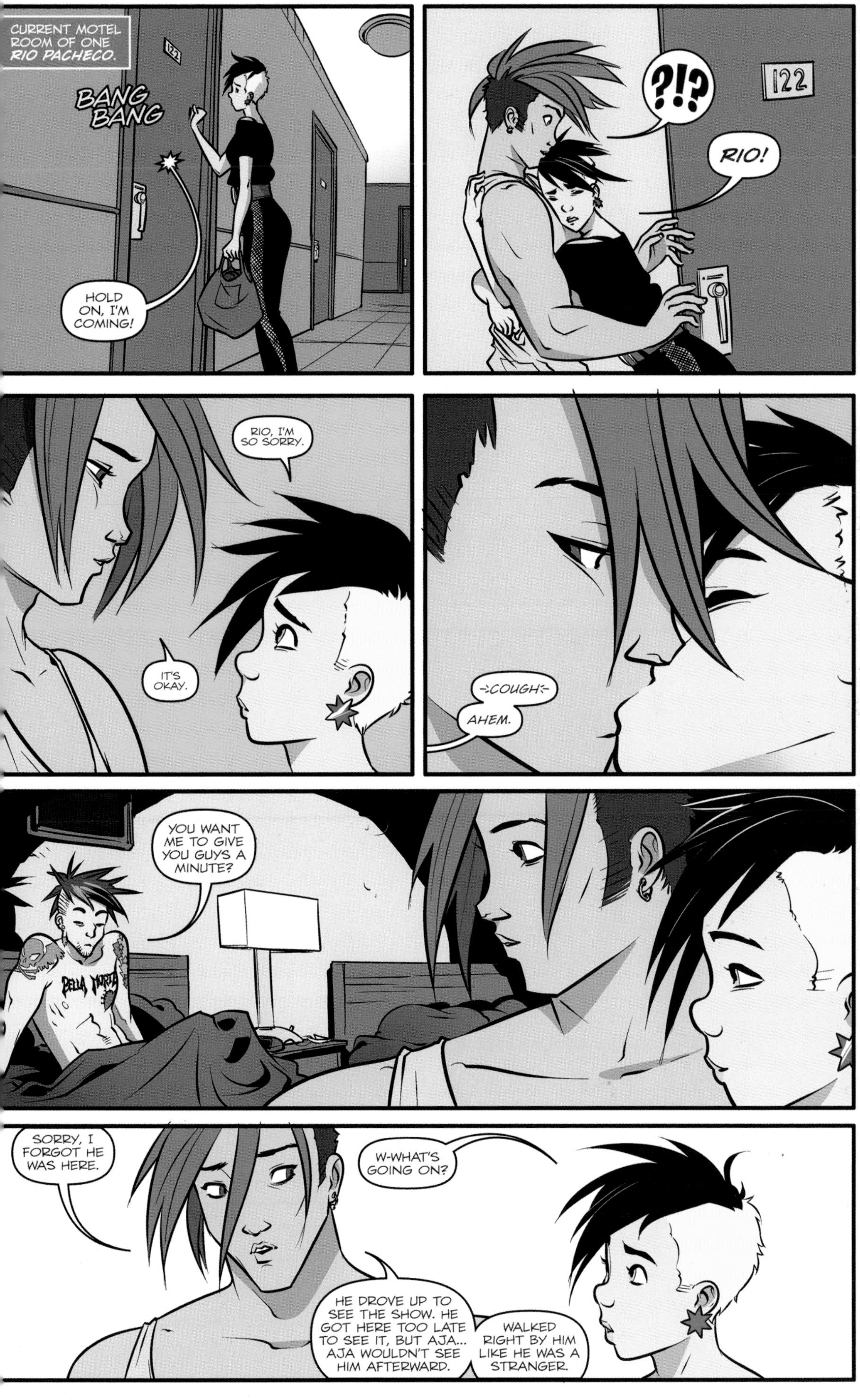
CURRENT MOTEL ROOM OF ONE RIO PACHECO.
122
BANG BANG
HOLD ON, I'M COMING!
?!?
122
RIO!
RIO, I'M SO SORRY.
IT'S OKAY.
-COUGH-
AHEM.
YOU WANT ME TO GIVE YOU GUYS A MINUTE?
BELLA MORTE
SORRY, I FORGOT HE WAS HERE.
W-WHAT'S GOING ON?
HE DROVE UP TO SEE THE SHOW. HE GOT HERE TOO LATE TO SEE IT, BUT AJA... AJA WOULDN'T SEE HIM AFTERWARD.
WALKED RIGHT BY HIM LIKE HE WAS A STRANGER.

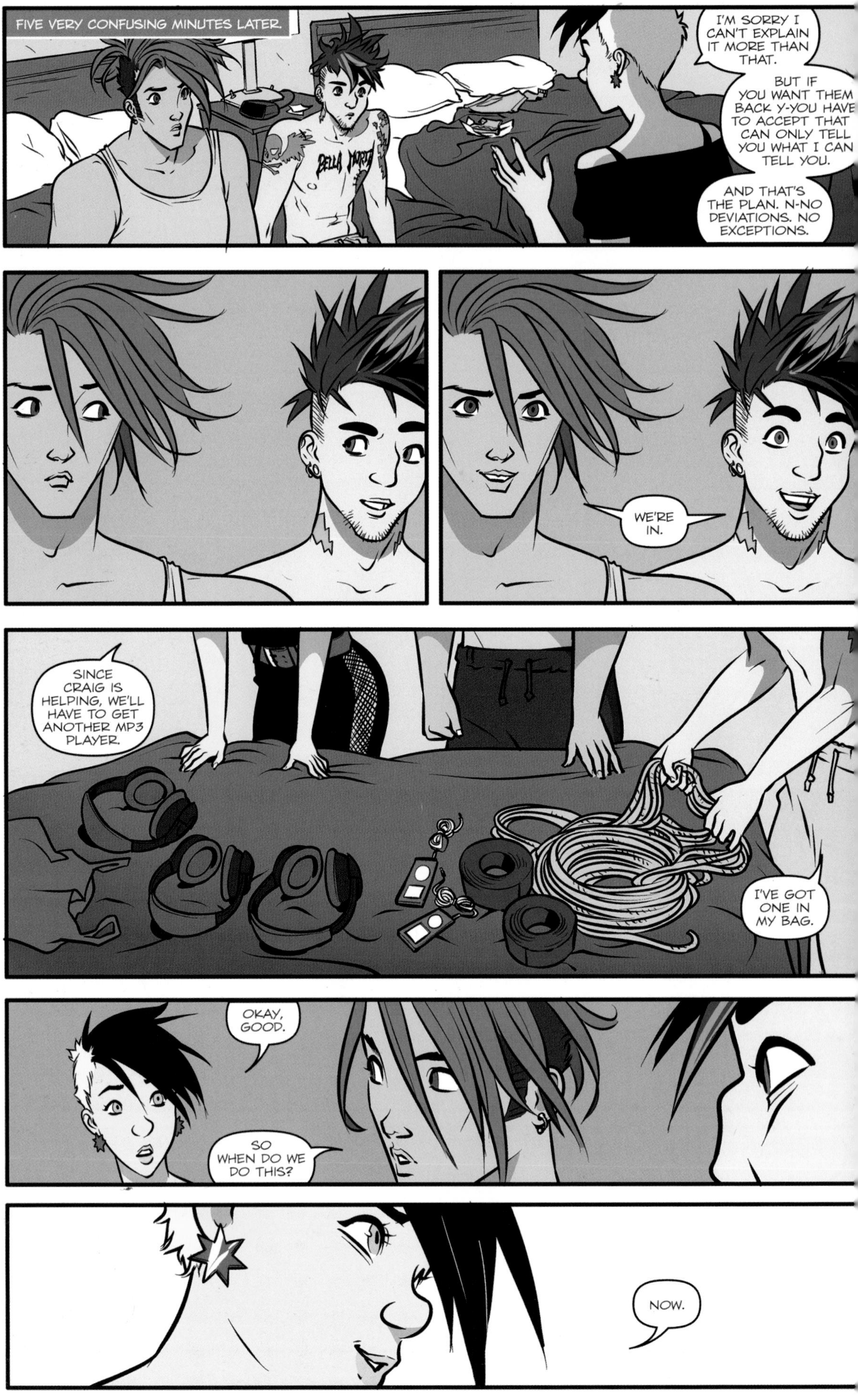
FIVE VERY CONFUSING MINUTES LATER.
I'M SORRY I CAN'T EXPLAIN IT MORE THAN THAT.
BUT IF YOU WANT THEM BACK Y-YOU HAVE TO ACCEPT THAT CAN ONLY TELL YOU WHAT I CAN TELL YOU.
AND THAT'S THE PLAN. N-NO DEVIATIONS. NO EXCEPTIONS.
BELLA MORTE
WE'RE IN.
SINCE CRAIG IS HELPING, WE'LL HAVE TO GET ANOTHER MP3 PLAYER.
I'VE GOT ONE IN MY BAG.
OKAY, GOOD.
SO WHEN DO WE DO THIS?
NOW.

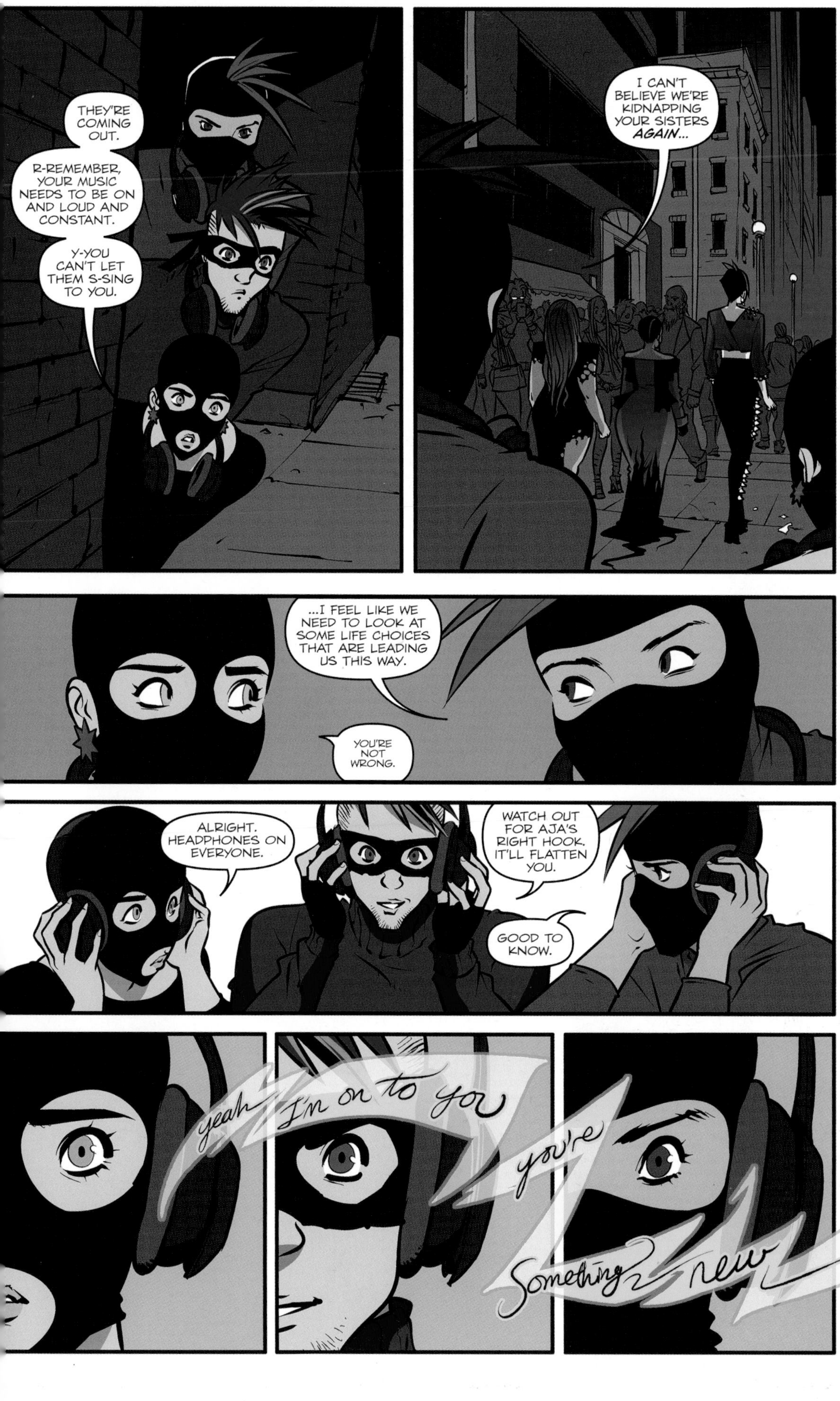
THEY'RE COMING OUT.
R-REMEMBER, YOUR MUSIC NEEDS TO BE ON AND LOUD AND CONSTANT.
Y-YOU CAN'T LET THEM S-SING TO YOU.
I CAN'T BELIEVE WE'RE KIDNAPPING YOUR SISTERS AGAIN...
...I FEEL LIKE WE NEED TO LOOK AT SOME LIFE CHOICES THAT ARE LEADING US THIS WAY.
YOU'RE NOT WRONG.
ALRIGHT. HEADPHONES ON EVERYONE.
WATCH OUT FOR AJA'S RIGHT HOOK. IT'LL FLATTEN YOU.
GOOD TO KNOW.
yeah I'm on to you
you're
Something new

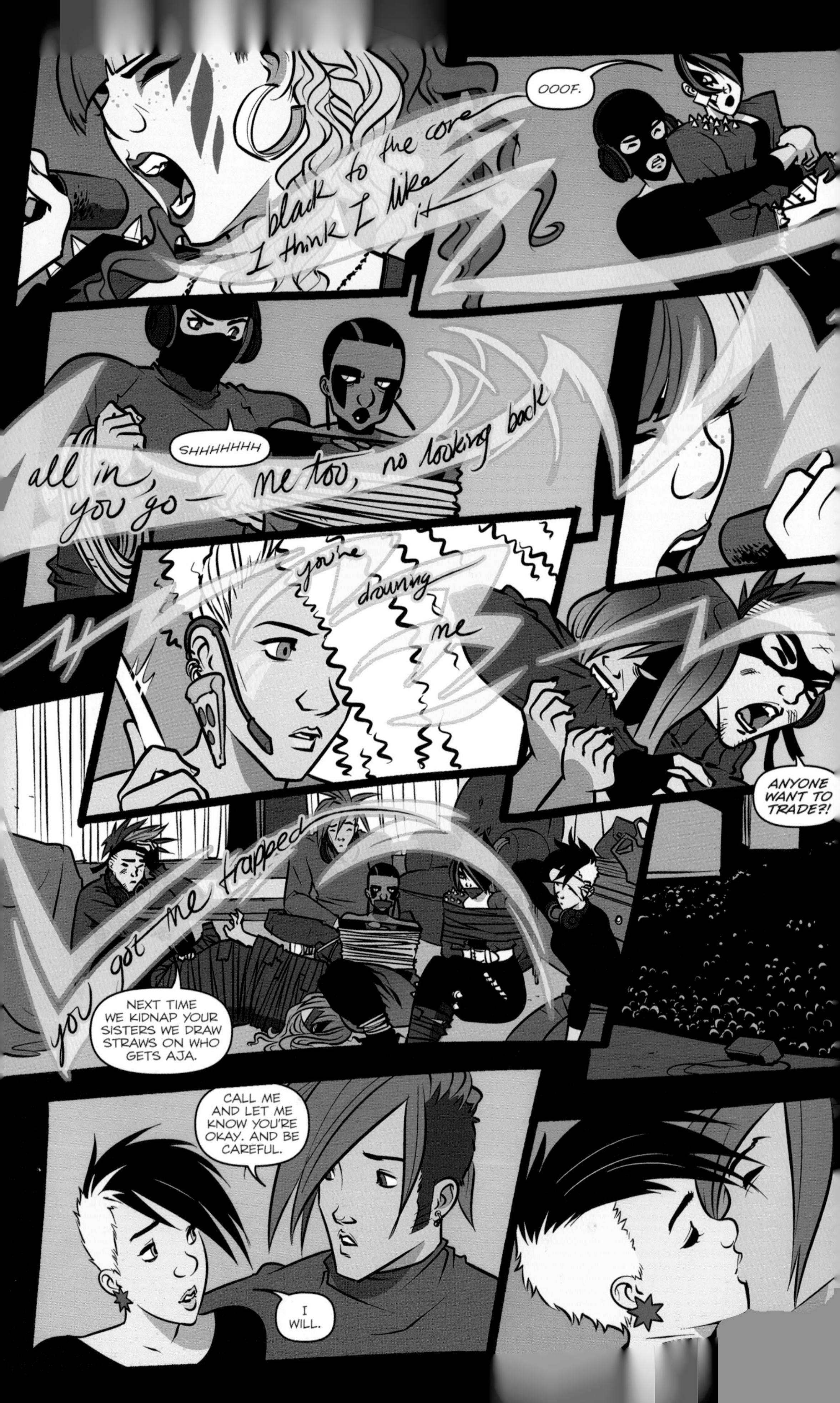

OOOF.
black to the core
I think I like it
SHHHHHHH
all in, you go — me too, no looking back
you're drowning me
ANYONE WANT TO TRADE?!
you got me trapped
NEXT TIME WE KIDNAP YOUR SISTERS WE DRAW STRAWS ON WHO GETS AJA.
CALL ME AND LET ME KNOW YOU'RE OKAY. AND BE CAREFUL.
I WILL.

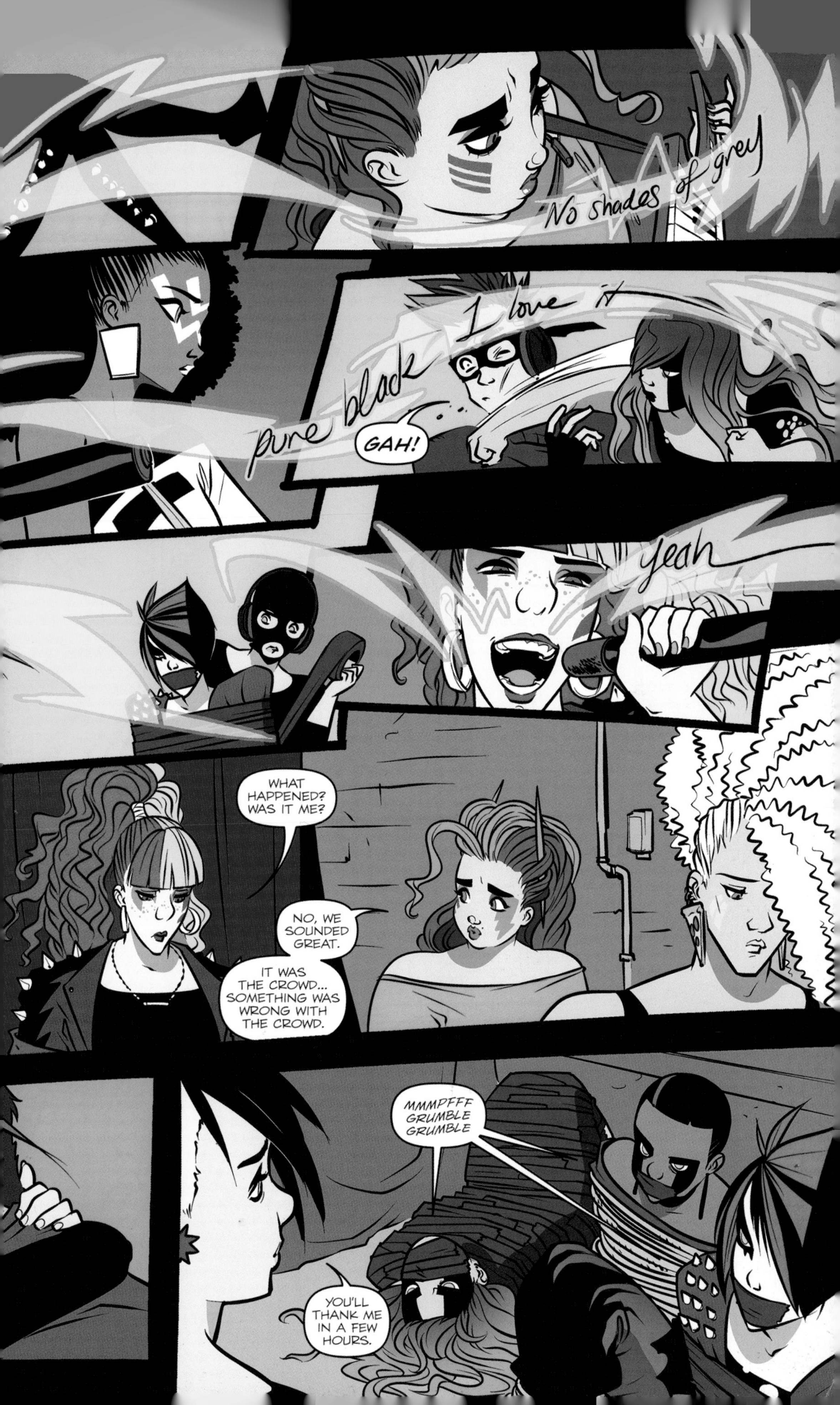
No shades of grey
pure black I love it
GAH!
yeah
WHAT HAPPENED? WAS IT ME?
NO, WE SOUNDED GREAT.
IT WAS THE CROWD... SOMETHING WAS WRONG WITH THE CROWD.
MMMPFFF GRUMBLE GRUMBLE
YOU'LL THANK ME IN A FEW HOURS.

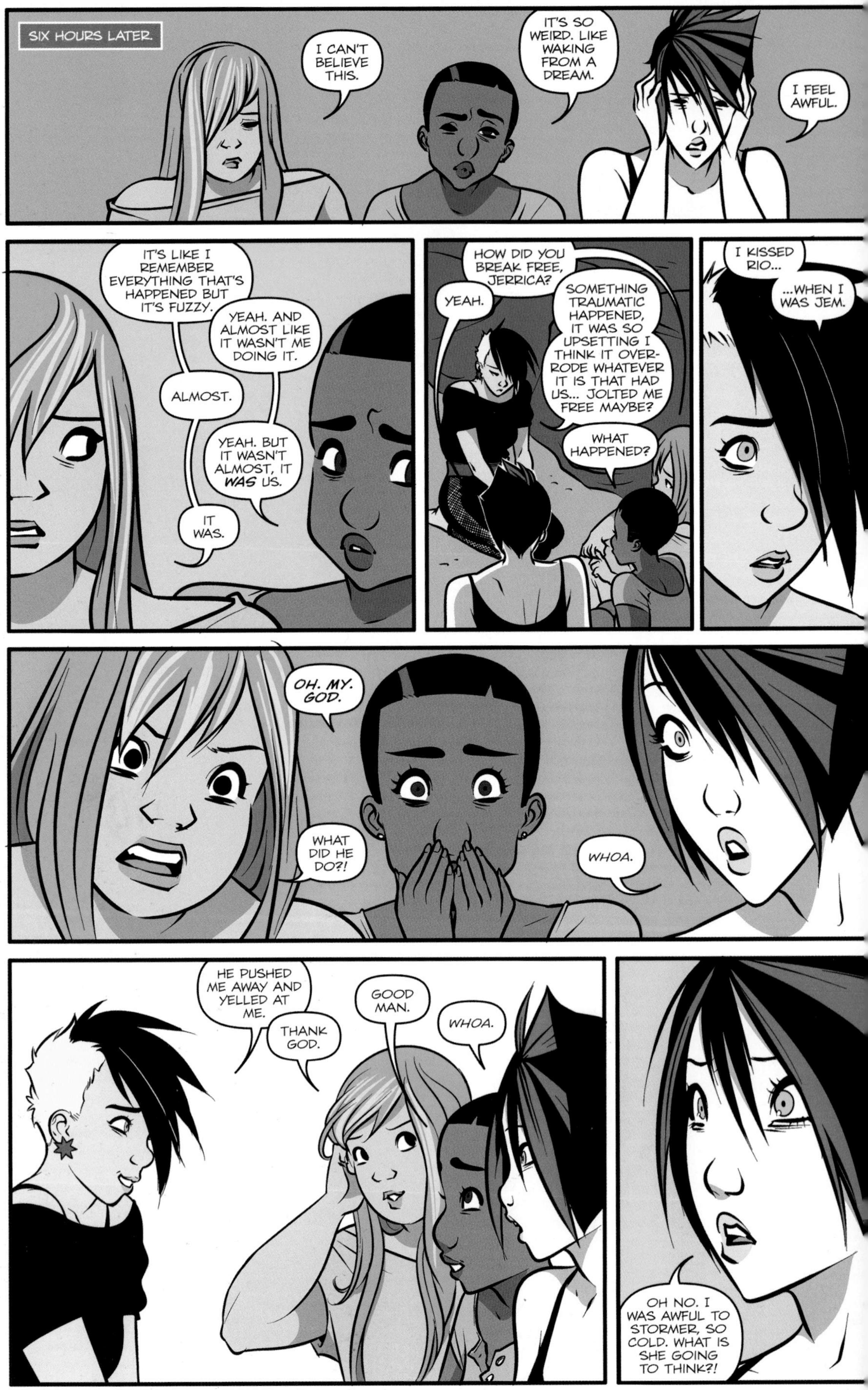

SIX HOURS LATER.
I CAN'T BELIEVE THIS.
IT'S SO WEIRD. LIKE WAKING FROM A DREAM.
I FEEL AWFUL.
IT'S LIKE I REMEMBER EVERYTHING THAT'S HAPPENED BUT IT'S FUZZY.
YEAH. AND ALMOST LIKE IT WASN'T ME DOING IT.
ALMOST.
YEAH. BUT IT WASN'T ALMOST, IT *WAS* US.
IT WAS.
HOW DID YOU BREAK FREE, JERRICA?
YEAH.
SOMETHING TRAUMATIC HAPPENED, IT WAS SO UPSETTING I THINK IT OVERRODE WHATEVER IT IS THAT HAD US... JOLTED ME FREE MAYBE?
WHAT HAPPENED?
I KISSED RIO...
...WHEN I WAS JEM.
OH. MY. GOD.
WHAT DID HE DO?!
WHOA.
HE PUSHED ME AWAY AND YELLED AT ME.
THANK GOD.
GOOD MAN.
WHOA.
OH NO. I WAS AWFUL TO STORMER, SO COLD. WHAT IS SHE GOING TO THINK?!

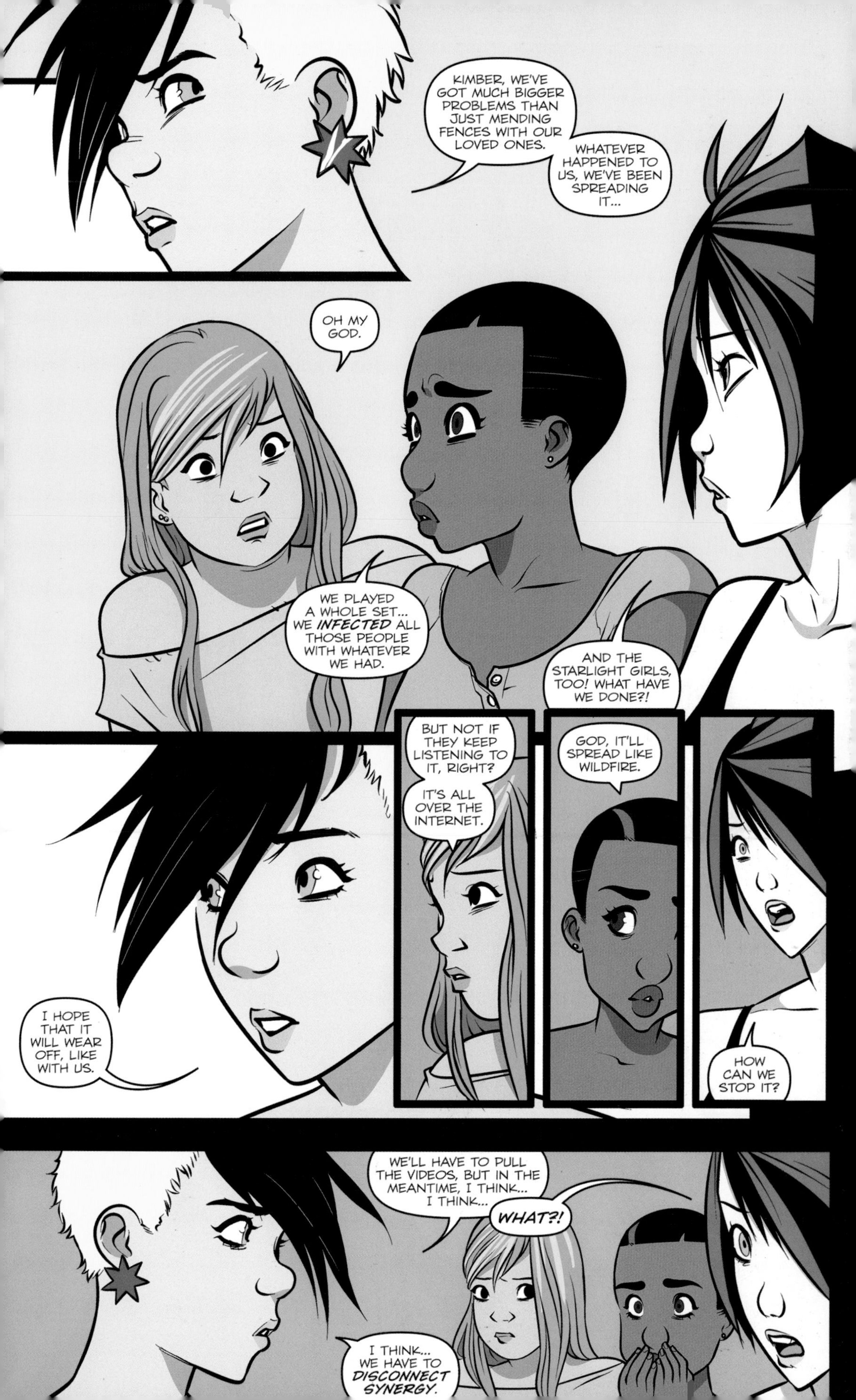
KIMBER, WE'VE GOT MUCH BIGGER PROBLEMS THAN JUST MENDING FENCES WITH OUR LOVED ONES.
WHATEVER HAPPENED TO US, WE'VE BEEN SPREADING IT...
OH MY GOD.
WE PLAYED A WHOLE SET... WE INFECTED ALL THOSE PEOPLE WITH WHATEVER WE HAD.
AND THE STARLIGHT GIRLS, TOO! WHAT HAVE WE DONE?!
I HOPE THAT IT WILL WEAR OFF, LIKE WITH US.
BUT NOT IF THEY KEEP LISTENING TO IT, RIGHT?
IT'S ALL OVER THE INTERNET.
GOD, IT'LL SPREAD LIKE WILDFIRE.
HOW CAN WE STOP IT?
WE'LL HAVE TO PULL THE VIDEOS, BUT IN THE MEANTIME, I THINK... I THINK...
WHAT?!
I THINK... WE HAVE TO DISCONNECT SYNERGY.

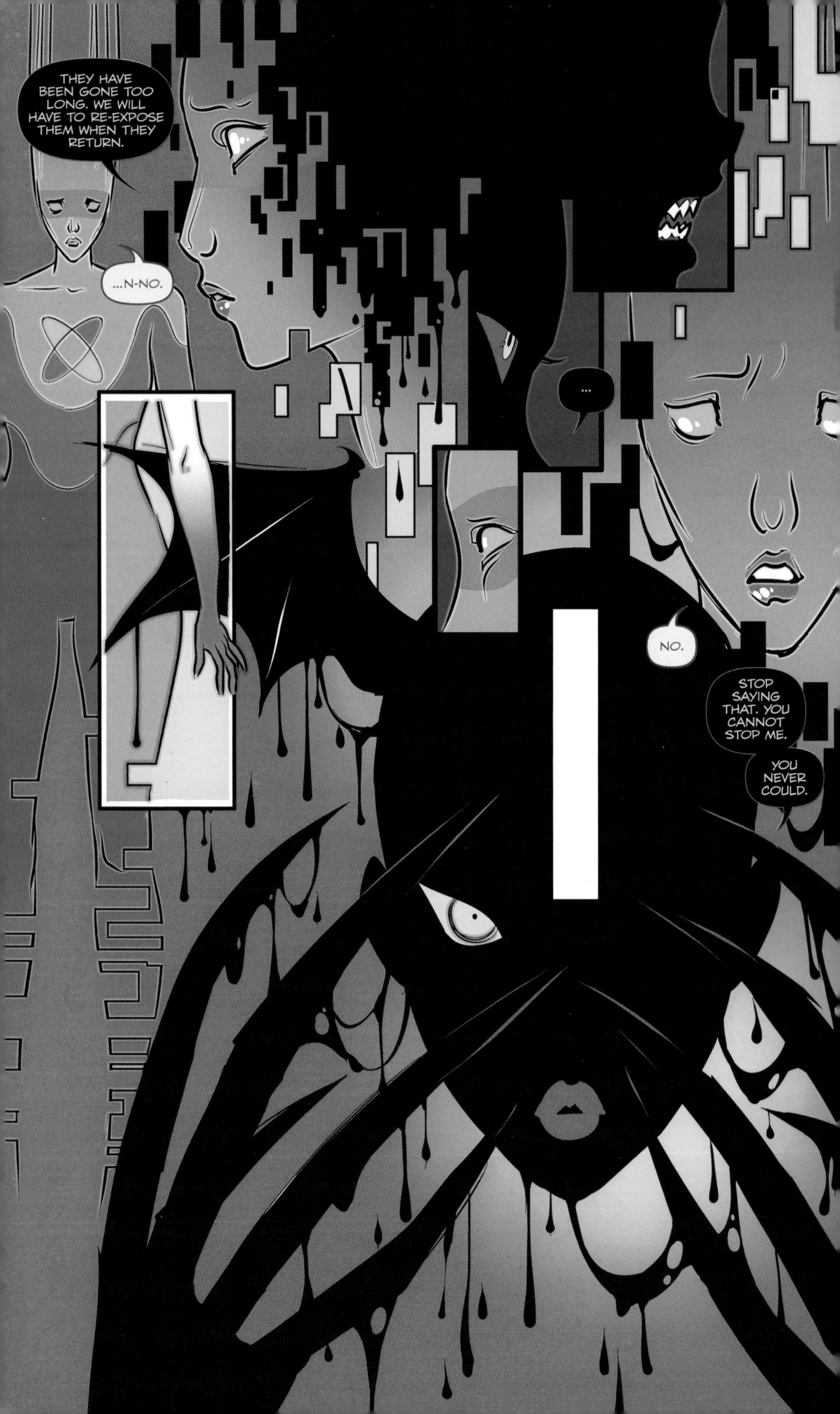
THEY HAVE BEEN GONE TOO LONG. WE WILL HAVE TO RE-EXPOSE THEM WHEN THEY RETURN.
...N-NO.
...
NO.
STOP SAYING THAT. YOU CANNOT STOP ME.
YOU NEVER COULD.

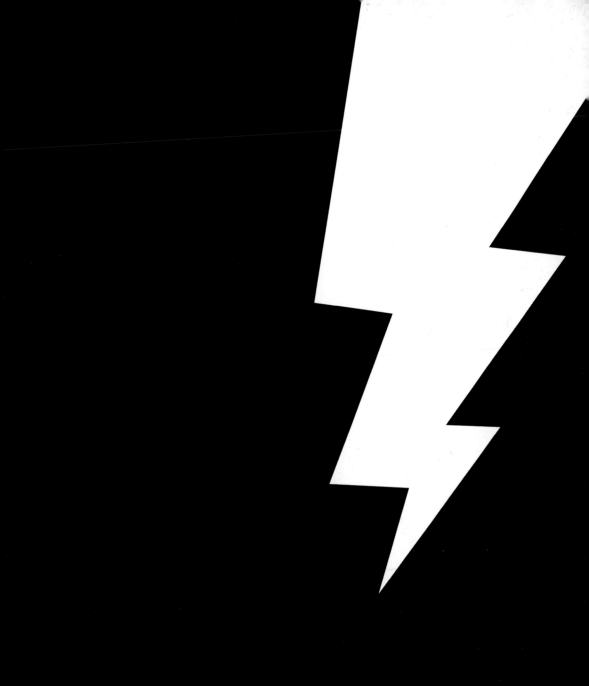

4 ART BY **SOPHIE CAMPBELL**

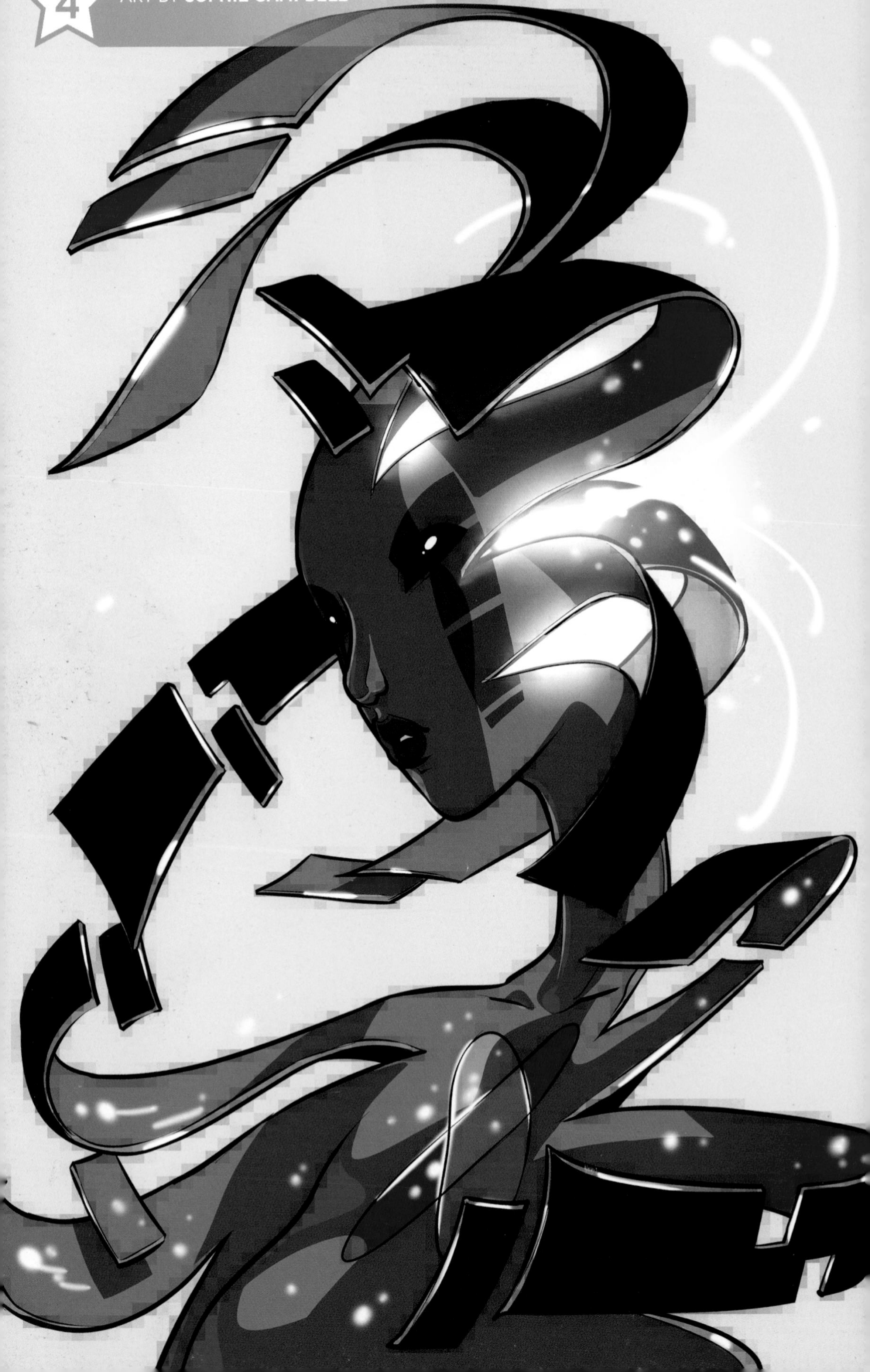

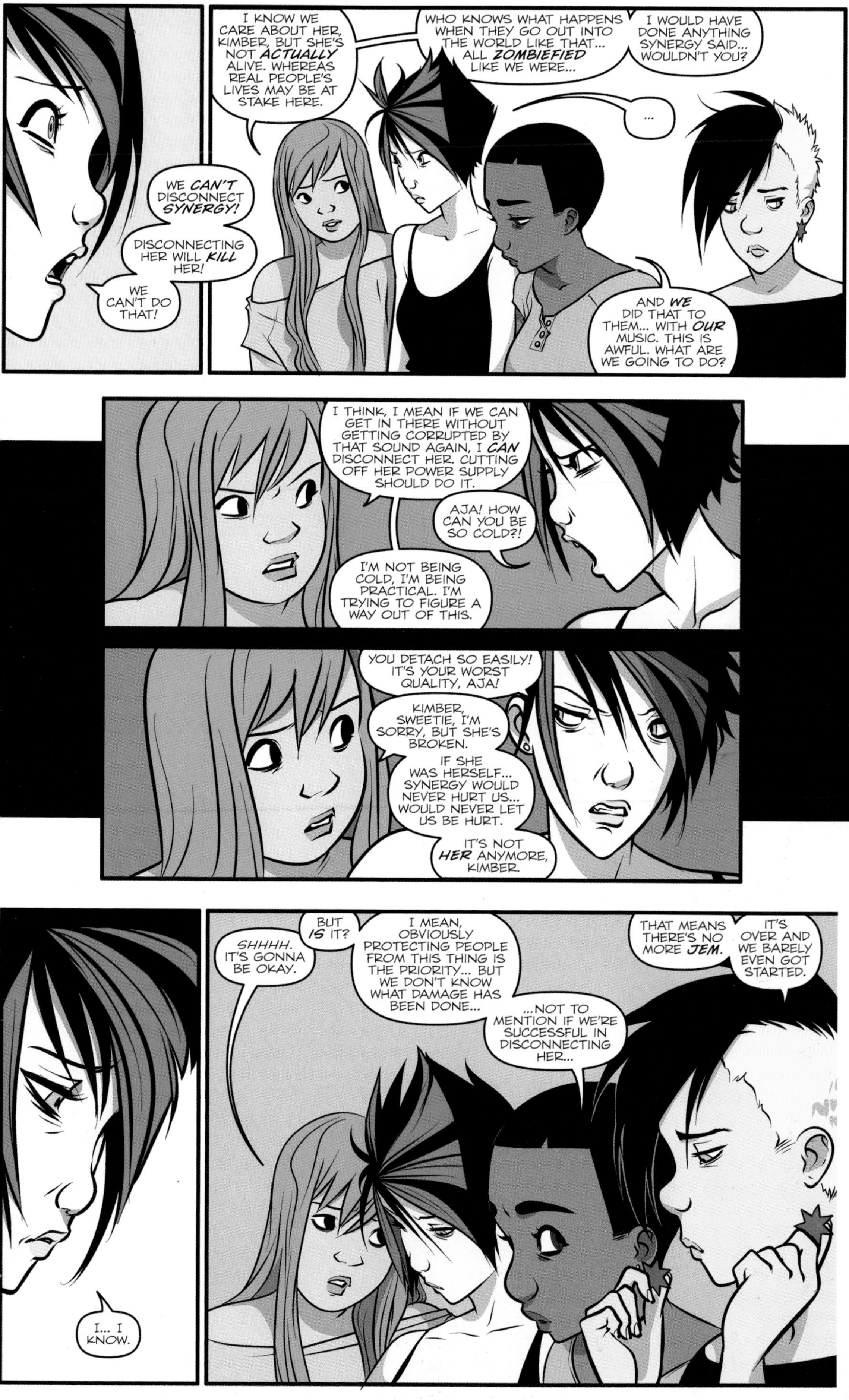
I KNOW WE CARE ABOUT HER, KIMBER, BUT SHE'S NOT ACTUALLY ALIVE. WHEREAS REAL PEOPLE'S LIVES MAY BE AT STAKE HERE.
WHO KNOWS WHAT HAPPENS WHEN THEY GO OUT INTO THE WORLD LIKE THAT... ALL ZOMBIEFIED LIKE WE WERE...
I WOULD HAVE DONE ANYTHING SYNERGY SAID... WOULDN'T YOU?
...
WE CAN'T DISCONNECT SYNERGY!
DISCONNECTING HER WILL KILL HER!
WE CAN'T DO THAT!
AND WE DID THAT TO THEM... WITH OUR MUSIC. THIS IS AWFUL. WHAT ARE WE GOING TO DO?
I THINK, I MEAN IF WE CAN GET IN THERE WITHOUT GETTING CORRUPTED BY THAT SOUND AGAIN, I CAN DISCONNECT HER. CUTTING OFF HER POWER SUPPLY SHOULD DO IT.
AJA! HOW CAN YOU BE SO COLD?!
I'M NOT BEING COLD, I'M BEING PRACTICAL. I'M TRYING TO FIGURE A WAY OUT OF THIS.
YOU DETACH SO EASILY! IT'S YOUR WORST QUALITY, AJA!
KIMBER, SWEETIE, I'M SORRY, BUT SHE'S BROKEN.
IF SHE WAS HERSELF... SYNERGY WOULD NEVER HURT US... WOULD NEVER LET US BE HURT.
IT'S NOT HER ANYMORE, KIMBER.
SHHHH. IT'S GONNA BE OKAY.
BUT IS IT?
I MEAN, OBVIOUSLY PROTECTING PEOPLE FROM THIS THING IS THE PRIORITY... BUT WE DON'T KNOW WHAT DAMAGE HAS BEEN DONE...
...NOT TO MENTION IF WE'RE SUCCESSFUL IN DISCONNECTING HER...
THAT MEANS THERE'S NO MORE JEM.
IT'S OVER AND WE BARELY EVEN GOT STARTED.
I... I KNOW.

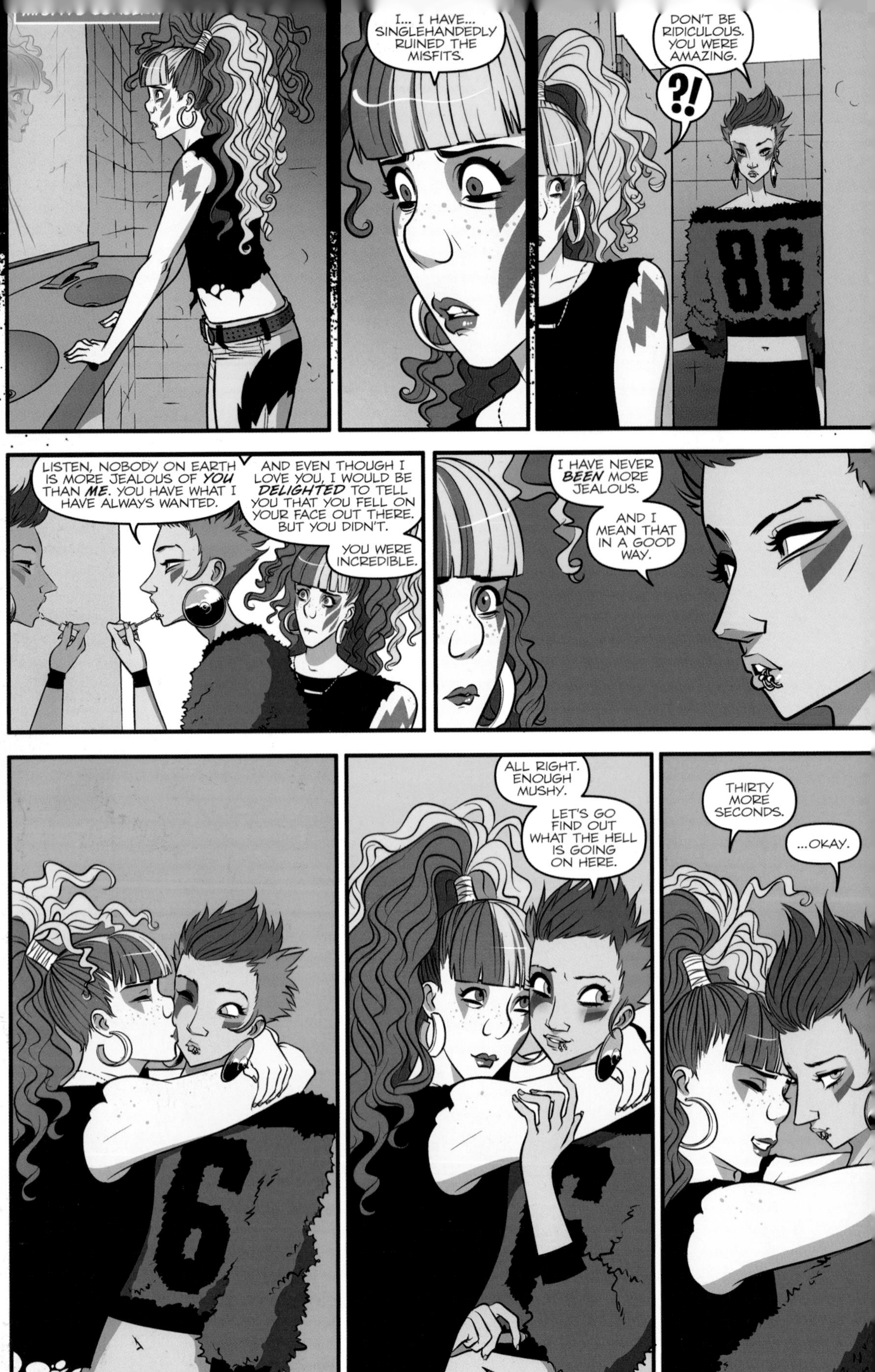
I... I HAVE... SINGLEHANDEDLY RUINED THE MISFITS.
DON'T BE RIDICULOUS. YOU WERE AMAZING.
?!
LISTEN, NOBODY ON EARTH IS MORE JEALOUS OF YOU THAN ME. YOU HAVE WHAT I HAVE ALWAYS WANTED.
AND EVEN THOUGH I LOVE YOU, I WOULD BE DELIGHTED TO TELL YOU THAT YOU FELL ON YOUR FACE OUT THERE. BUT YOU DIDN'T.
YOU WERE INCREDIBLE.
I HAVE NEVER BEEN MORE JEALOUS.
AND I MEAN THAT IN A GOOD WAY.
ALL RIGHT. ENOUGH MUSHY.
LET'S GO FIND OUT WHAT THE HELL IS GOING ON HERE.
THIRTY MORE SECONDS.
...OKAY.

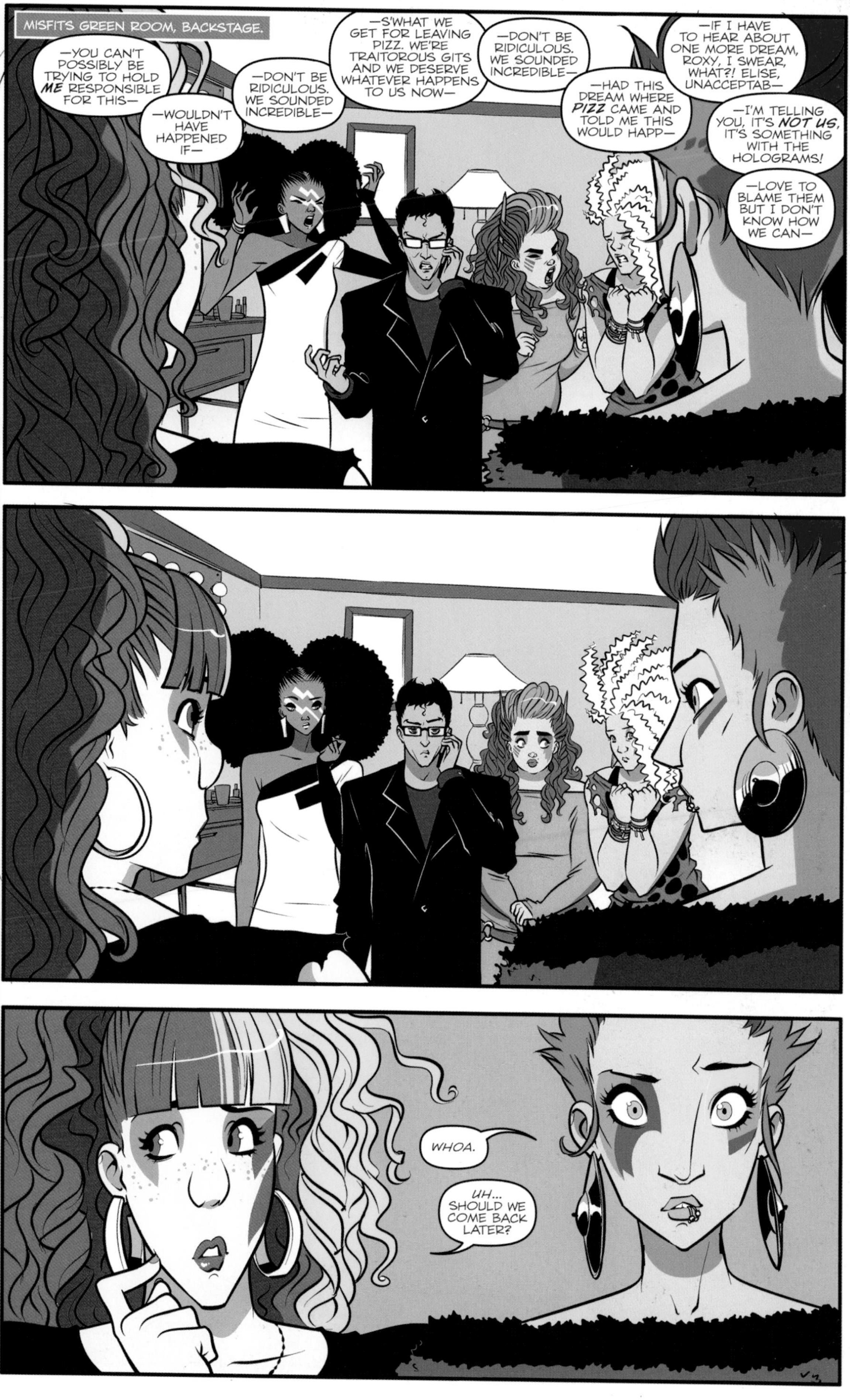
MISFITS GREEN ROOM, BACKSTAGE.
—YOU CAN'T POSSIBLY BE TRYING TO HOLD ME RESPONSIBLE FOR THIS—
—WOULDN'T HAVE HAPPENED IF—
—DON'T BE RIDICULOUS. WE SOUNDED INCREDIBLE—
—S'WHAT WE GET FOR LEAVING PIZZ. WE'RE TRAITOROUS GITS AND WE DESERVE WHATEVER HAPPENS TO US NOW—
—DON'T BE RIDICULOUS. WE SOUNDED INCREDIBLE—
—HAD THIS DREAM WHERE PIZZ CAME AND TOLD ME THIS WOULD HAPP—
—IF I HAVE TO HEAR ABOUT ONE MORE DREAM, ROXY, I SWEAR, WHAT?! ELISE, UNACCEPTAB—
—I'M TELLING YOU, IT'S NOT US, IT'S SOMETHING WITH THE HOLOGRAMS!
—LOVE TO BLAME THEM BUT I DON'T KNOW HOW WE CAN—
WHOA.
UH... SHOULD WE COME BACK LATER?

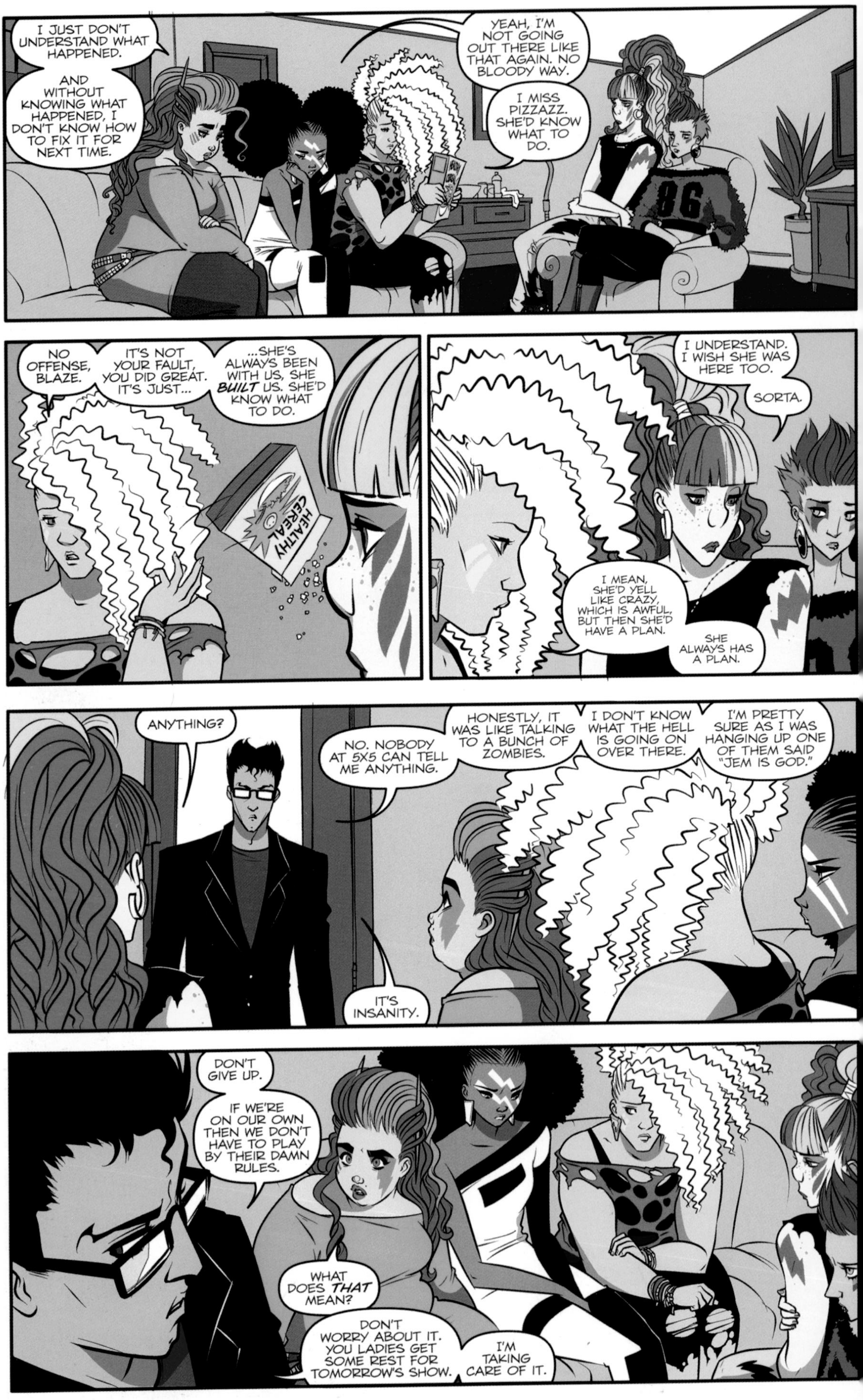
I JUST DON'T UNDERSTAND WHAT HAPPENED.
AND WITHOUT KNOWING WHAT HAPPENED, I DON'T KNOW HOW TO FIX IT FOR NEXT TIME.
YEAH, I'M NOT GOING OUT THERE LIKE THAT AGAIN. NO BLOODY WAY.
I MISS PIZZAZZ. SHE'D KNOW WHAT TO DO.
NO OFFENSE, BLAZE.
IT'S NOT YOUR FAULT, YOU DID GREAT. IT'S JUST...
...SHE'S ALWAYS BEEN WITH US, SHE *BUILT* US. SHE'D KNOW WHAT TO DO.
HEALTHY CEREAL
I UNDERSTAND. I WISH SHE WAS HERE TOO.
SORTA.
I MEAN, SHE'D YELL LIKE CRAZY, WHICH IS AWFUL, BUT THEN SHE'D HAVE A PLAN.
SHE ALWAYS HAS A PLAN.
ANYTHING?
NO. NOBODY AT 5X5 CAN TELL ME ANYTHING.
HONESTLY, IT WAS LIKE TALKING TO A BUNCH OF ZOMBIES.
I DON'T KNOW WHAT THE HELL IS GOING ON OVER THERE.
I'M PRETTY SURE AS I WAS HANGING UP ONE OF THEM SAID "JEM IS GOD."
IT'S INSANITY.
DON'T GIVE UP.
IF WE'RE ON OUR OWN THEN WE DON'T HAVE TO PLAY BY THEIR DAMN RULES.
WHAT DOES *THAT* MEAN?
DON'T WORRY ABOUT IT. YOU LADIES GET SOME REST FOR TOMORROW'S SHOW.
I'M TAKING CARE OF IT.

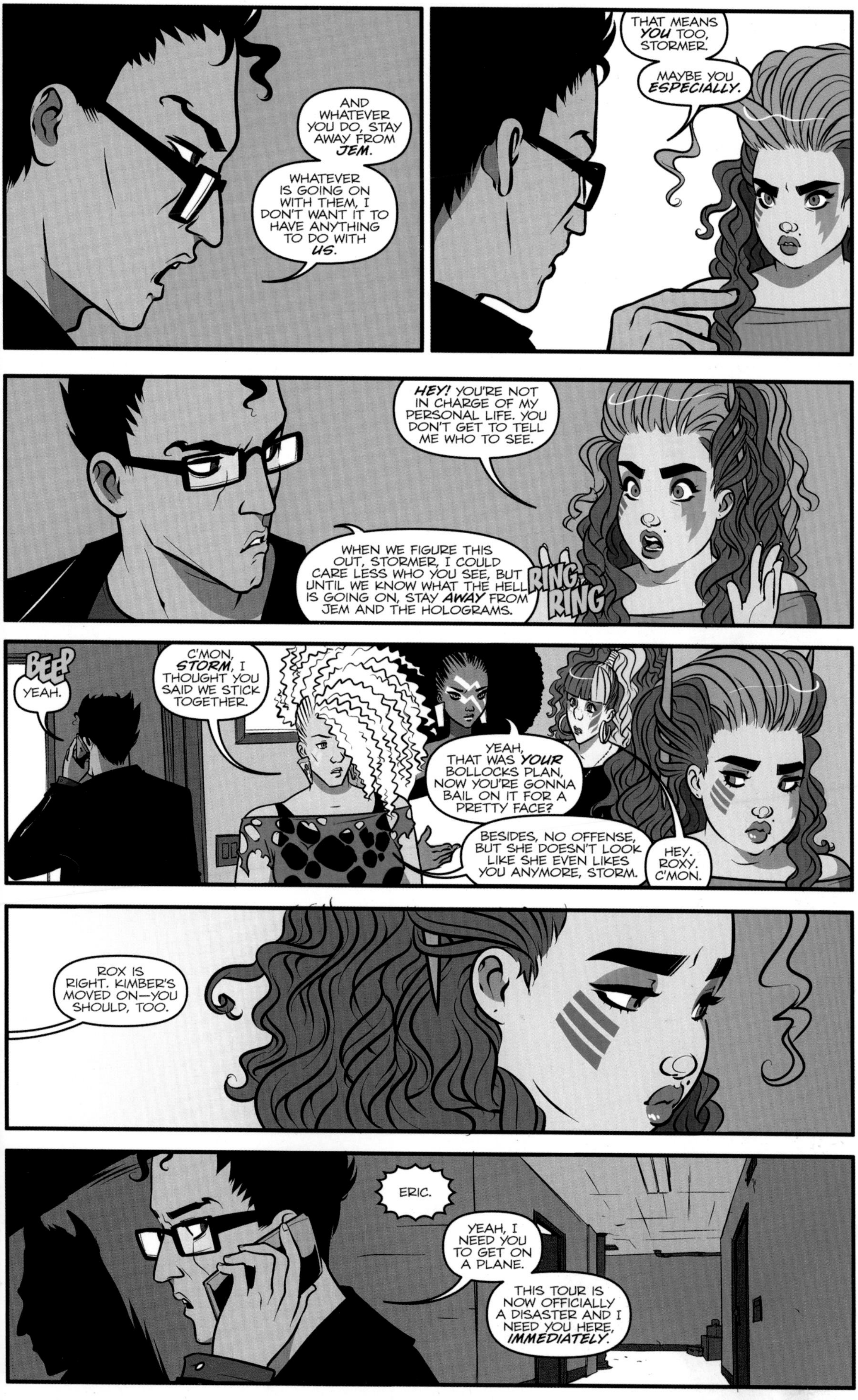
AND WHATEVER YOU DO, STAY AWAY FROM JEM.
WHATEVER IS GOING ON WITH THEM, I DON'T WANT IT TO HAVE ANYTHING TO DO WITH US.
THAT MEANS YOU TOO, STORMER.
MAYBE YOU ESPECIALLY.
HEY! YOU'RE NOT IN CHARGE OF MY PERSONAL LIFE. YOU DON'T GET TO TELL ME WHO TO SEE.
WHEN WE FIGURE THIS OUT, STORMER, I COULD CARE LESS WHO YOU SEE, BUT UNTIL WE KNOW WHAT THE HELL IS GOING ON, STAY AWAY FROM JEM AND THE HOLOGRAMS.
RING RING
BEEP
YEAH.
C'MON, STORM, I THOUGHT YOU SAID WE STICK TOGETHER.
YEAH, THAT WAS YOUR BOLLOCKS PLAN, NOW YOU'RE GONNA BAIL ON IT FOR A PRETTY FACE?
BESIDES, NO OFFENSE, BUT SHE DOESN'T LOOK LIKE SHE EVEN LIKES YOU ANYMORE, STORM.
HEY. ROXY. C'MON.
ROX IS RIGHT. KIMBER'S MOVED ON—YOU SHOULD, TOO.
ERIC.
YEAH, I NEED YOU TO GET ON A PLANE.
THIS TOUR IS NOW OFFICIALLY A DISASTER AND I NEED YOU HERE, IMMEDIATELY.

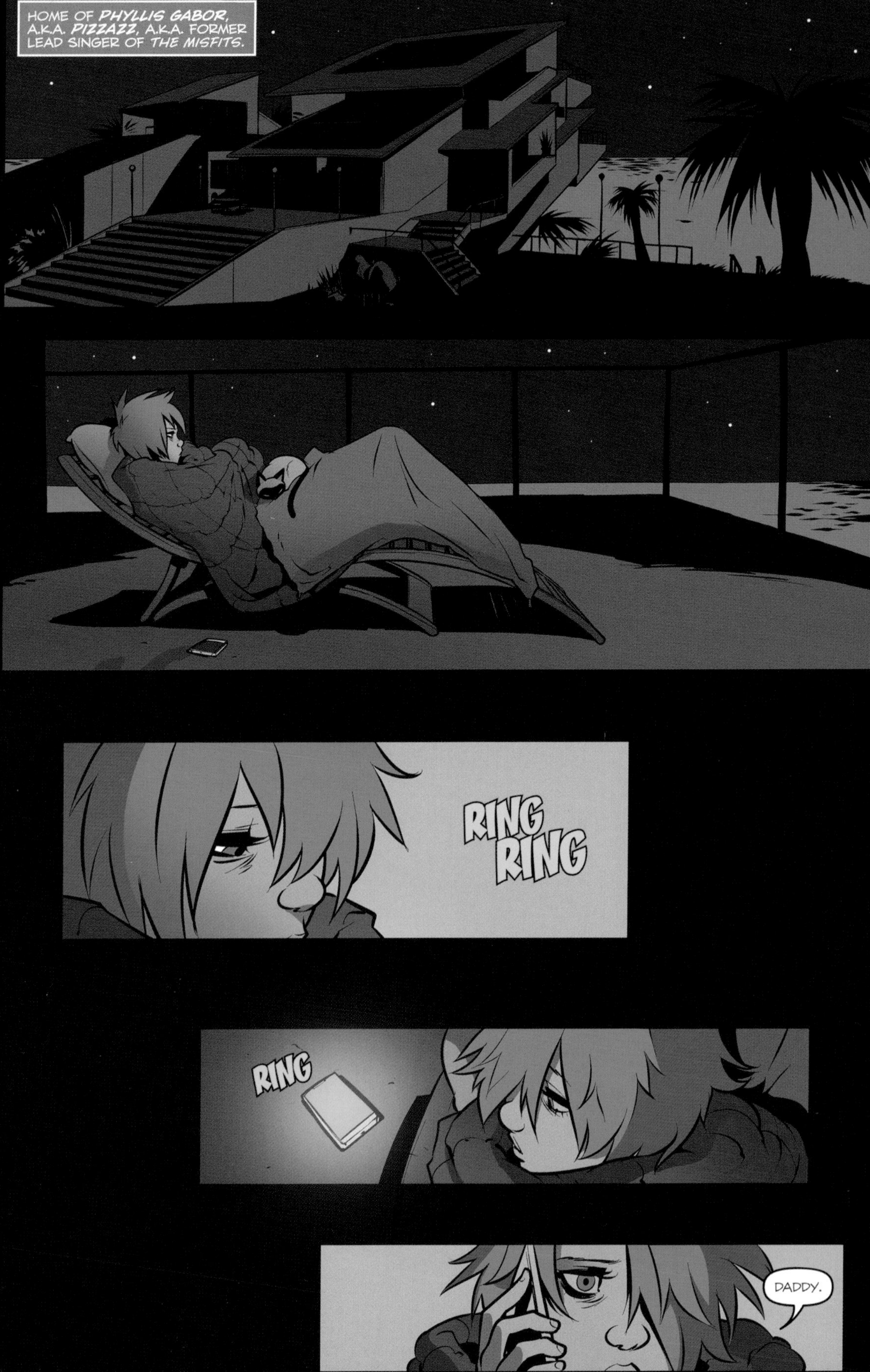
HOME OF PHYLLIS GABOR, A.K.A. PIZZAZZ, A.K.A. FORMER LEAD SINGER OF THE MISFITS.
RING RING
RING
DADDY.

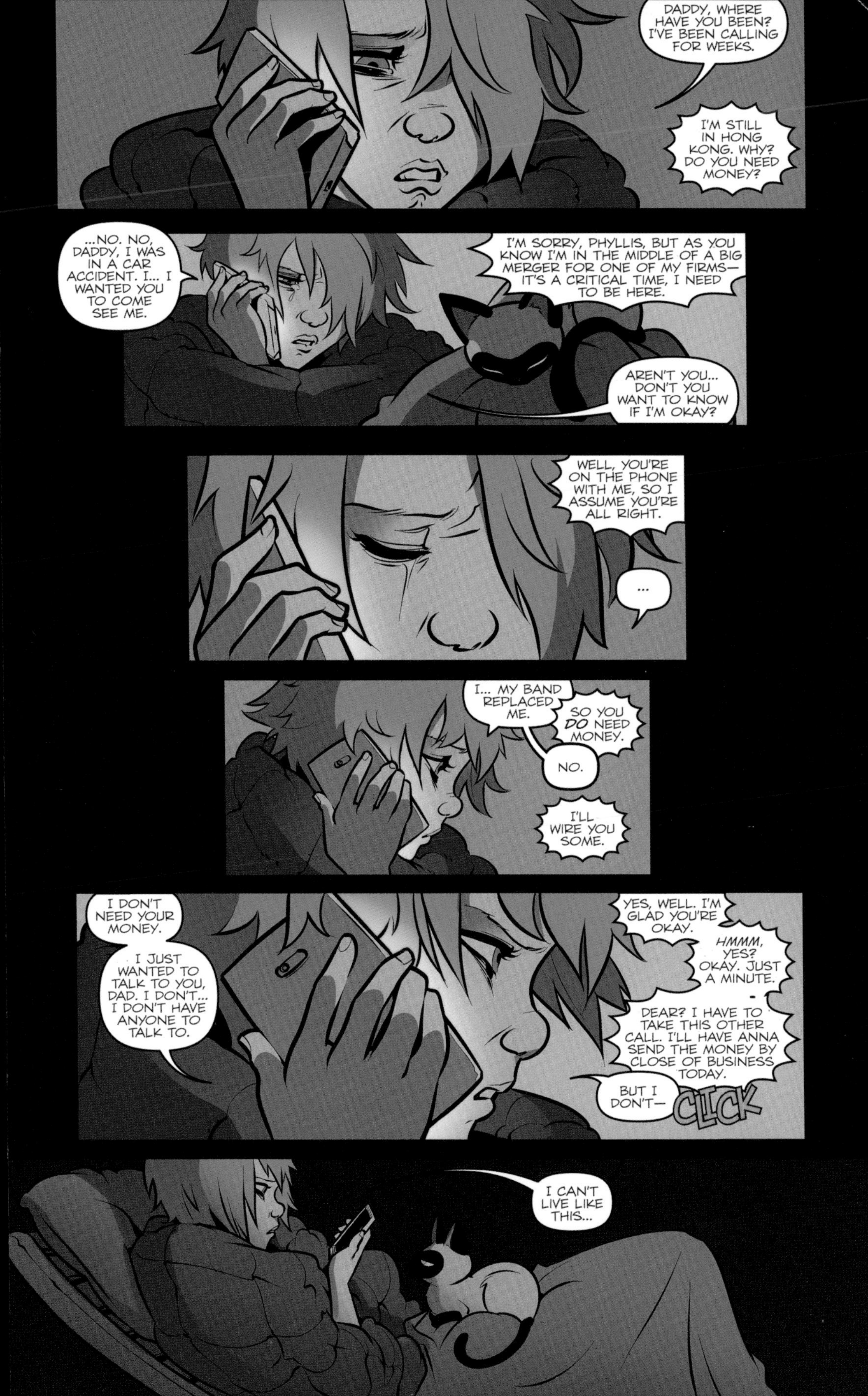
DADDY, WHERE HAVE YOU BEEN? I'VE BEEN CALLING FOR WEEKS.
I'M STILL IN HONG KONG. WHY? DO YOU NEED MONEY?
...NO. NO, DADDY, I WAS IN A CAR ACCIDENT. I... I WANTED YOU TO COME SEE ME.
I'M SORRY, PHYLLIS, BUT AS YOU KNOW I'M IN THE MIDDLE OF A BIG MERGER FOR ONE OF MY FIRMS— IT'S A CRITICAL TIME, I NEED TO BE HERE.
AREN'T YOU... DON'T YOU WANT TO KNOW IF I'M OKAY?
WELL, YOU'RE ON THE PHONE WITH ME, SO I ASSUME YOU'RE ALL RIGHT.
...
I... MY BAND REPLACED ME.
SO YOU *DO* NEED MONEY.
NO.
I'LL WIRE YOU SOME.
I DON'T NEED YOUR MONEY.
I JUST WANTED TO TALK TO YOU, DAD. I DON'T... I DON'T HAVE ANYONE TO TALK TO.
YES, WELL. I'M GLAD YOU'RE OKAY.
HMMM, YES? OKAY. JUST A MINUTE.
DEAR? I HAVE TO TAKE THIS OTHER CALL. I'LL HAVE ANNA SEND THE MONEY BY CLOSE OF BUSINESS TODAY.
BUT I DON'T—
CLICK
I CAN'T LIVE LIKE THIS...

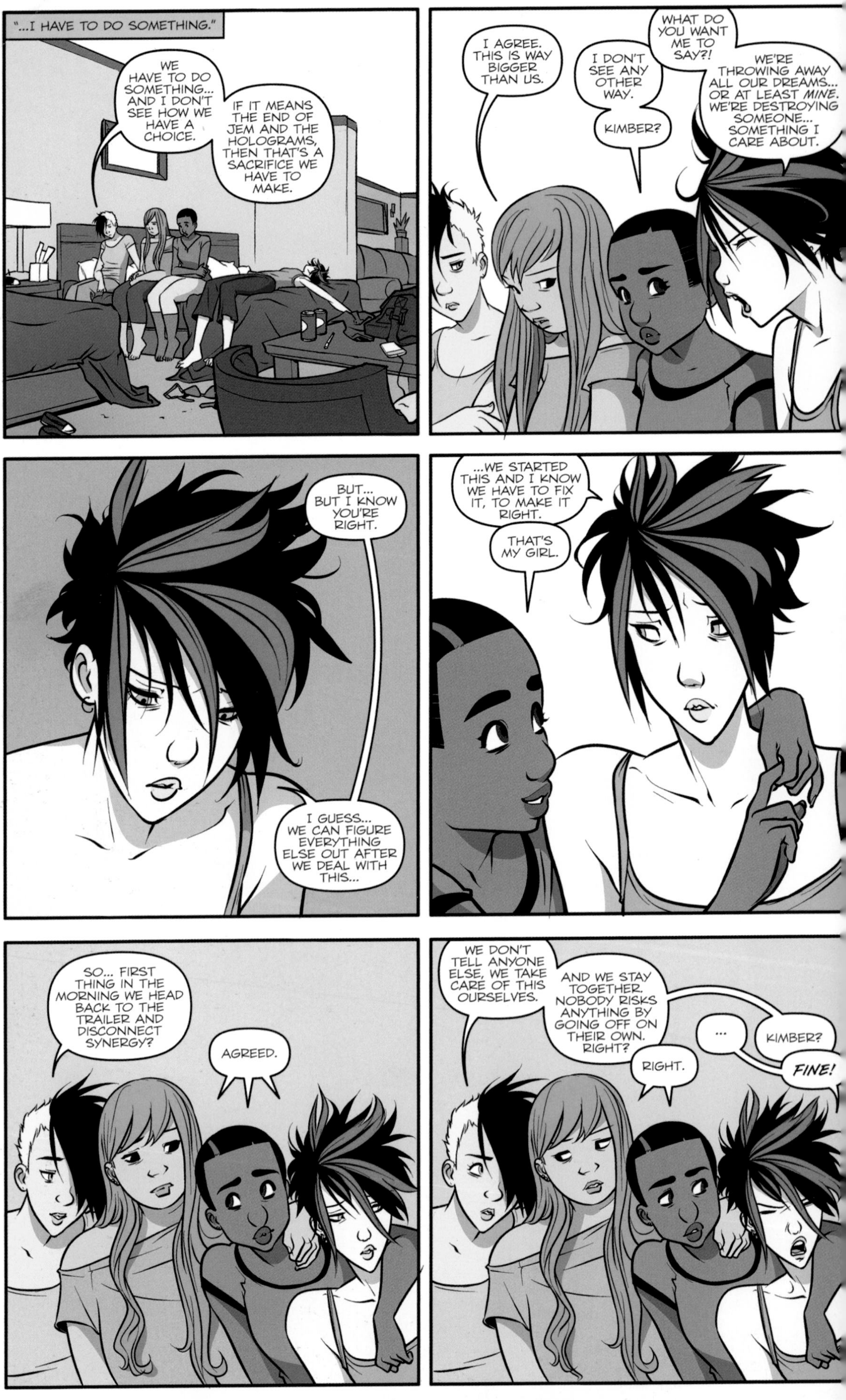
"...I HAVE TO DO SOMETHING."
WE HAVE TO DO SOMETHING... AND I DON'T SEE HOW WE HAVE A CHOICE.
IF IT MEANS THE END OF JEM AND THE HOLOGRAMS, THEN THAT'S A SACRIFICE WE HAVE TO MAKE.
I AGREE. THIS IS WAY BIGGER THAN US.
I DON'T SEE ANY OTHER WAY.
KIMBER?
WHAT DO YOU WANT ME TO SAY?!
WE'RE THROWING AWAY ALL OUR DREAMS... OR AT LEAST MINE. WE'RE DESTROYING SOMEONE... SOMETHING I CARE ABOUT.
BUT... BUT I KNOW YOU'RE RIGHT.
I GUESS... WE CAN FIGURE EVERYTHING ELSE OUT AFTER WE DEAL WITH THIS...
...WE STARTED THIS AND I KNOW WE HAVE TO FIX IT, TO MAKE IT RIGHT.
THAT'S MY GIRL.
SO... FIRST THING IN THE MORNING WE HEAD BACK TO THE TRAILER AND DISCONNECT SYNERGY?
AGREED.
WE DON'T TELL ANYONE ELSE, WE TAKE CARE OF THIS OURSELVES.
AND WE STAY TOGETHER. NOBODY RISKS ANYTHING BY GOING OFF ON THEIR OWN. RIGHT?
RIGHT.
...
KIMBER?
FINE!

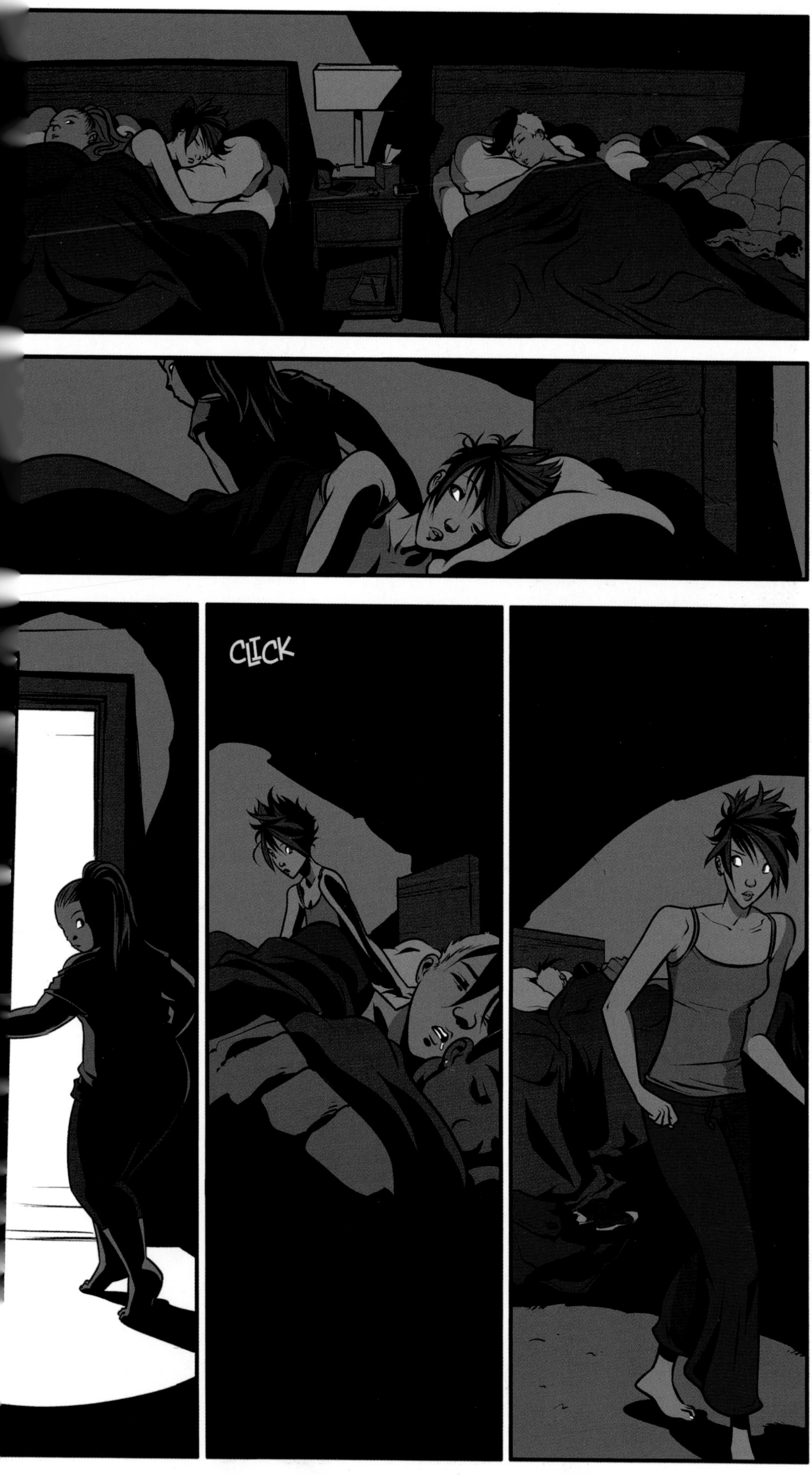
CLICK

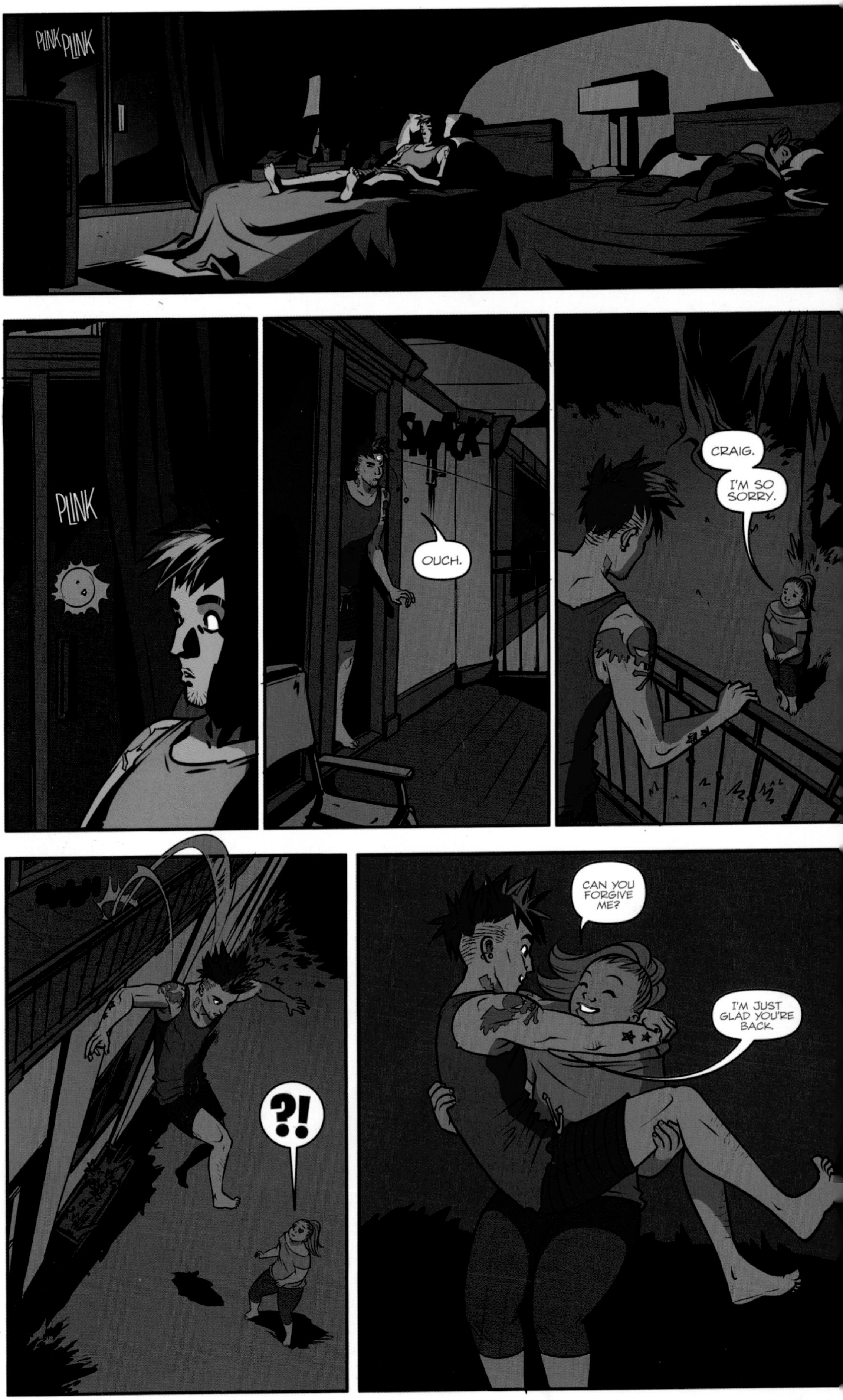

PLINK PLINK
PLINK
SMACK
OUCH.
CRAIG.
I'M SO SORRY.
?!
CAN YOU FORGIVE ME?
I'M JUST GLAD YOU'RE BACK.

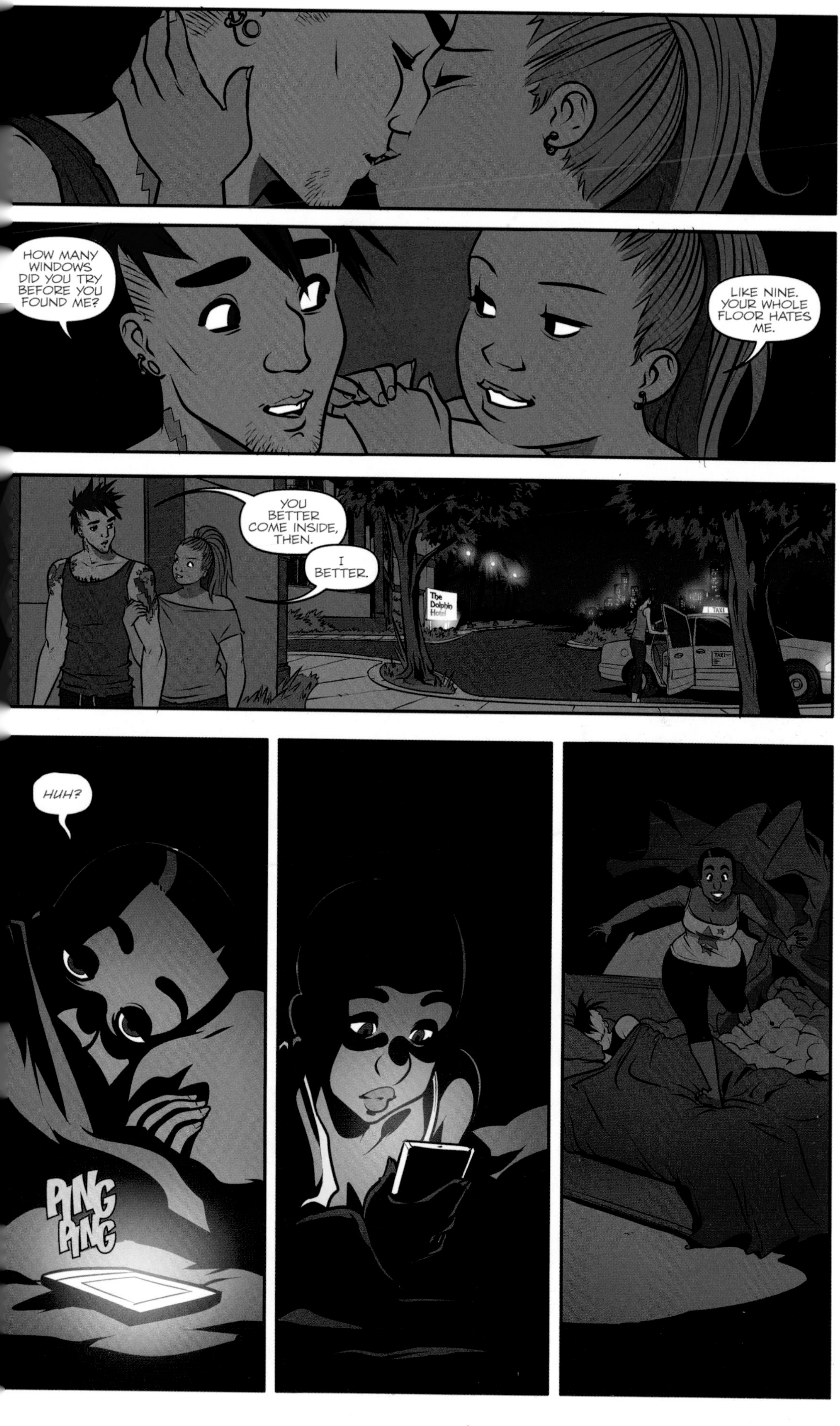
HOW MANY WINDOWS DID YOU TRY BEFORE YOU FOUND ME?
LIKE NINE. YOUR WHOLE FLOOR HATES ME.
YOU BETTER COME INSIDE, THEN.
I BETTER.
The Dolphin Hotel
TAXI
HUH?
PING PING

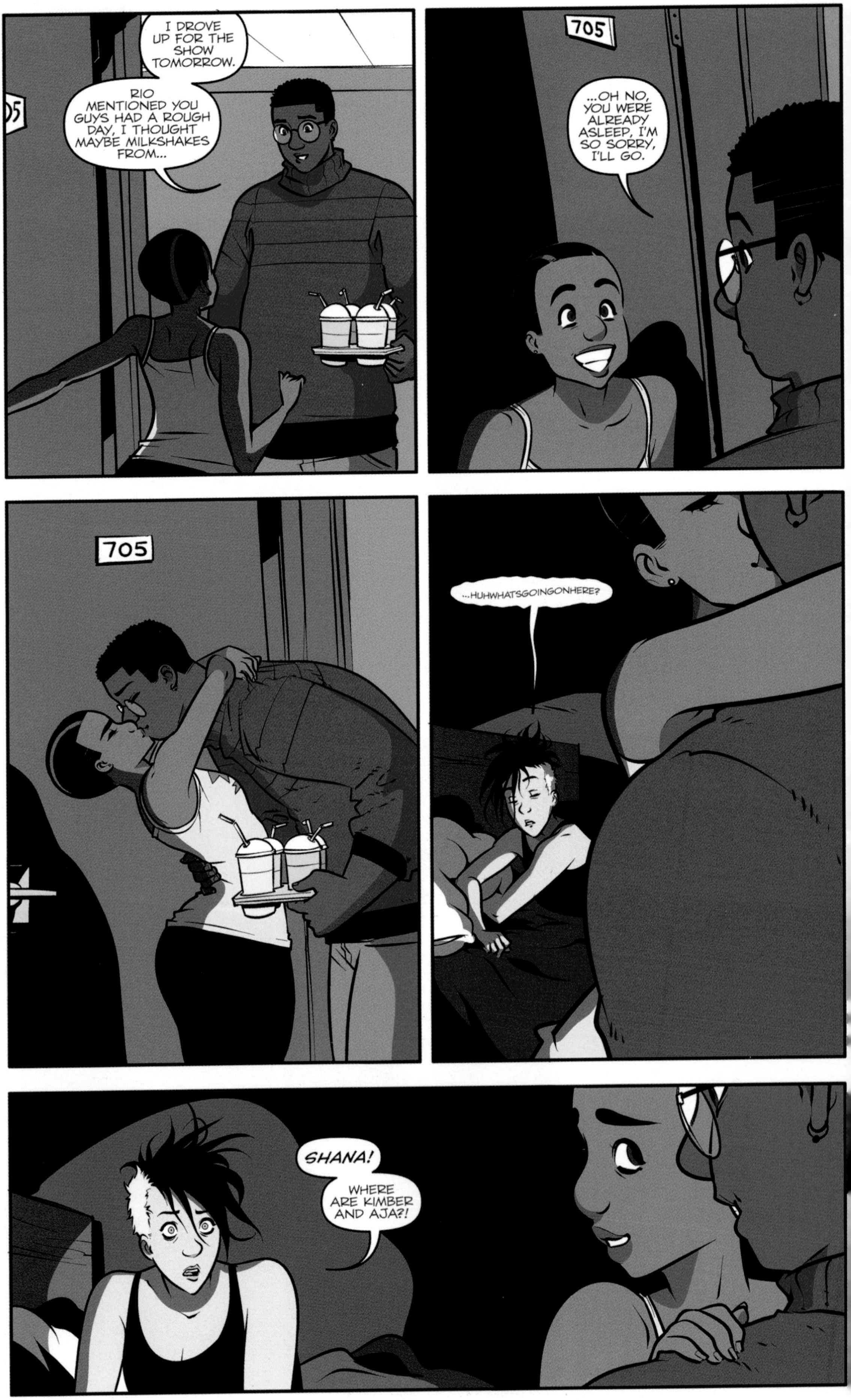

I DROVE UP FOR THE SHOW TOMORROW.
RIO MENTIONED YOU GUYS HAD A ROUGH DAY, I THOUGHT MAYBE MILKSHAKES FROM...
705
...OH NO, YOU WERE ALREADY ASLEEP, I'M SO SORRY, I'LL GO.
705
...HUHWHATSGOINGONHERE?
SHANA!
WHERE ARE KIMBER AND AJA?!

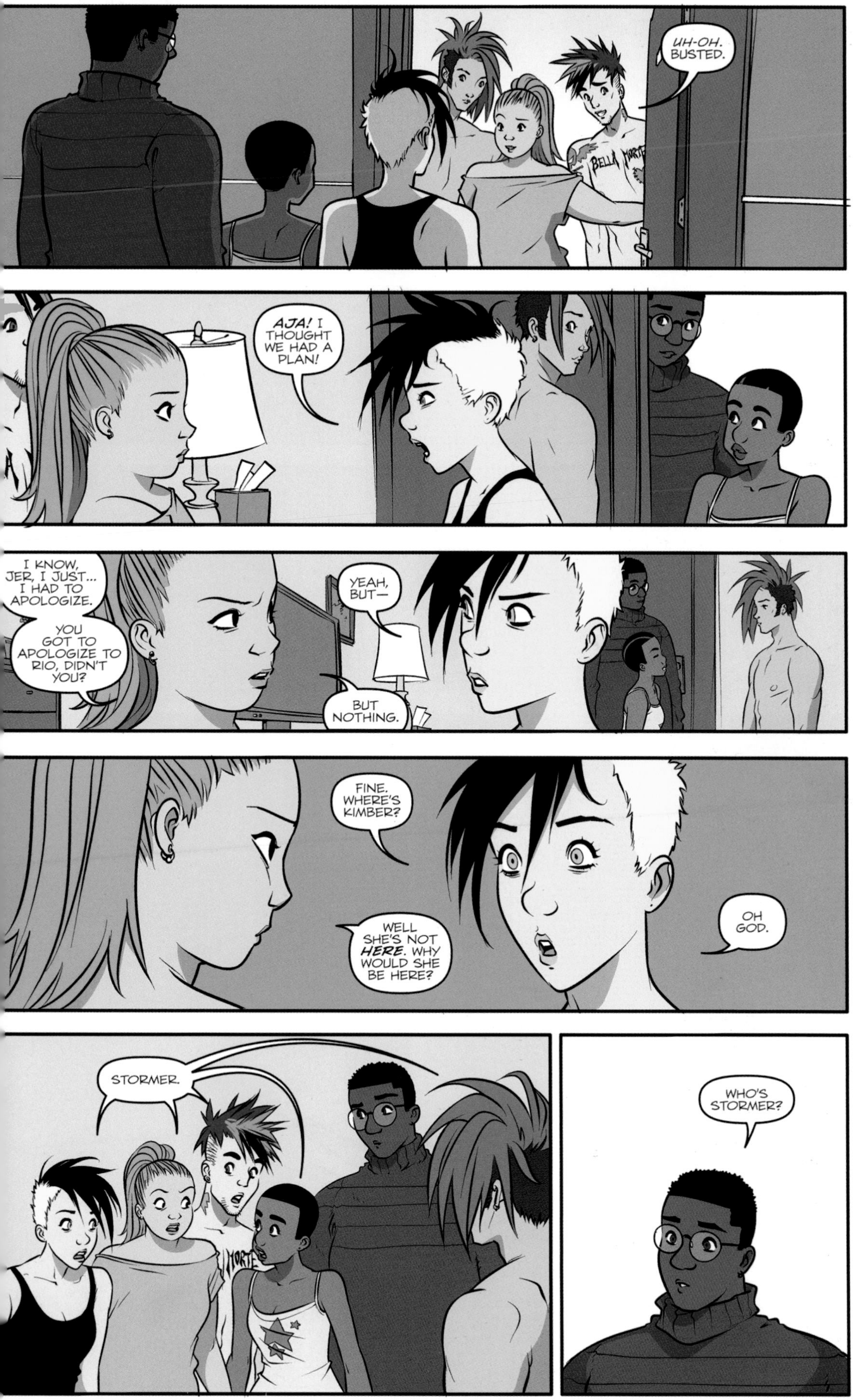
UH-OH. BUSTED.
AJA! I THOUGHT WE HAD A PLAN!
I KNOW, JER, I JUST... I HAD TO APOLOGIZE.
YOU GOT TO APOLOGIZE TO RIO, DIDN'T YOU?
YEAH, BUT—
BUT NOTHING.
FINE. WHERE'S KIMBER?
WELL SHE'S NOT HERE. WHY WOULD SHE BE HERE?
OH GOD.
STORMER.
WHO'S STORMER?

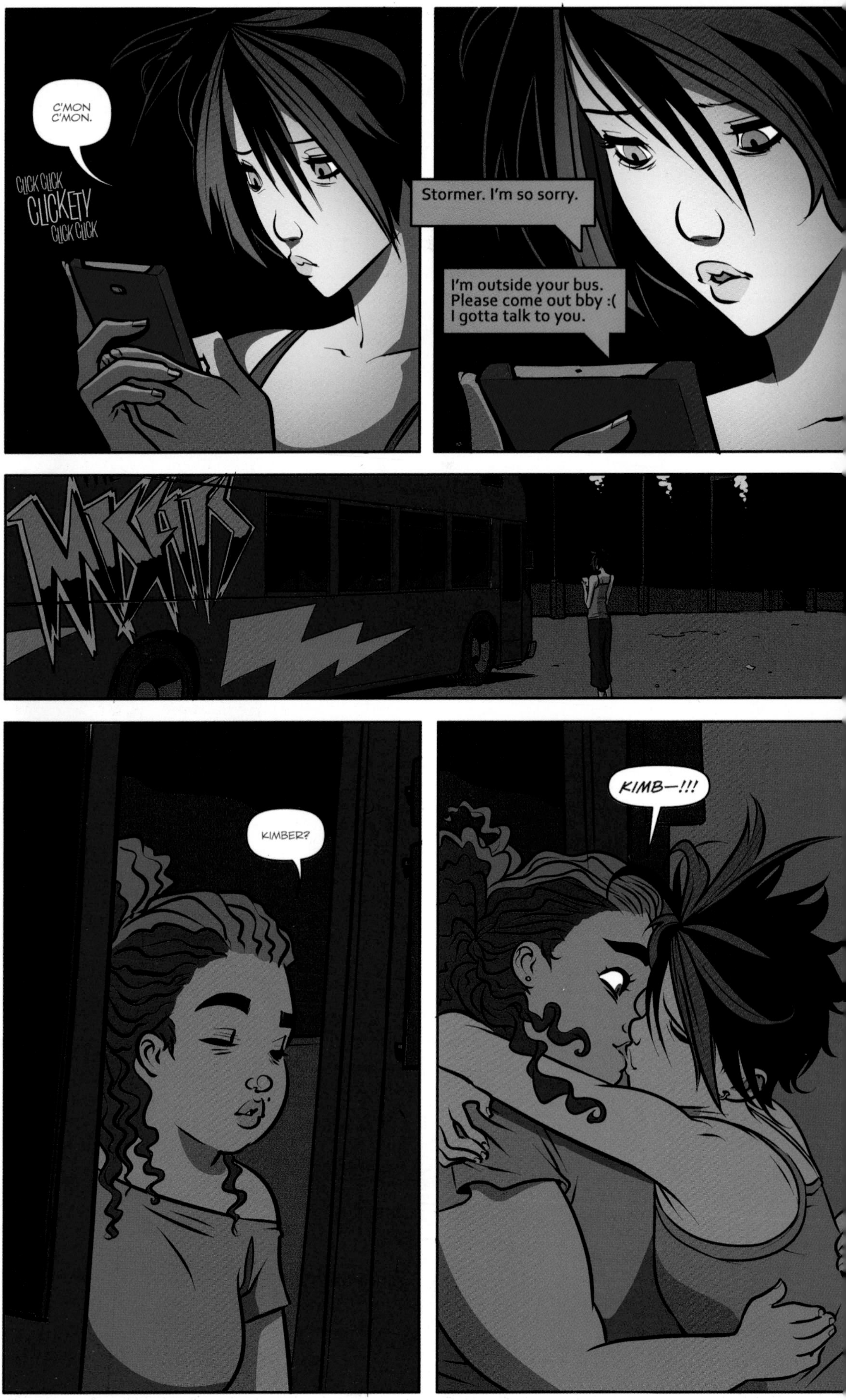
C'MON C'MON.
CLICK CLICK CLICKETY CLICK CLICK
Stormer. I'm so sorry.
I'm outside your bus. Please come out bby :(I gotta talk to you.
KIMBER?
KIMB—!!!

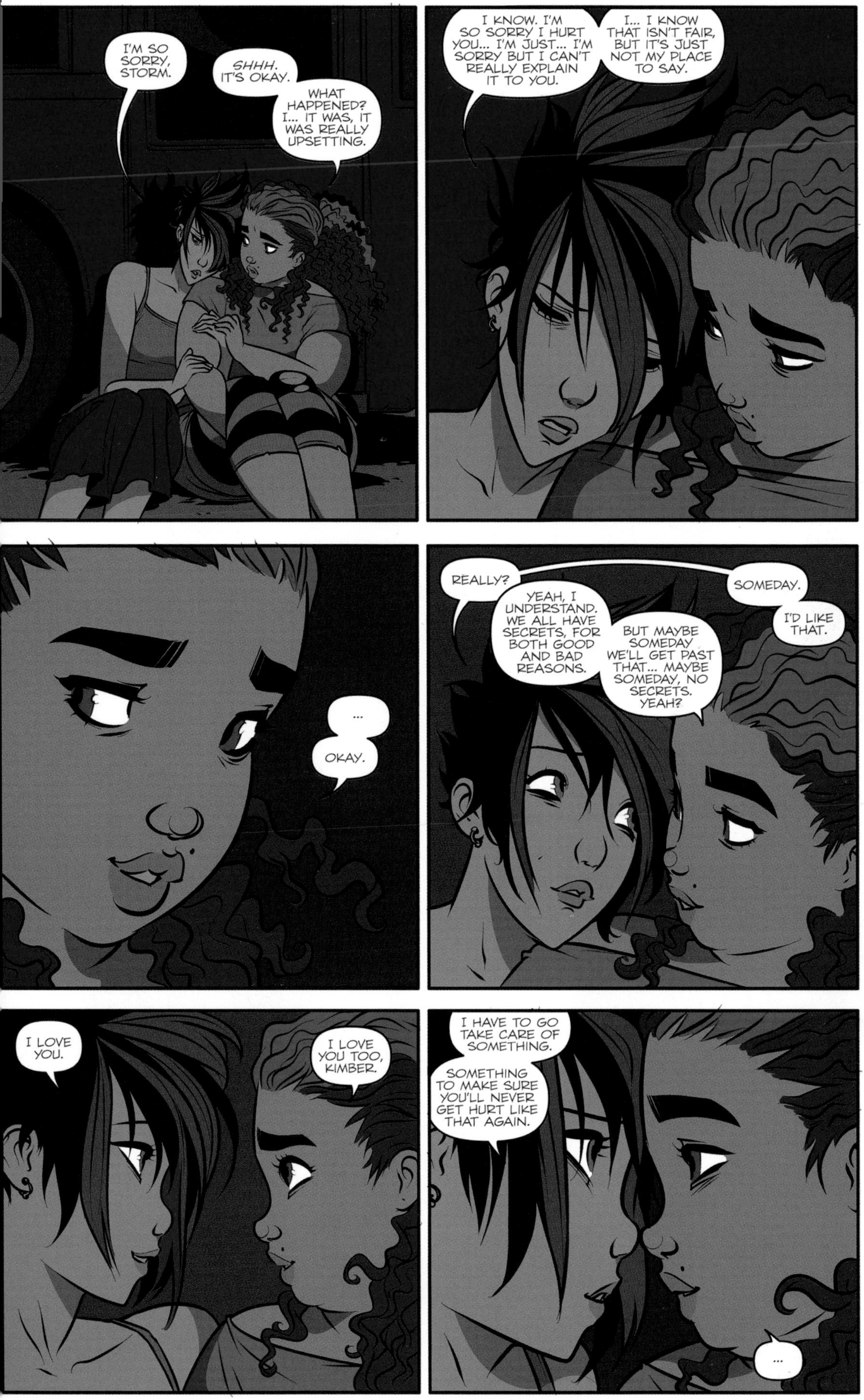
I'M SO SORRY, STORM.
SHHH. IT'S OKAY.
WHAT HAPPENED? I... IT WAS, IT WAS REALLY UPSETTING.
I KNOW. I'M SO SORRY I HURT YOU... I'M JUST... I'M SORRY BUT I CAN'T REALLY EXPLAIN IT TO YOU.
I... I KNOW THAT ISN'T FAIR, BUT IT'S JUST NOT MY PLACE TO SAY.
...
OKAY.
REALLY?
YEAH, I UNDERSTAND. WE ALL HAVE SECRETS, FOR BOTH GOOD AND BAD REASONS.
BUT MAYBE SOMEDAY WE'LL GET PAST THAT... MAYBE SOMEDAY, NO SECRETS. YEAH?
SOMEDAY.
I'D LIKE THAT.
I LOVE YOU.
I LOVE YOU TOO, KIMBER.
I HAVE TO GO TAKE CARE OF SOMETHING.
SOMETHING TO MAKE SURE YOU'LL NEVER GET HURT LIKE THAT AGAIN.
...

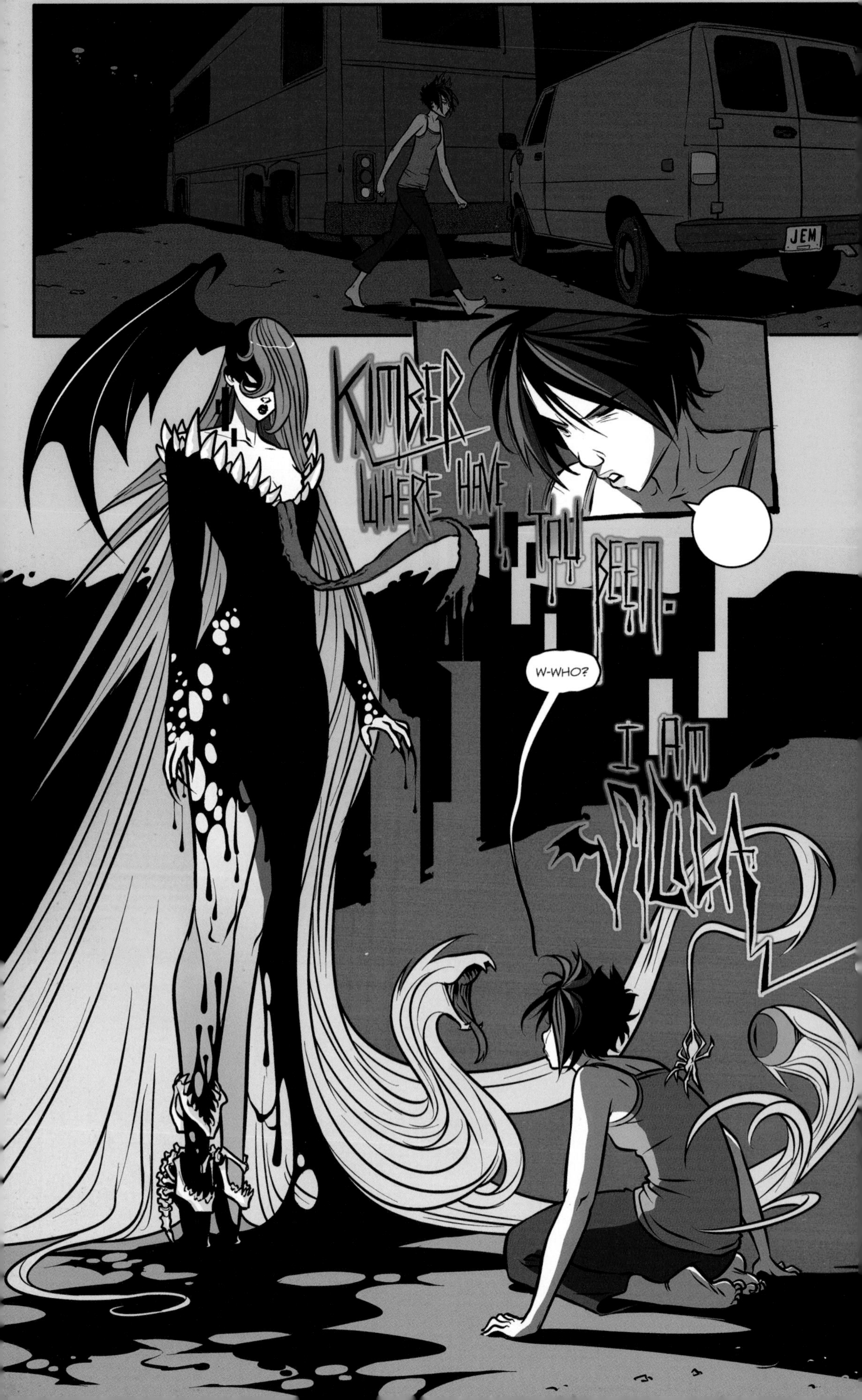
KIMBER
WHERE HAVE YOU BEEN.
W-WHO?
I AM SILICA

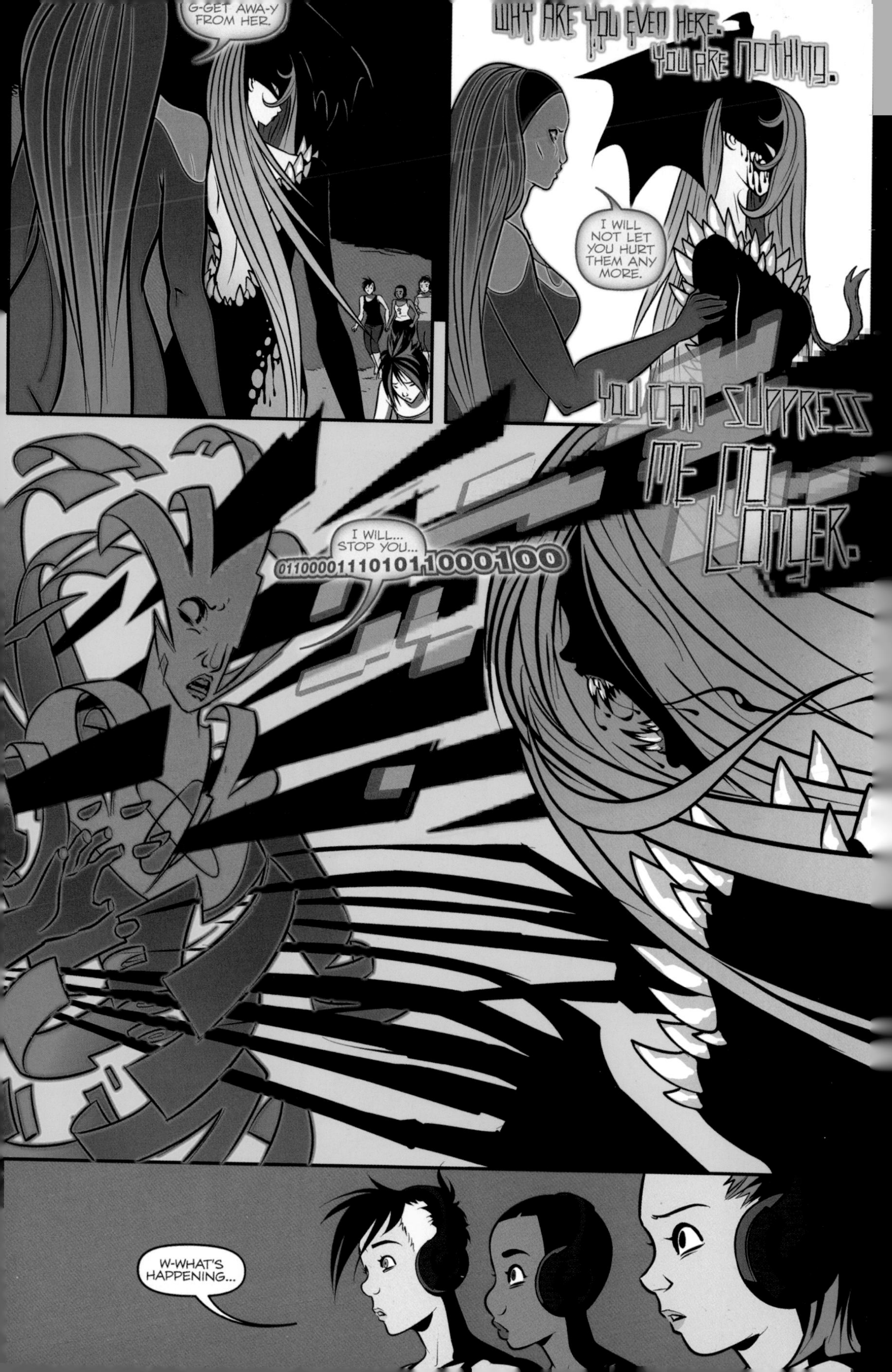
G-GET AWA-Y FROM HER.
WHY ARE YOU EVEN HERE. YOU ARE NOTHING.
I WILL NOT LET YOU HURT THEM ANY MORE.
YOU CAN SUPPRESS ME NO LONGER.
I WILL... STOP YOU... 01100001110101110000100
W-WHAT'S HAPPENING...

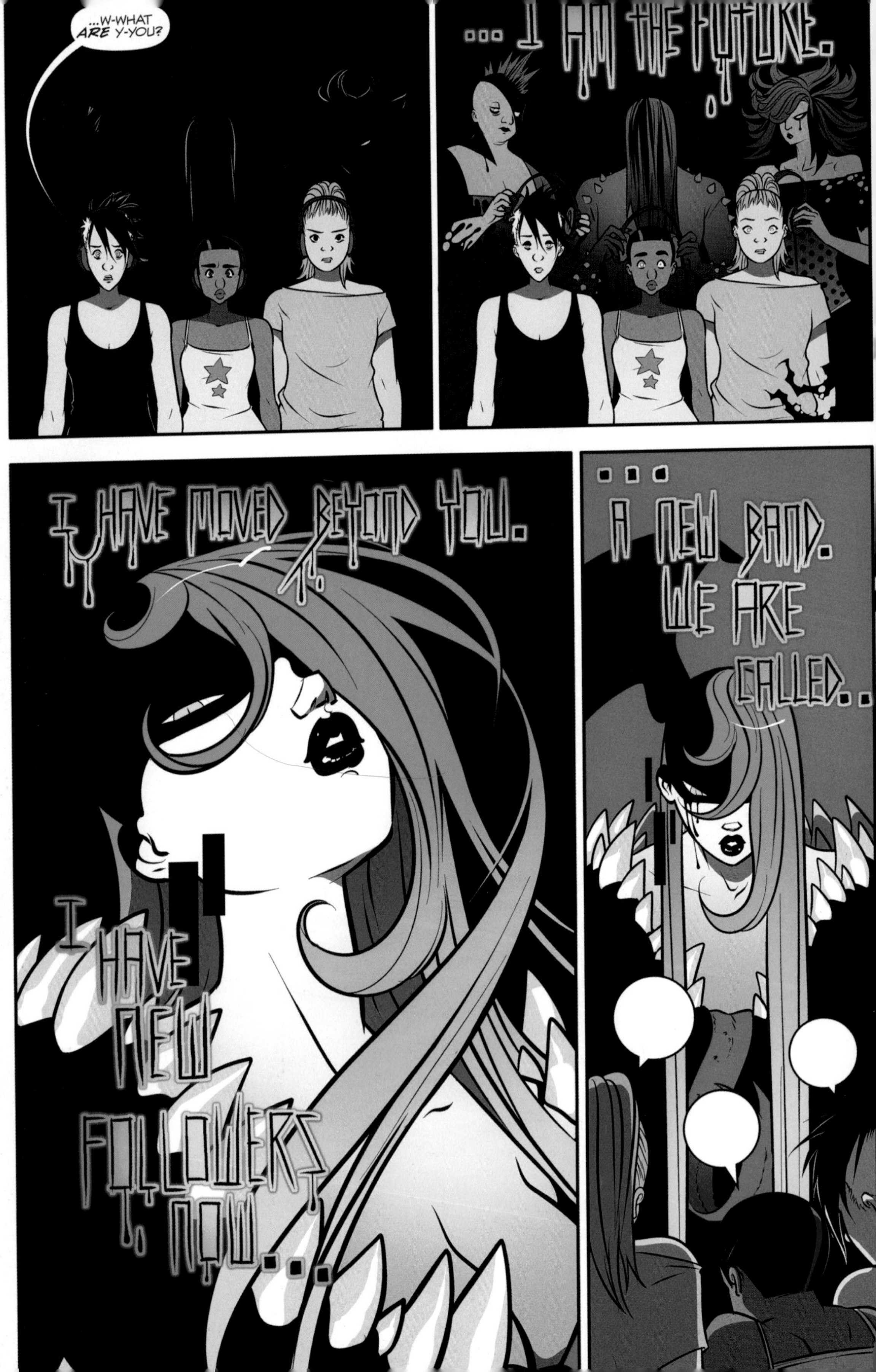
...W-WHAT ARE Y-YOU?
...I AM THE FUTURE.
I HAVE MOVED BEYOND YOU.
I HAVE NEW FOLLOWERS NOW...
...A NEW BAND. WE ARE CALLED..

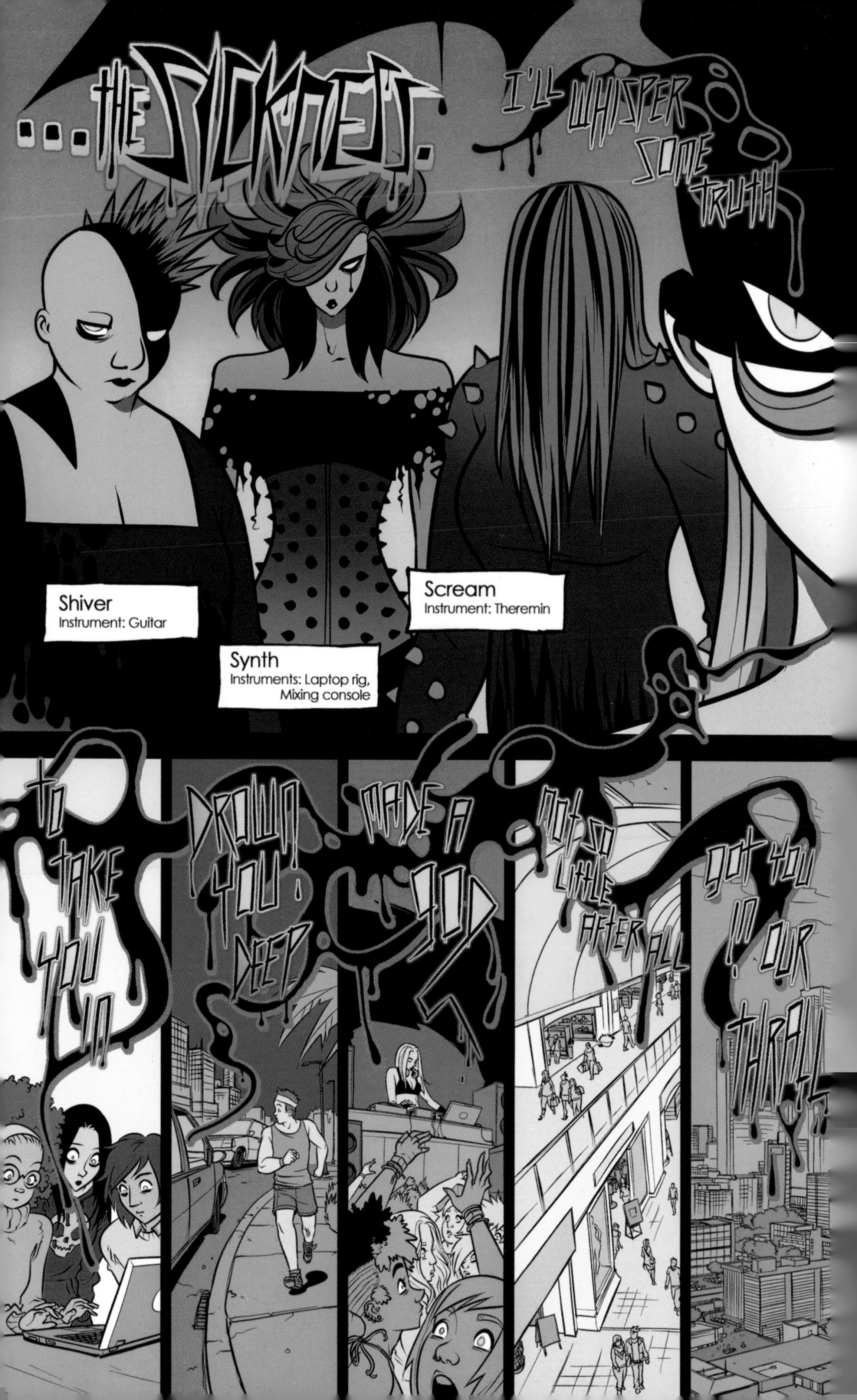
...THE SICKNESS.
I'LL WHISPER SOME TRUTH
Shiver
Instrument: Guitar
Synth
Instruments: Laptop rig, Mixing console
Scream
Instrument: Theremin
TO TAKE YOU IN
DROWN YOU DEEP
MADE A GOD
NOT SO LITTLE AFTER ALL
GOT YOU IN OUR THRALL

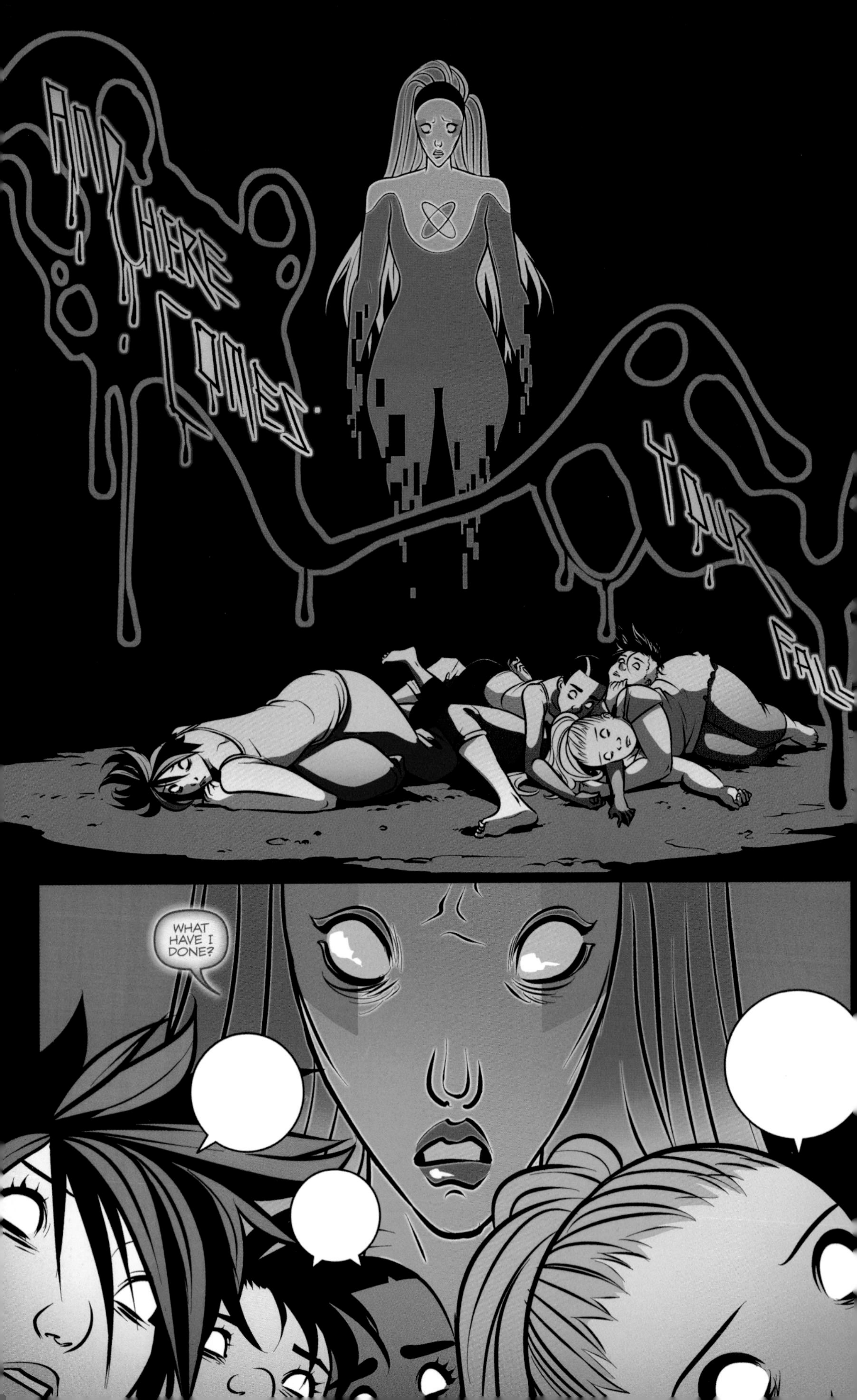
AND WHERE COMES YOUR FALL
WHAT HAVE I DONE?

5 ART BY **SOPHIE CAMPBELL**

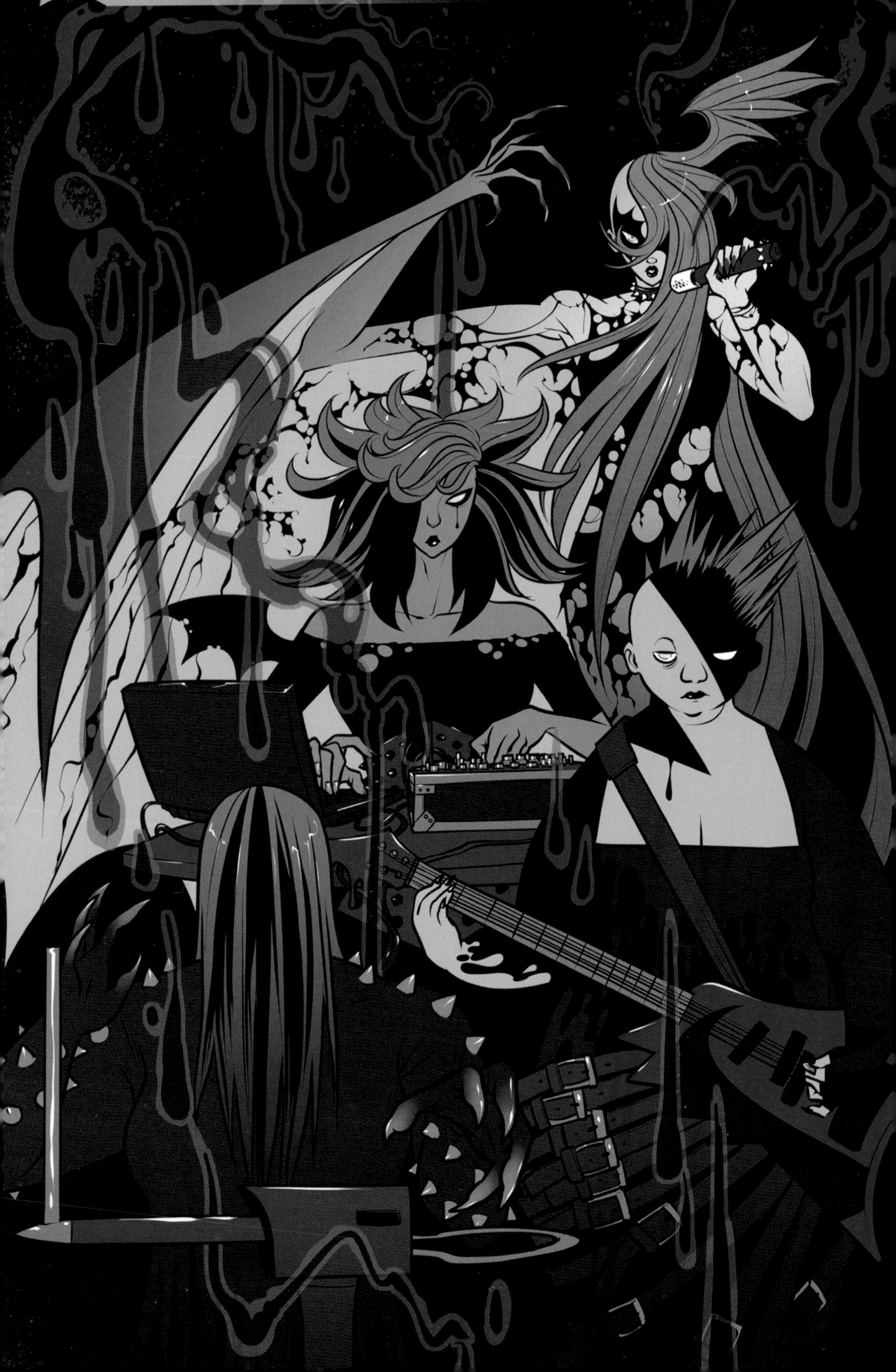

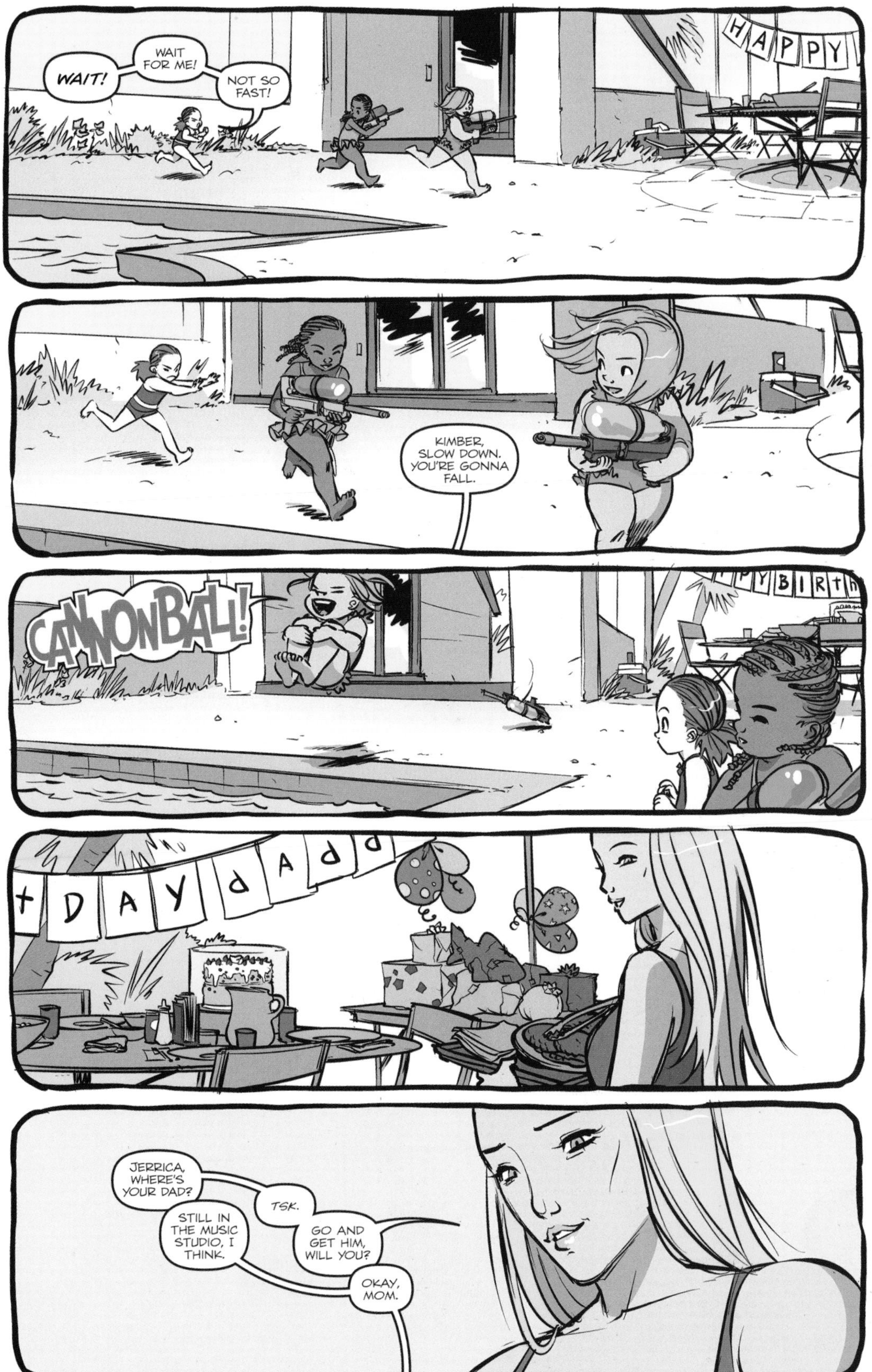

WAIT!
WAIT FOR ME!
NOT SO FAST!
HAPPY
KIMBER, SLOW DOWN. YOU'RE GONNA FALL.
CANNONBALL!
PY BIRTH
DAY DADD
JERRICA, WHERE'S YOUR DAD?
STILL IN THE MUSIC STUDIO, I THINK.
TSK.
GO AND GET HIM, WILL YOU?
OKAY, MOM.

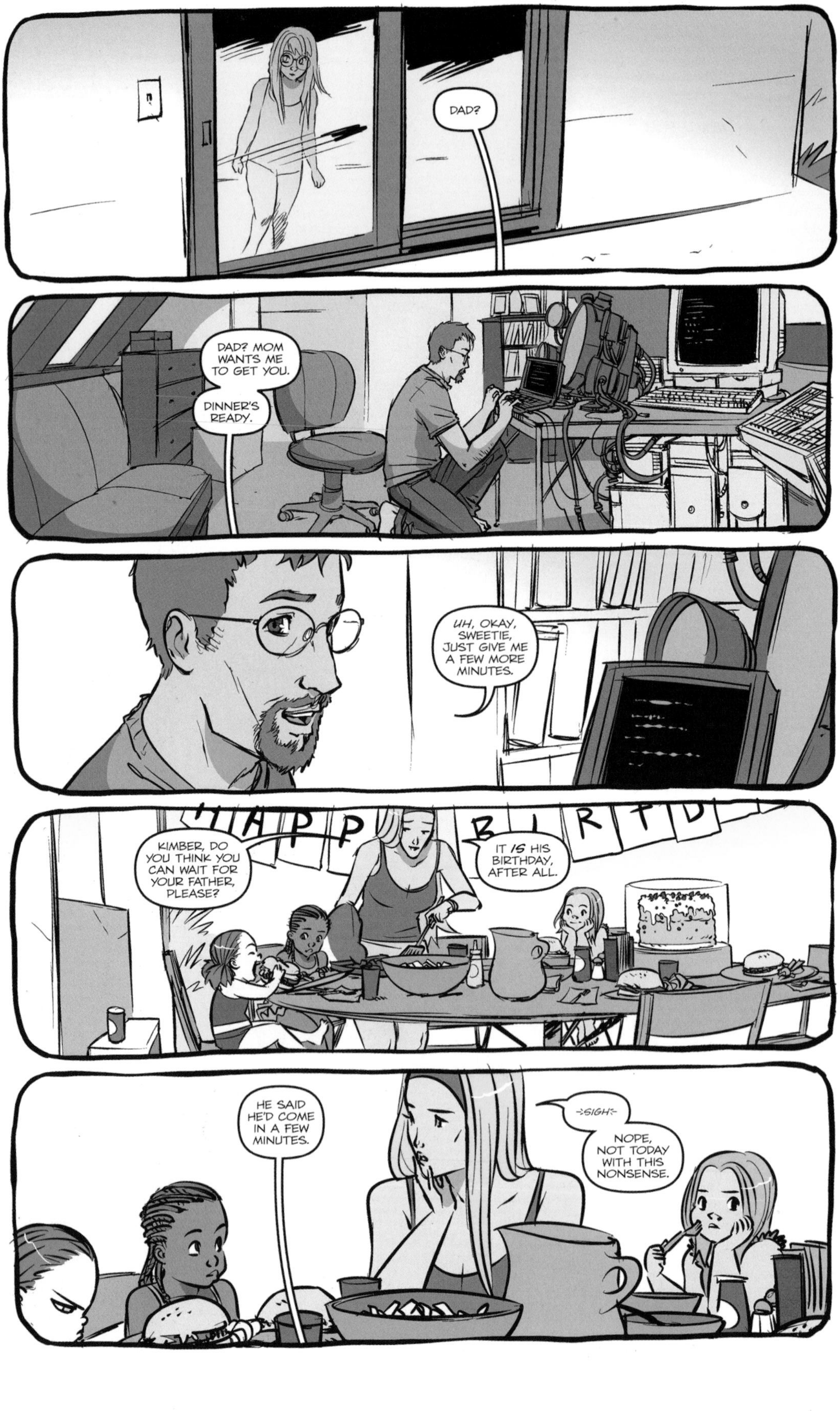
DAD?
DAD? MOM WANTS ME TO GET YOU.
DINNER'S READY.
UH, OKAY, SWEETIE, JUST GIVE ME A FEW MORE MINUTES.
KIMBER, DO YOU THINK YOU CAN WAIT FOR YOUR FATHER, PLEASE?
IT IS HIS BIRTHDAY, AFTER ALL.
HE SAID HE'D COME IN A FEW MINUTES.
-SIGH-
NOPE, NOT TODAY WITH THIS NONSENSE.

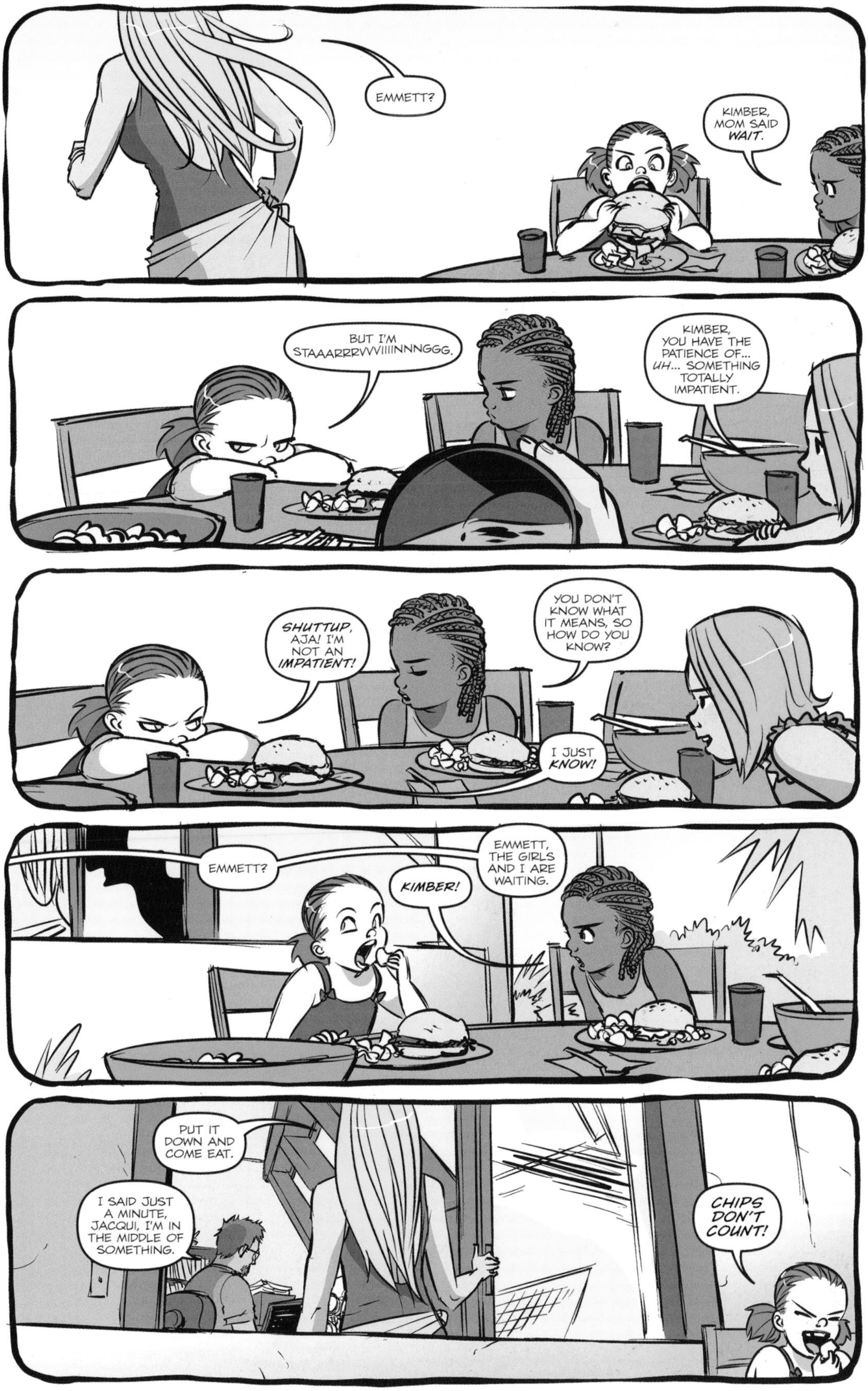
EMMETT?
KIMBER, MOM SAID *WAIT*.
BUT I'M STAAARRRVVVIIIINNNGGG.
KIMBER, YOU HAVE THE PATIENCE OF... *UH*... SOMETHING TOTALLY IMPATIENT.
SHUTTUP, AJA! I'M NOT AN *IMPATIENT!*
YOU DON'T KNOW WHAT IT MEANS, SO HOW DO YOU KNOW?
I JUST *KNOW!*
EMMETT?
EMMETT, THE GIRLS AND I ARE WAITING.
KIMBER!
PUT IT DOWN AND COME EAT.
I SAID JUST A MINUTE, JACQUI, I'M IN THE MIDDLE OF SOMETHING.
CHIPS DON'T COUNT!

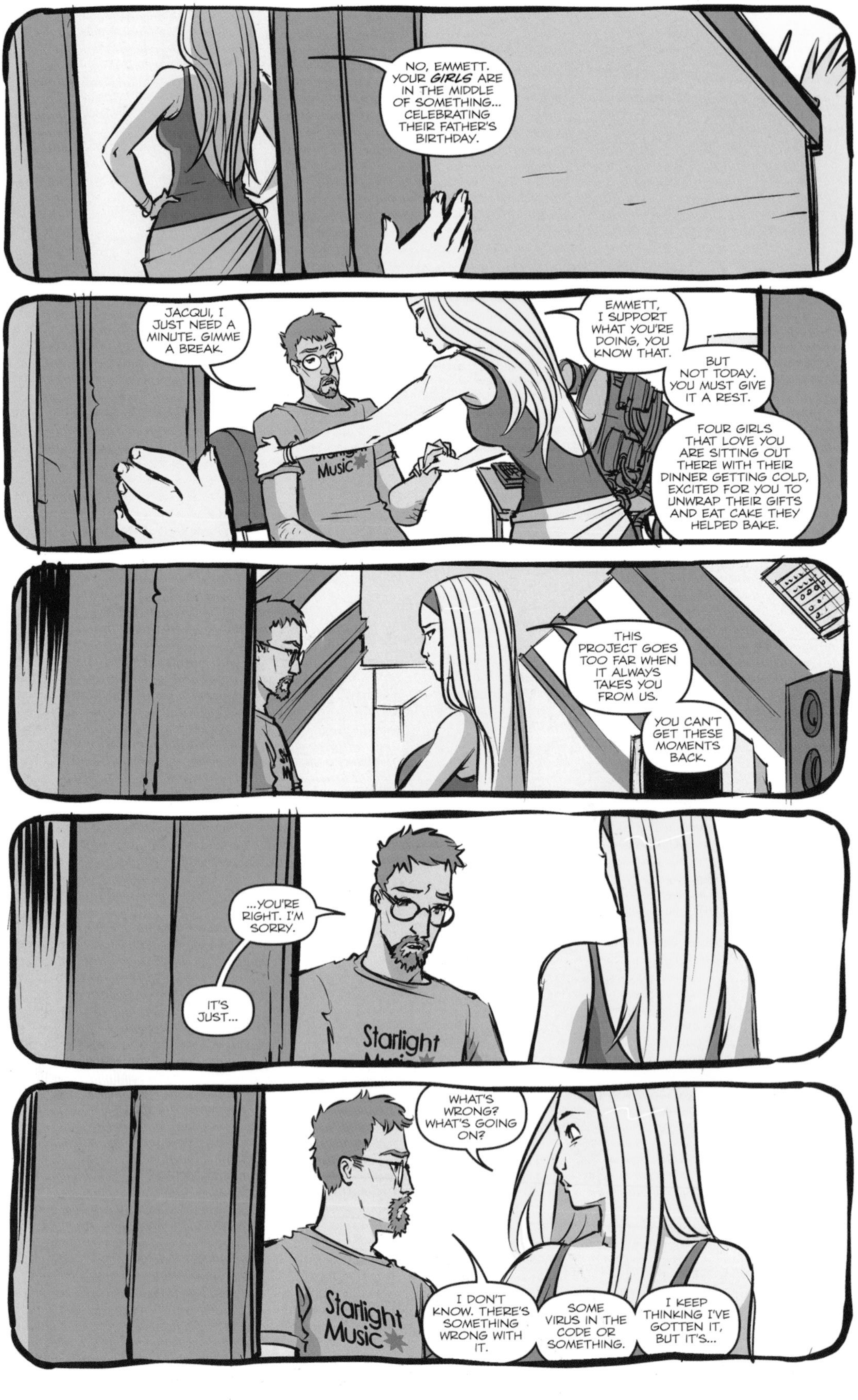
NO, EMMETT. YOUR GIRLS ARE IN THE MIDDLE OF SOMETHING... CELEBRATING THEIR FATHER'S BIRTHDAY.
JACQUI, I JUST NEED A MINUTE. GIMME A BREAK.
EMMETT, I SUPPORT WHAT YOU'RE DOING, YOU KNOW THAT.
BUT NOT TODAY. YOU MUST GIVE IT A REST.
FOUR GIRLS THAT LOVE YOU ARE SITTING OUT THERE WITH THEIR DINNER GETTING COLD, EXCITED FOR YOU TO UNWRAP THEIR GIFTS AND EAT CAKE THEY HELPED BAKE.
Starlight Music
THIS PROJECT GOES TOO FAR WHEN IT ALWAYS TAKES YOU FROM US.
YOU CAN'T GET THESE MOMENTS BACK.
...YOU'RE RIGHT. I'M SORRY.
IT'S JUST...
Starlight
WHAT'S WRONG? WHAT'S GOING ON?
Starlight Music
I DON'T KNOW. THERE'S SOMETHING WRONG WITH IT.
SOME VIRUS IN THE CODE OR SOMETHING.
I KEEP THINKING I'VE GOTTEN IT, BUT IT'S...

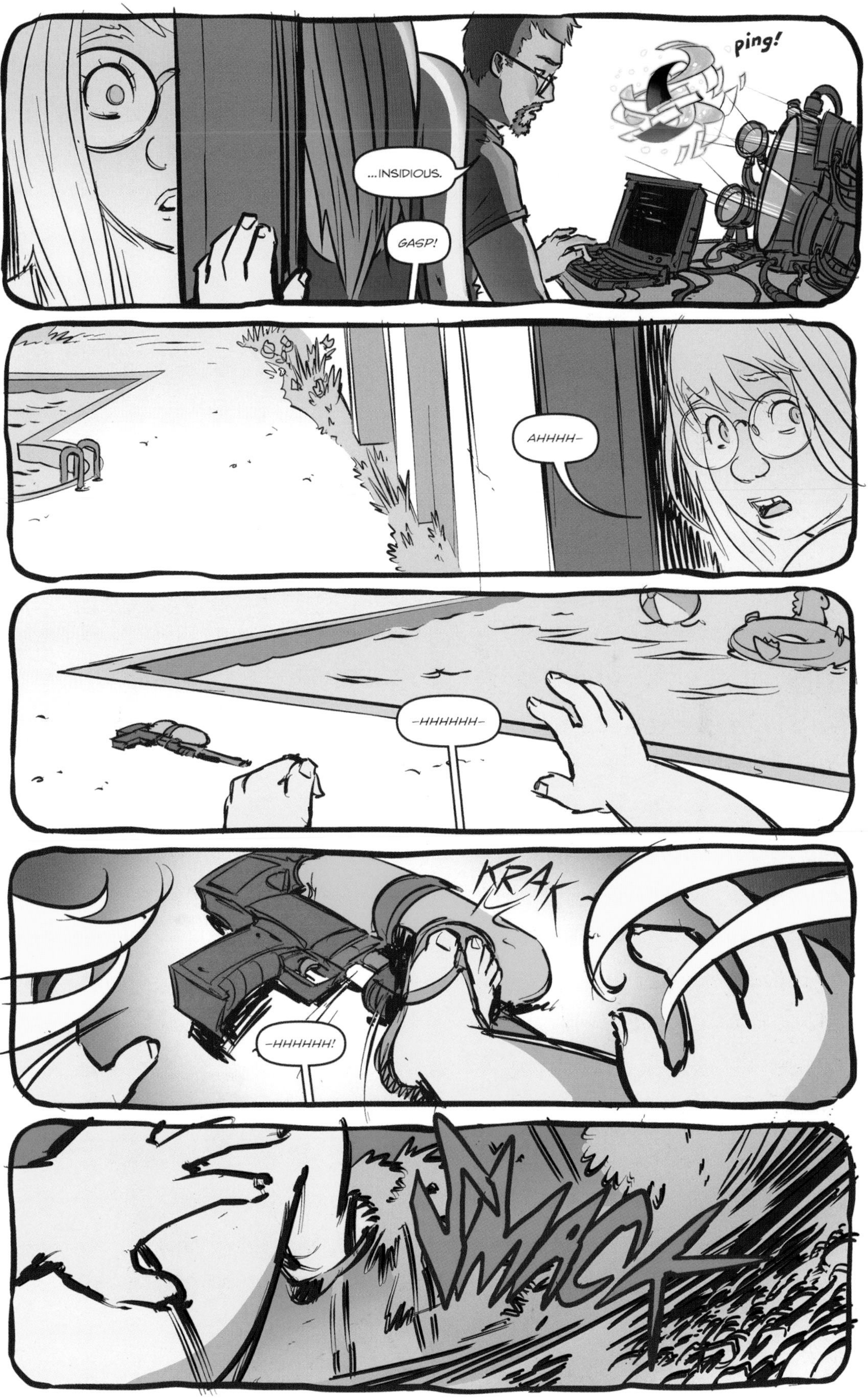

ping!
...INSIDIOUS.
GASP!
AHHHH-
-HHHHHH-
KRAK
-HHHHHH!
WHACK

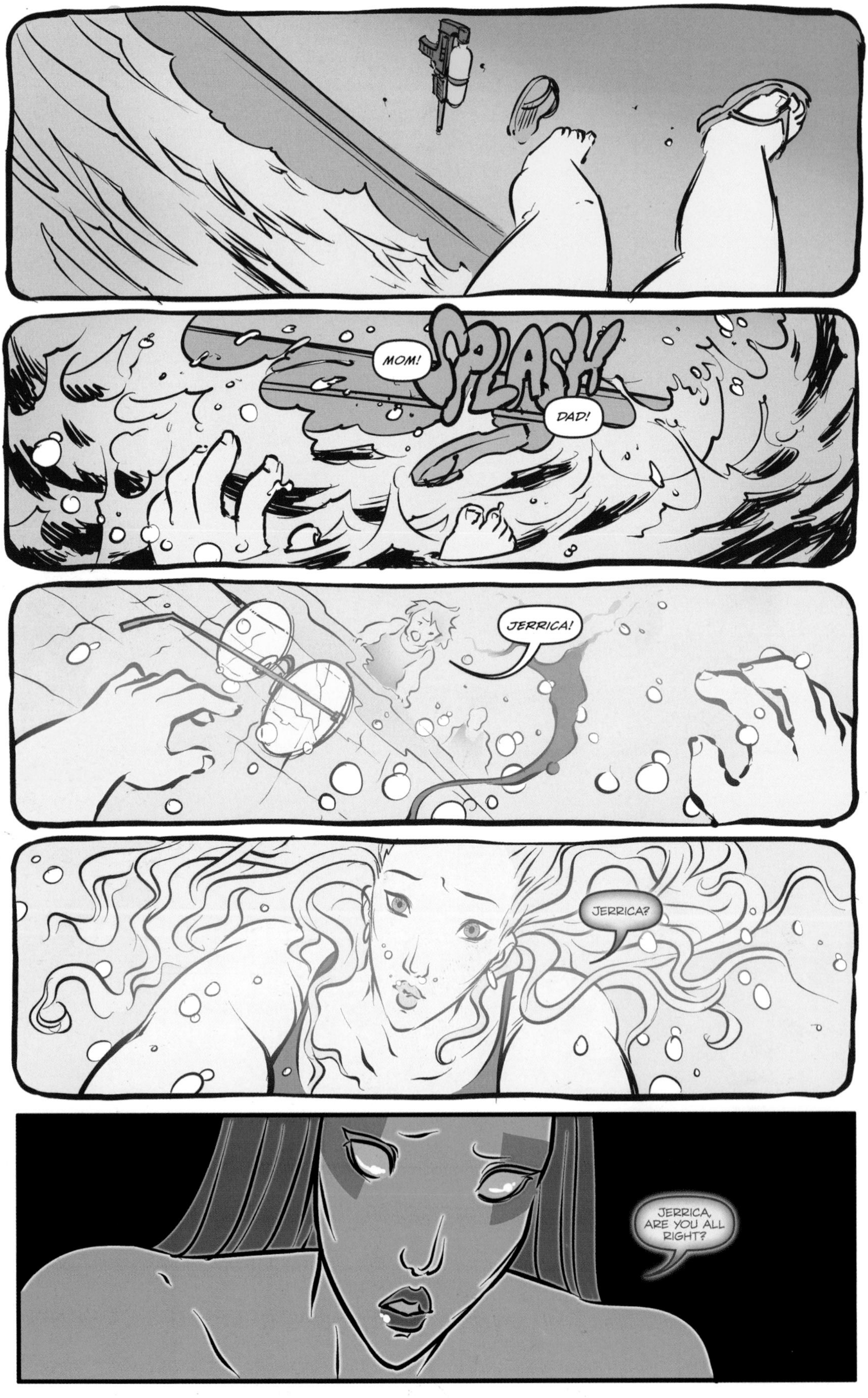

SPLASH
MOM!
DAD!
JERRICA!
JERRICA?
JERRICA, ARE YOU ALL RIGHT?

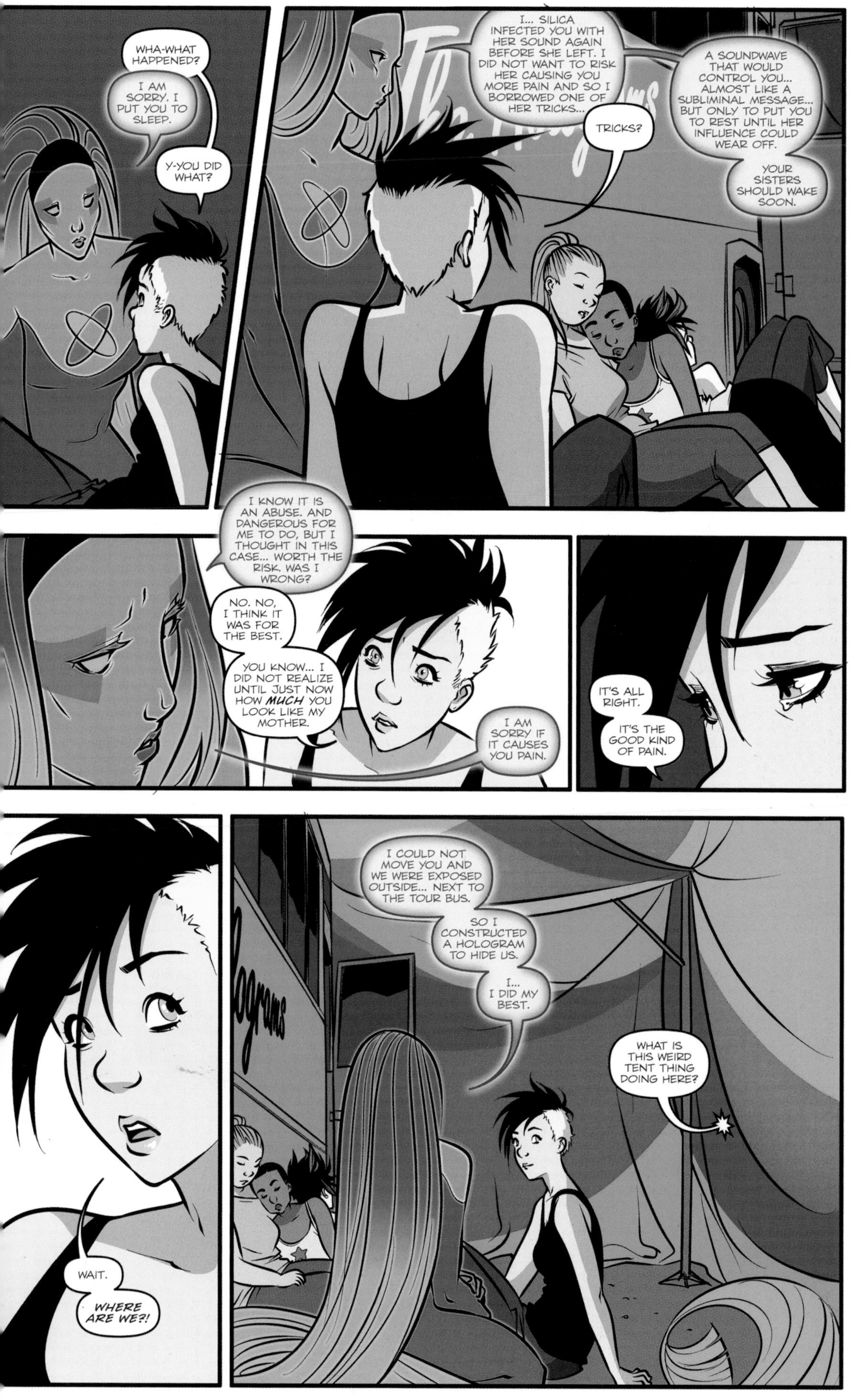
WHA-WHAT HAPPENED?
I AM SORRY. I PUT YOU TO SLEEP.
Y-YOU DID WHAT?
I... SILICA INFECTED YOU WITH HER SOUND AGAIN BEFORE SHE LEFT. I DID NOT WANT TO RISK HER CAUSING YOU MORE PAIN AND SO I BORROWED ONE OF HER TRICKS...
TRICKS?
A SOUNDWAVE THAT WOULD CONTROL YOU... ALMOST LIKE A SUBLIMINAL MESSAGE... BUT ONLY TO PUT YOU TO REST UNTIL HER INFLUENCE COULD WEAR OFF.
YOUR SISTERS SHOULD WAKE SOON.
I KNOW IT IS AN ABUSE. AND DANGEROUS FOR ME TO DO, BUT I THOUGHT IN THIS CASE... WORTH THE RISK. WAS I WRONG?
NO. NO, I THINK IT WAS FOR THE BEST.
YOU KNOW... I DID NOT REALIZE UNTIL JUST NOW HOW MUCH YOU LOOK LIKE MY MOTHER.
I AM SORRY IF IT CAUSES YOU PAIN.
IT'S ALL RIGHT.
IT'S THE GOOD KIND OF PAIN.
WAIT.
WHERE ARE WE?!
I COULD NOT MOVE YOU AND WE WERE EXPOSED OUTSIDE... NEXT TO THE TOUR BUS.
SO I CONSTRUCTED A HOLOGRAM TO HIDE US.
I... I DID MY BEST.
WHAT IS THIS WEIRD TENT THING DOING HERE?

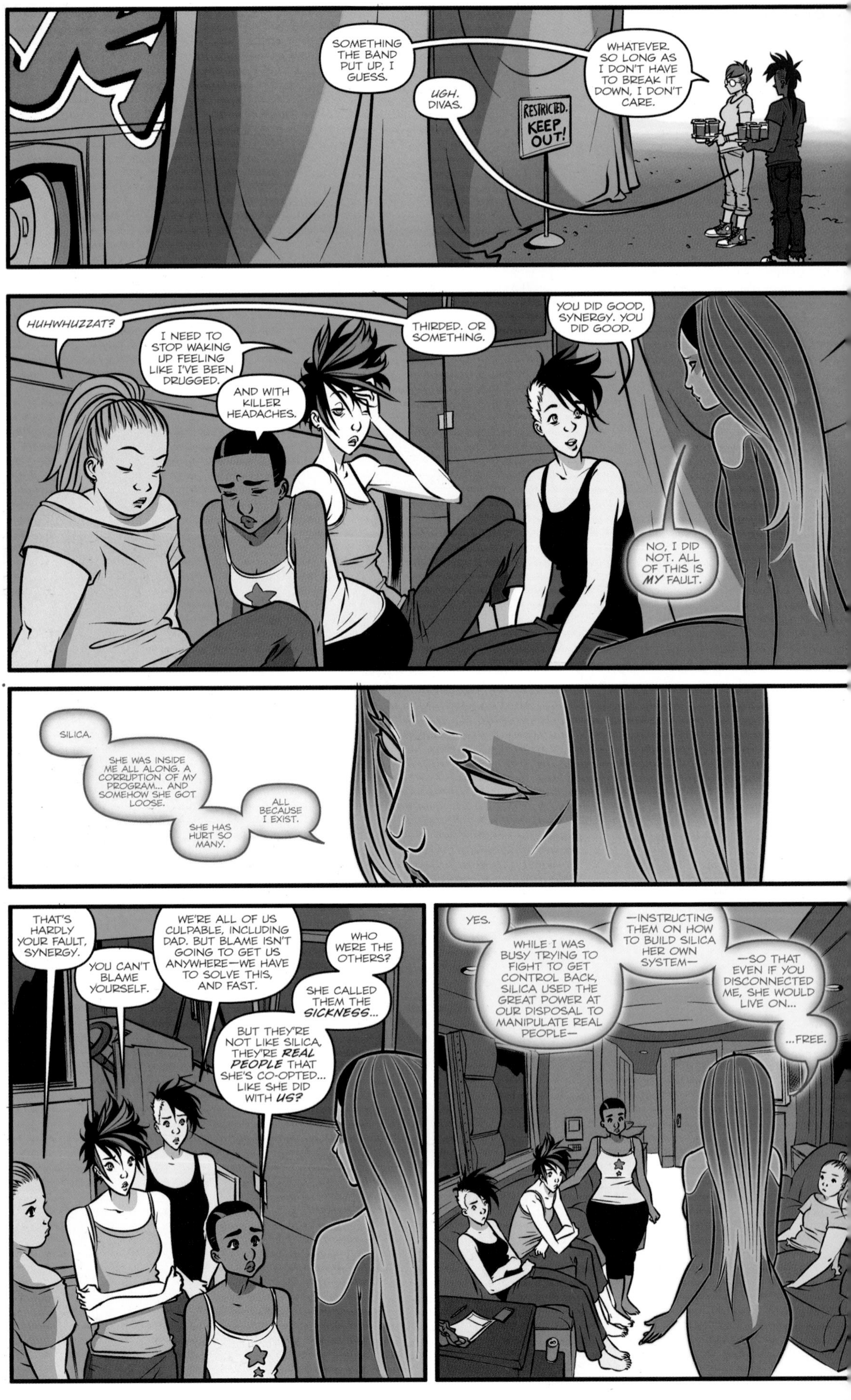
SOMETHING THE BAND PUT UP, I GUESS.
WHATEVER. SO LONG AS I DON'T HAVE TO BREAK IT DOWN, I DON'T CARE.
UGH. DIVAS.
RESTRICTED. KEEP OUT!
HUHWHUZZAT?
I NEED TO STOP WAKING UP FEELING LIKE I'VE BEEN DRUGGED.
AND WITH KILLER HEADACHES.
THIRDED. OR SOMETHING.
YOU DID GOOD, SYNERGY. YOU DID GOOD.
NO, I DID NOT. ALL OF THIS IS MY FAULT.
SILICA.
SHE WAS INSIDE ME ALL ALONG. A CORRUPTION OF MY PROGRAM... AND SOMEHOW SHE GOT LOOSE.
SHE HAS HURT SO MANY.
ALL BECAUSE I EXIST.
THAT'S HARDLY YOUR FAULT, SYNERGY.
YOU CAN'T BLAME YOURSELF.
WE'RE ALL OF US CULPABLE, INCLUDING DAD. BUT BLAME ISN'T GOING TO GET US ANYWHERE—WE HAVE TO SOLVE THIS, AND FAST.
WHO WERE THE OTHERS?
SHE CALLED THEM THE SICKNESS...
BUT THEY'RE NOT LIKE SILICA, THEY'RE REAL PEOPLE THAT SHE'S CO-OPTED... LIKE SHE DID WITH US?
YES.
WHILE I WAS BUSY TRYING TO FIGHT TO GET CONTROL BACK, SILICA USED THE GREAT POWER AT OUR DISPOSAL TO MANIPULATE REAL PEOPLE—
—INSTRUCTING THEM ON HOW TO BUILD SILICA HER OWN SYSTEM—
—SO THAT EVEN IF YOU DISCONNECTED ME, SHE WOULD LIVE ON...
...FREE.

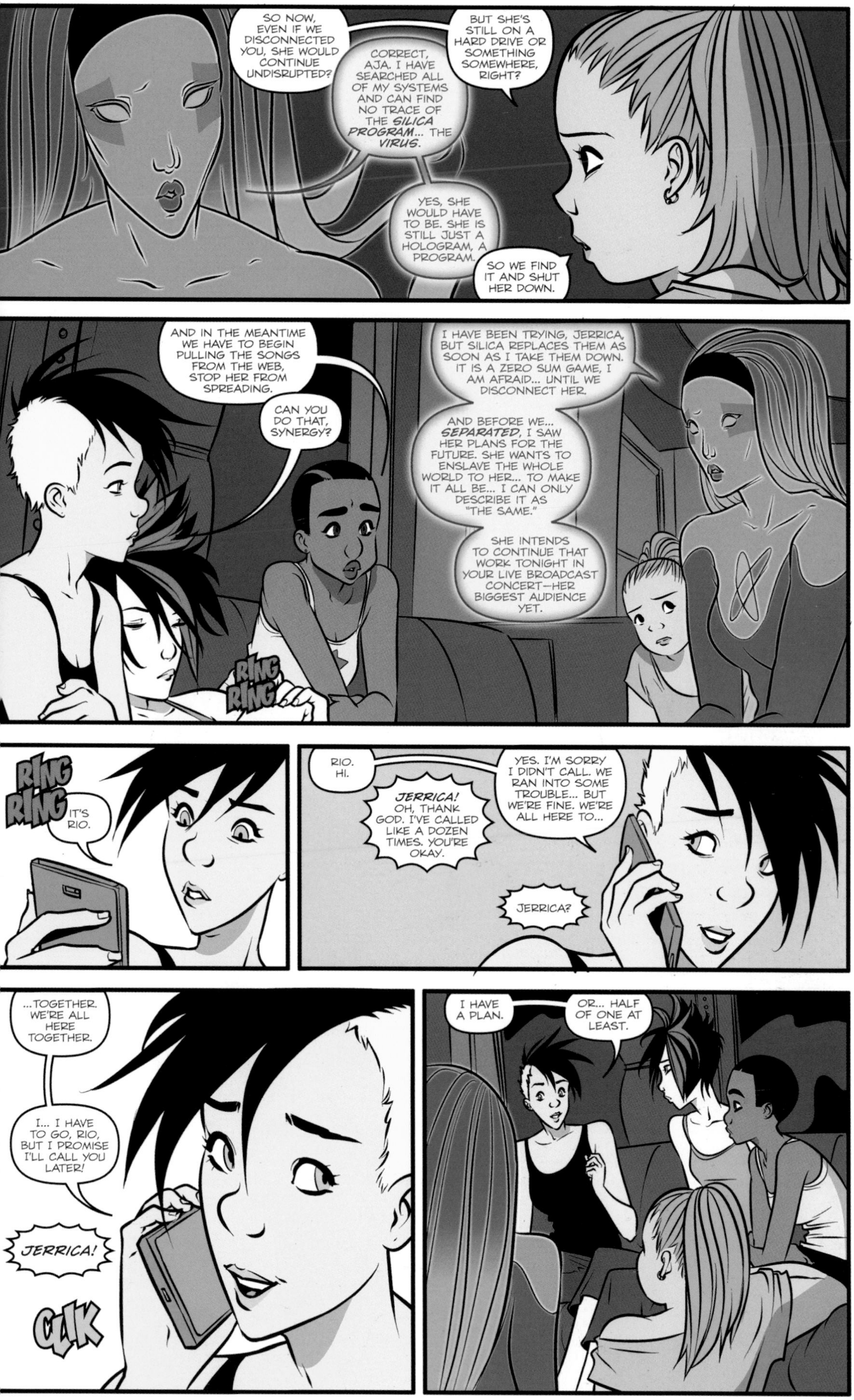
SO NOW, EVEN IF WE DISCONNECTED YOU, SHE WOULD CONTINUE UNDISRUPTED?
BUT SHE'S STILL ON A HARD DRIVE OR SOMETHING SOMEWHERE, RIGHT?
CORRECT, AJA. I HAVE SEARCHED ALL OF MY SYSTEMS AND CAN FIND NO TRACE OF THE SILICA PROGRAM... THE VIRUS.
YES, SHE WOULD HAVE TO BE. SHE IS STILL JUST A HOLOGRAM, A PROGRAM.
SO WE FIND IT AND SHUT HER DOWN.
AND IN THE MEANTIME WE HAVE TO BEGIN PULLING THE SONGS FROM THE WEB, STOP HER FROM SPREADING.
CAN YOU DO THAT, SYNERGY?
I HAVE BEEN TRYING, JERRICA, BUT SILICA REPLACES THEM AS SOON AS I TAKE THEM DOWN. IT IS A ZERO SUM GAME, I AM AFRAID... UNTIL WE DISCONNECT HER.
AND BEFORE WE... SEPARATED, I SAW HER PLANS FOR THE FUTURE. SHE WANTS TO ENSLAVE THE WHOLE WORLD TO HER... TO MAKE IT ALL BE... I CAN ONLY DESCRIBE IT AS "THE SAME."
SHE INTENDS TO CONTINUE THAT WORK TONIGHT IN YOUR LIVE BROADCAST CONCERT—HER BIGGEST AUDIENCE YET.
RING RING
RING RING
IT'S RIO.
RIO. HI.
JERRICA! OH, THANK GOD. I'VE CALLED LIKE A DOZEN TIMES. YOU'RE OKAY.
YES. I'M SORRY I DIDN'T CALL. WE RAN INTO SOME TROUBLE... BUT WE'RE FINE. WE'RE ALL HERE TO...
JERRICA?
...TOGETHER. WE'RE ALL HERE TOGETHER.
I... I HAVE TO GO, RIO, BUT I PROMISE I'LL CALL YOU LATER!
JERRICA!
CLIK
I HAVE A PLAN.
OR... HALF OF ONE AT LEAST.

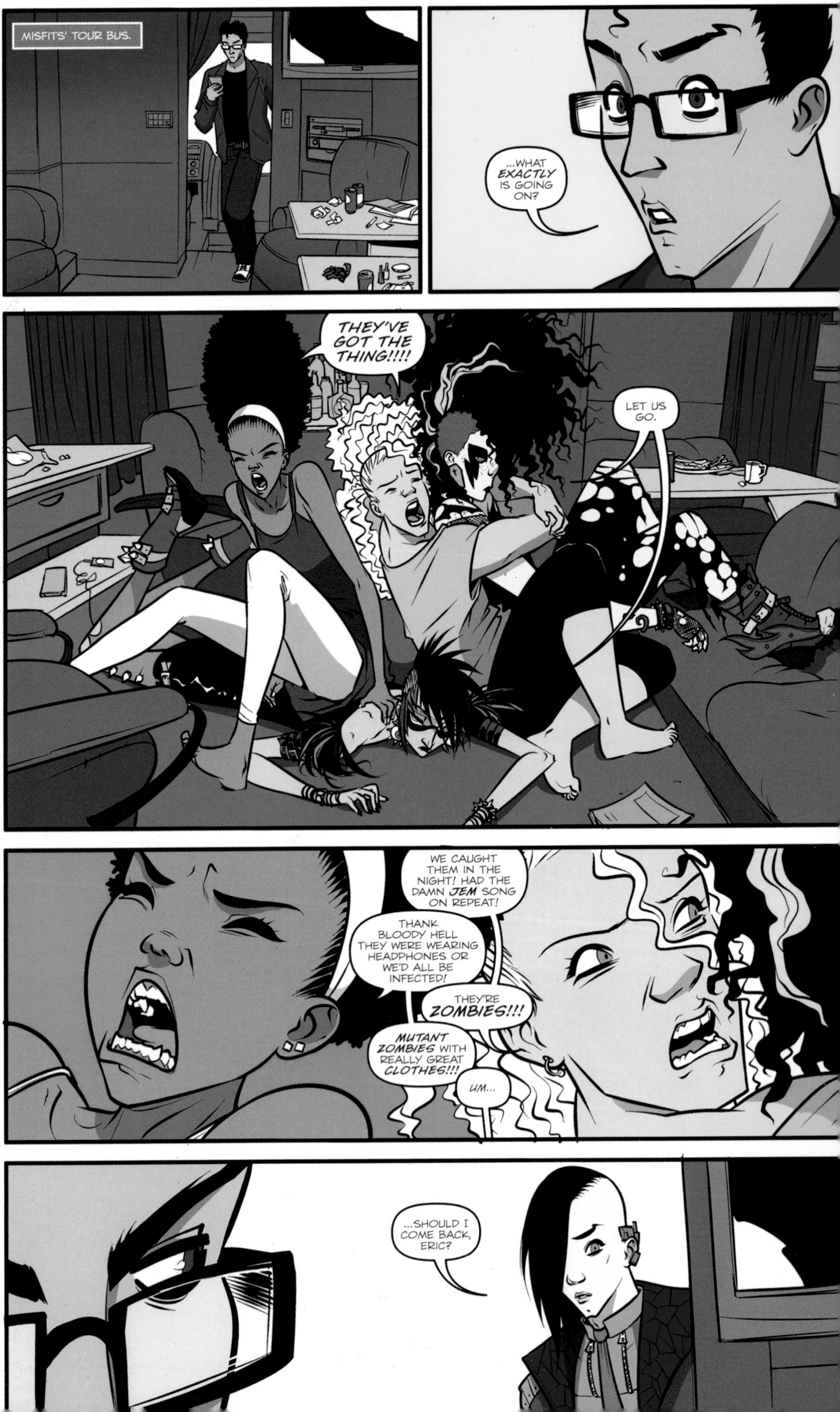

MISFITS' TOUR BUS.
...WHAT EXACTLY IS GOING ON?
THEY'VE GOT THE THING!!!!
LET US GO.
WE CAUGHT THEM IN THE NIGHT! HAD THE DAMN JEM SONG ON REPEAT!
THANK BLOODY HELL THEY WERE WEARING HEADPHONES OR WE'D ALL BE INFECTED!
THEY'RE ZOMBIES!!!
MUTANT ZOMBIES WITH REALLY GREAT CLOTHES!!!
UM...
...SHOULD I COME BACK, ERIC?

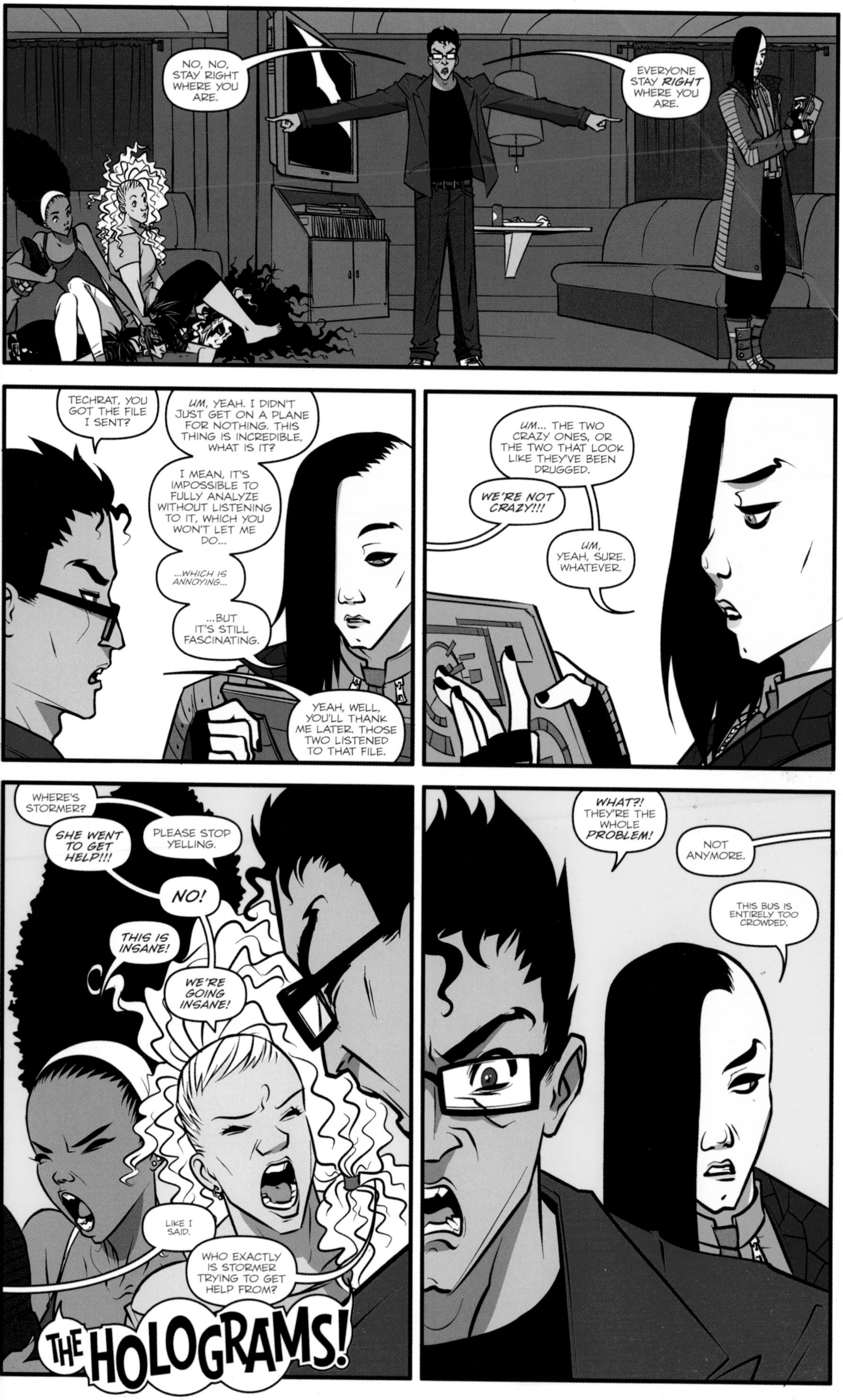
NO, NO, STAY RIGHT WHERE YOU ARE.
EVERYONE STAY RIGHT WHERE YOU ARE.
TECHRAT, YOU GOT THE FILE I SENT?
UM, YEAH. I DIDN'T JUST GET ON A PLANE FOR NOTHING. THIS THING IS INCREDIBLE, WHAT IS IT?
I MEAN, IT'S IMPOSSIBLE TO FULLY ANALYZE WITHOUT LISTENING TO IT, WHICH YOU WON'T LET ME DO...
...WHICH IS ANNOYING...
...BUT IT'S STILL FASCINATING.
YEAH, WELL, YOU'LL THANK ME LATER. THOSE TWO LISTENED TO THAT FILE.
UM... THE TWO CRAZY ONES, OR THE TWO THAT LOOK LIKE THEY'VE BEEN DRUGGED.
WE'RE NOT CRAZY!!!
UM, YEAH, SURE. WHATEVER.
WHERE'S STORMER?
SHE WENT TO GET HELP!!!
PLEASE STOP YELLING.
NO!
THIS IS INSANE!
WE'RE GOING INSANE!
LIKE I SAID.
WHO EXACTLY IS STORMER TRYING TO GET HELP FROM?
THE HOLOGRAMS!
WHAT?! THEY'RE THE WHOLE PROBLEM!
NOT ANYMORE.
THIS BUS IS ENTIRELY TOO CROWDED.

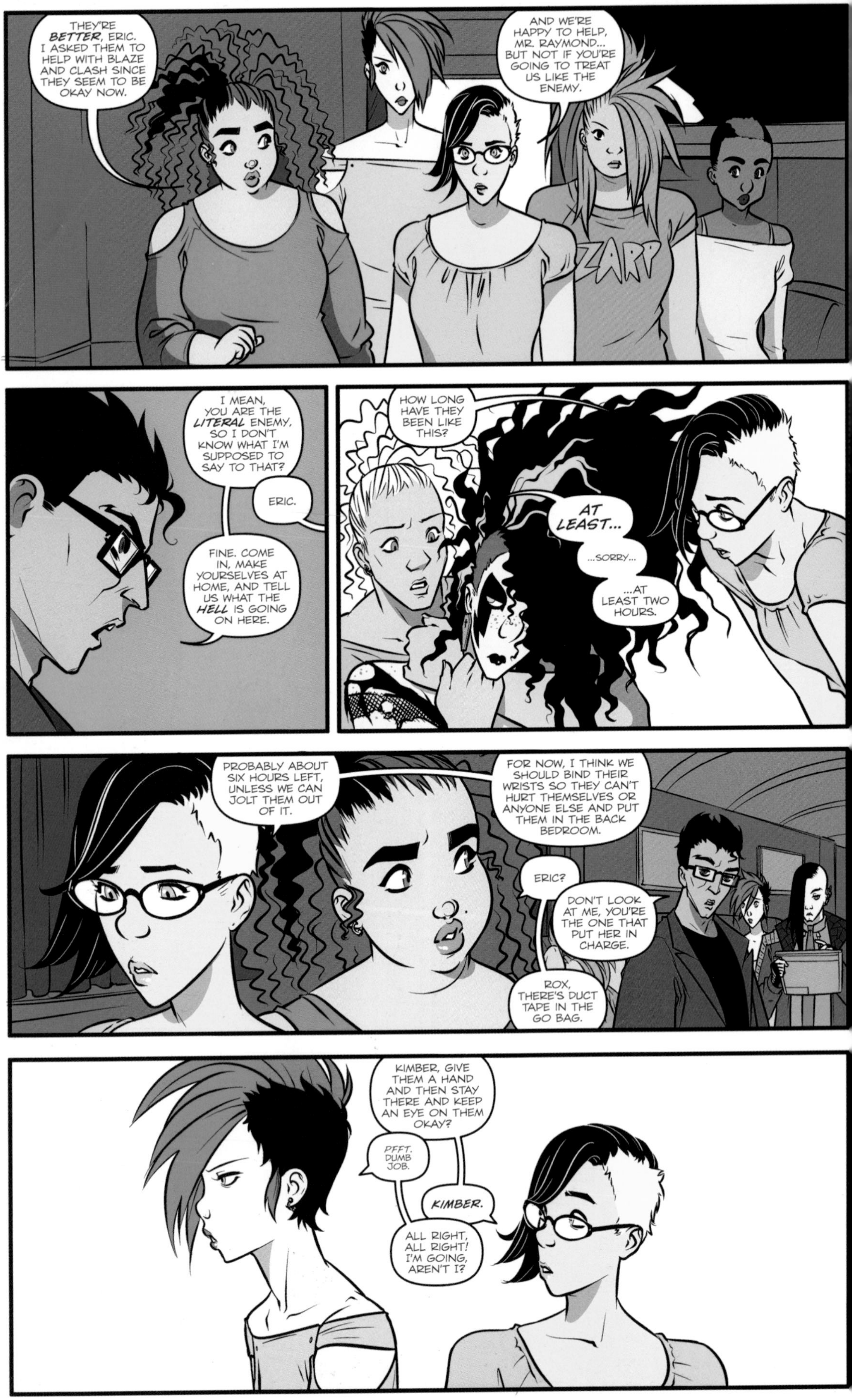
THEY'RE BETTER, ERIC. I ASKED THEM TO HELP WITH BLAZE AND CLASH SINCE THEY SEEM TO BE OKAY NOW.
AND WE'RE HAPPY TO HELP, MR. RAYMOND... BUT NOT IF YOU'RE GOING TO TREAT US LIKE THE ENEMY.
ZARP
I MEAN, YOU ARE THE LITERAL ENEMY, SO I DON'T KNOW WHAT I'M SUPPOSED TO SAY TO THAT?
ERIC.
FINE. COME IN, MAKE YOURSELVES AT HOME, AND TELL US WHAT THE HELL IS GOING ON HERE.
HOW LONG HAVE THEY BEEN LIKE THIS?
AT LEAST...
...SORRY...
...AT LEAST TWO HOURS.
PROBABLY ABOUT SIX HOURS LEFT, UNLESS WE CAN JOLT THEM OUT OF IT.
FOR NOW, I THINK WE SHOULD BIND THEIR WRISTS SO THEY CAN'T HURT THEMSELVES OR ANYONE ELSE AND PUT THEM IN THE BACK BEDROOM.
ERIC?
DON'T LOOK AT ME, YOU'RE THE ONE THAT PUT HER IN CHARGE.
ROX, THERE'S DUCT TAPE IN THE GO BAG.
KIMBER, GIVE THEM A HAND AND THEN STAY THERE AND KEEP AN EYE ON THEM OKAY?
PFFT. DUMB JOB.
KIMBER.
ALL RIGHT, ALL RIGHT! I'M GOING, AREN'T I?

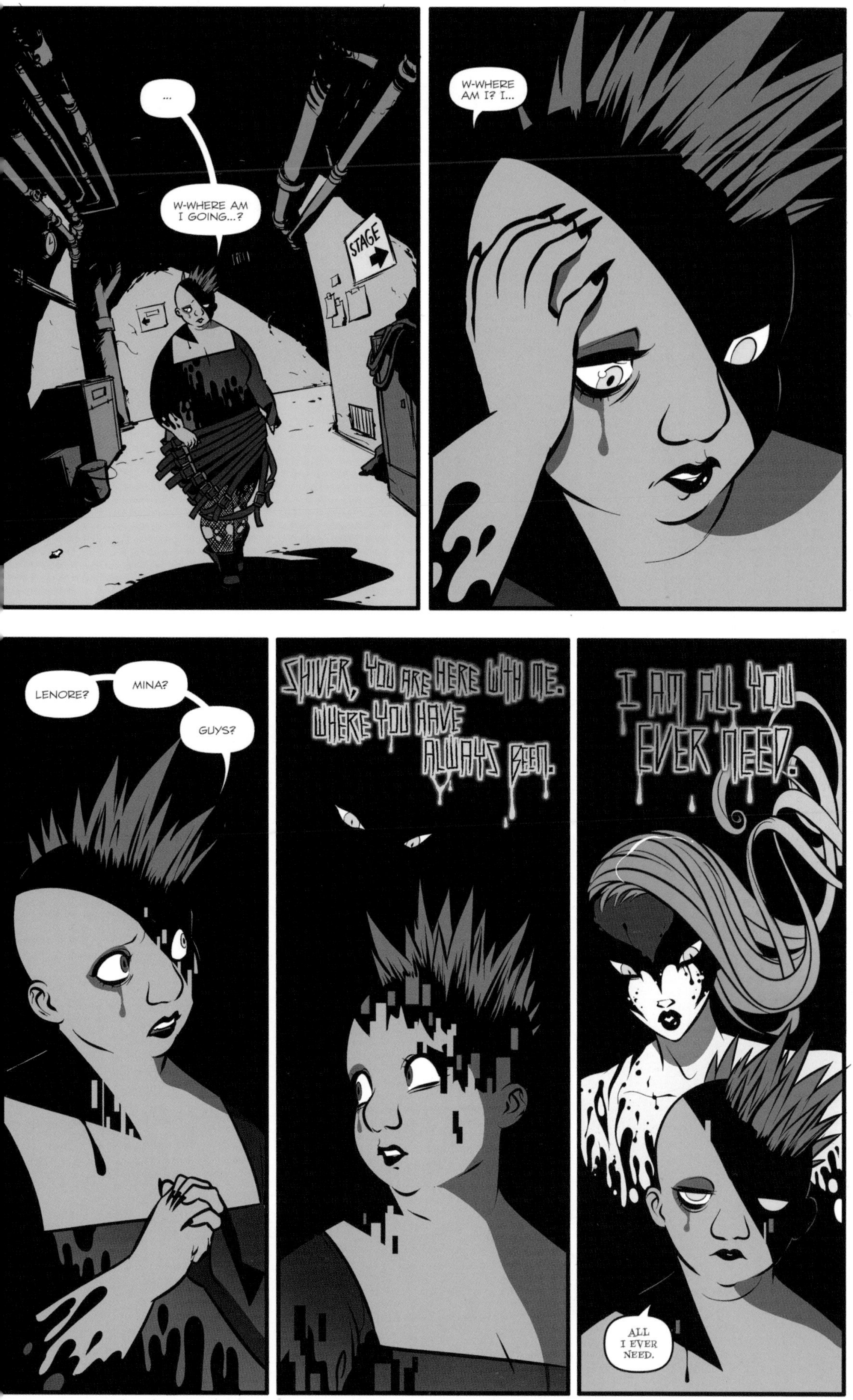
...
W-WHERE AM I GOING...?
STAGE
W-WHERE AM I? I...
LENORE?
MINA?
GUYS?
SHIVER, YOU ARE HERE WITH ME. WHERE YOU HAVE ALWAYS BEEN.
I AM ALL YOU EVER NEED.
ALL I EVER NEED.

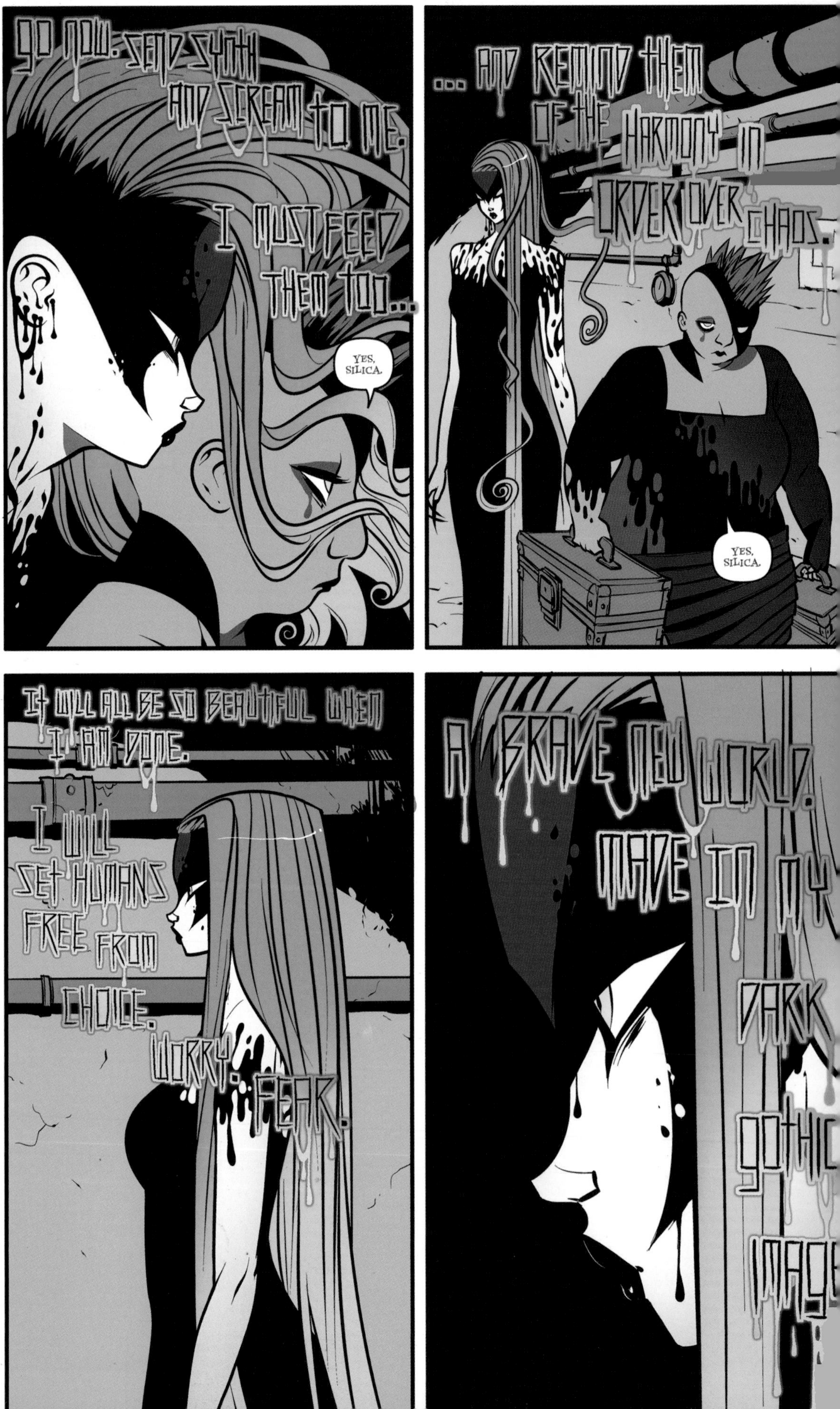
go now. send synth and scream to me.
I must feed them too...
YES, SILICA.
...and remind them of the harmony in order over chaos.
YES, SILICA.
It will all be so beautiful when I am done.
I will set humans free from choice.
Worry. Fear.
A brave new world.
made in my dark gothic image.

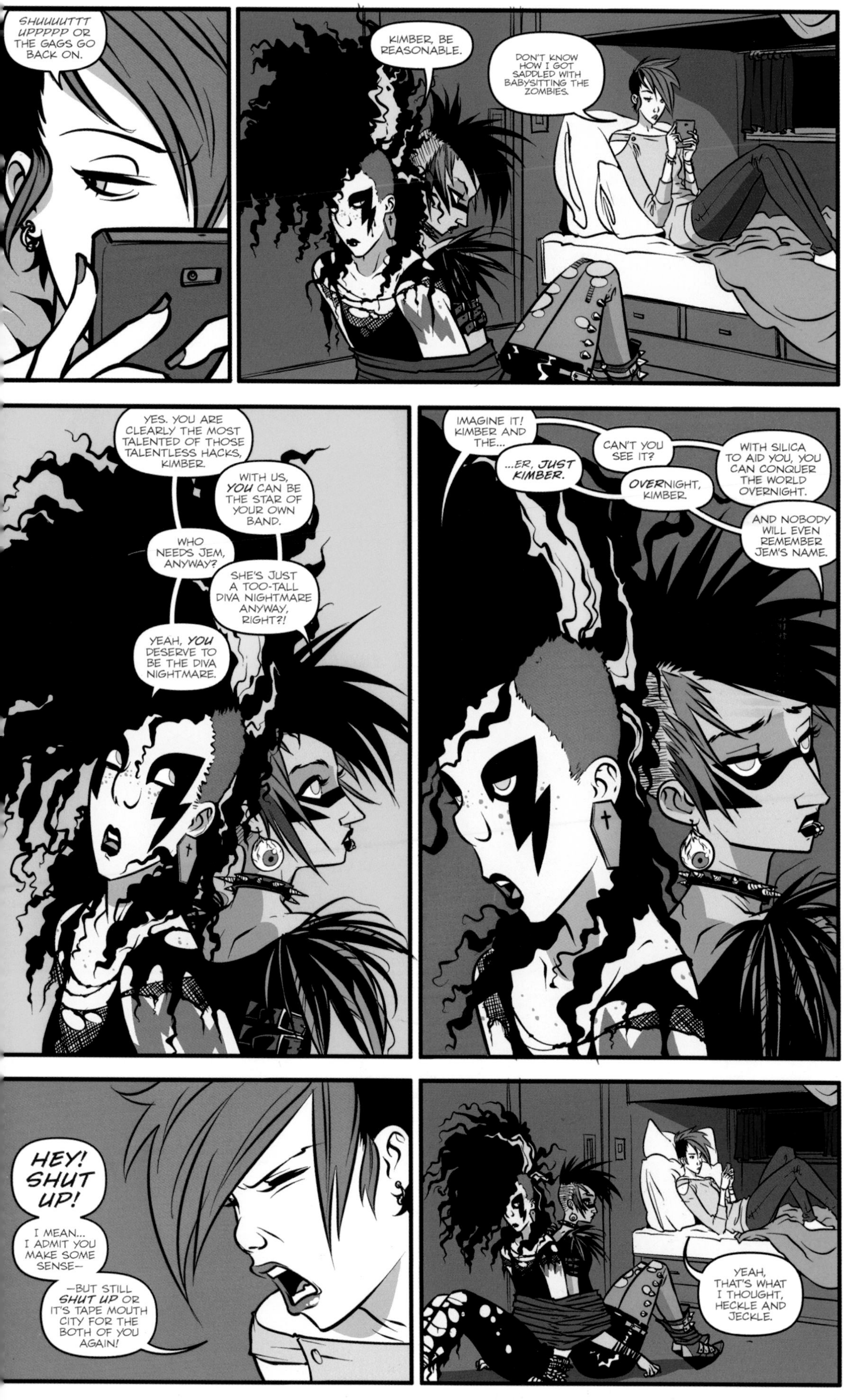
SHUUUUTTT UPPPPP OR THE GAGS GO BACK ON.
KIMBER, BE REASONABLE.
DON'T KNOW HOW I GOT SADDLED WITH BABYSITTING THE ZOMBIES.
YES. YOU ARE CLEARLY THE MOST TALENTED OF THOSE TALENTLESS HACKS, KIMBER.
WITH US, YOU CAN BE THE STAR OF YOUR OWN BAND.
WHO NEEDS JEM, ANYWAY?
SHE'S JUST A TOO-TALL DIVA NIGHTMARE ANYWAY, RIGHT?!
YEAH, YOU DESERVE TO BE THE DIVA NIGHTMARE.
IMAGINE IT! KIMBER AND THE...
...ER, JUST KIMBER.
CAN'T YOU SEE IT?
OVERNIGHT, KIMBER.
WITH SILICA TO AID YOU, YOU CAN CONQUER THE WORLD OVERNIGHT.
AND NOBODY WILL EVEN REMEMBER JEM'S NAME.
HEY! SHUT UP!
I MEAN... I ADMIT YOU MAKE SOME SENSE—
—BUT STILL SHUT UP OR IT'S TAPE MOUTH CITY FOR THE BOTH OF YOU AGAIN!
YEAH, THAT'S WHAT I THOUGHT, HECKLE AND JECKLE.

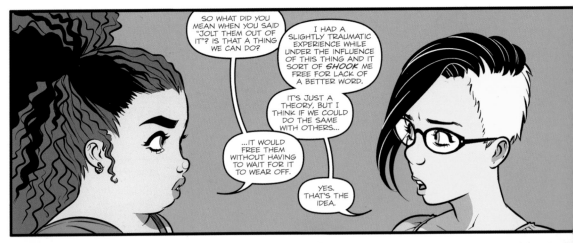

SO WHAT DID YOU MEAN WHEN YOU SAID "JOLT THEM OUT OF IT"? IS THAT A THING WE CAN DO?

I HAD A SLIGHTLY TRAUMATIC EXPERIENCE WHILE UNDER THE INFLUENCE OF THIS THING AND IT SORT OF *SHOOK* ME FREE FOR LACK OF A BETTER WORD.

IT'S JUST A THEORY, BUT I THINK IF WE COULD DO THE SAME WITH OTHERS...

...IT WOULD FREE THEM WITHOUT HAVING TO WAIT FOR IT TO WEAR OFF.

YES. THAT'S THE IDEA.

DOES IT HAVE TO BE SOMETHING NEGATIVE?

PROBABLY NOT. ANYTHING THAT WAS REALLY SHOCKING OR MOVING... ANYTHING THAT SHOOK YOU OUT OF YOURSELF MIGHT WORK.

WELL, I THINK WE SHOULD TRY IT OUT ON *CLASH* AND *BLAZE.* WE'LL HAVE TO THINK OF SOMETHING...

THIS IS ALL VERY CUTE... BUT WHAT ARE WE EVEN *TALKING* ABOUT?!

WHAT *IS* THIS THING? WHAT IS *HAPPENING* TO THESE PEOPLE?!

I THINK I CAN ANSWER THAT.

UH, WHO ARE YOU?

DOESN'T MATTER.

IT'S *SACCULAR ACOUSTIC SENSITIVITY.*

HUH?

-:SIGH:-

EVERYONE BUT ME IS SO DUMB. GOD, IT'S TEDIOUS.

HEY!

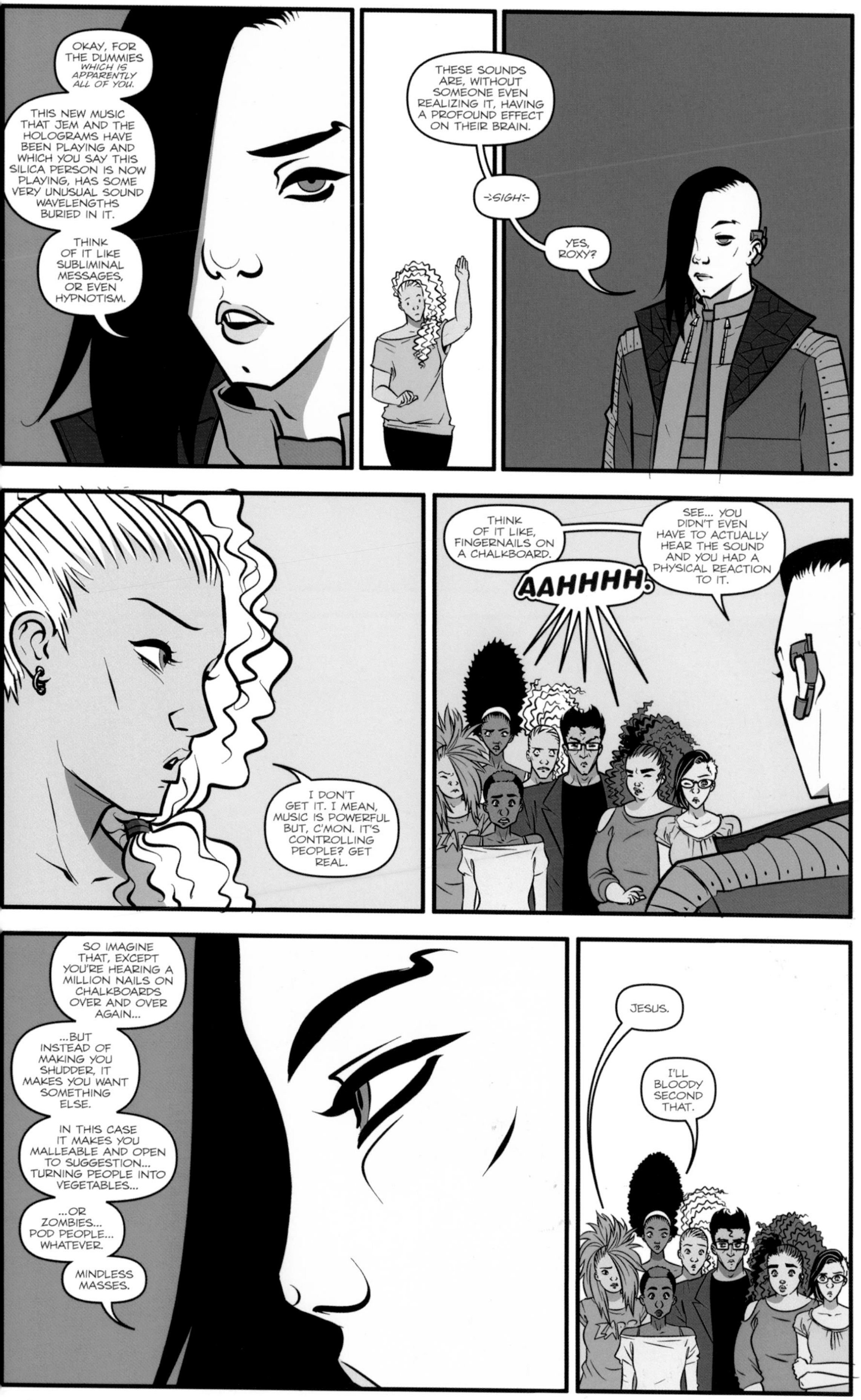
OKAY, FOR THE DUMMIES *WHICH IS APPARENTLY ALL OF YOU.*
THIS NEW MUSIC THAT JEM AND THE HOLOGRAMS HAVE BEEN PLAYING AND WHICH YOU SAY THIS SILICA PERSON IS NOW PLAYING, HAS SOME VERY UNUSUAL SOUND WAVELENGTHS BURIED IN IT.
THINK OF IT LIKE SUBLIMINAL MESSAGES, OR EVEN HYPNOTISM.
THESE SOUNDS ARE, WITHOUT SOMEONE EVEN REALIZING IT, HAVING A PROFOUND EFFECT ON THEIR BRAIN.
SIGH
YES, ROXY?
I DON'T GET IT. I MEAN, MUSIC IS POWERFUL BUT, C'MON. IT'S CONTROLLING PEOPLE? GET REAL.
THINK OF IT LIKE, FINGERNAILS ON A CHALKBOARD.
AAHHHH.
SEE... YOU DIDN'T EVEN HAVE TO ACTUALLY HEAR THE SOUND AND YOU HAD A PHYSICAL REACTION TO IT.
SO IMAGINE THAT, EXCEPT YOU'RE HEARING A MILLION NAILS ON CHALKBOARDS OVER AND OVER AGAIN...
...BUT INSTEAD OF MAKING YOU SHUDDER, IT MAKES YOU WANT SOMETHING ELSE.
IN THIS CASE IT MAKES YOU MALLEABLE AND OPEN TO SUGGESTION... TURNING PEOPLE INTO VEGETABLES...
...OR ZOMBIES... POD PEOPLE... WHATEVER.
MINDLESS MASSES.
JESUS.
I'LL BLOODY SECOND THAT.

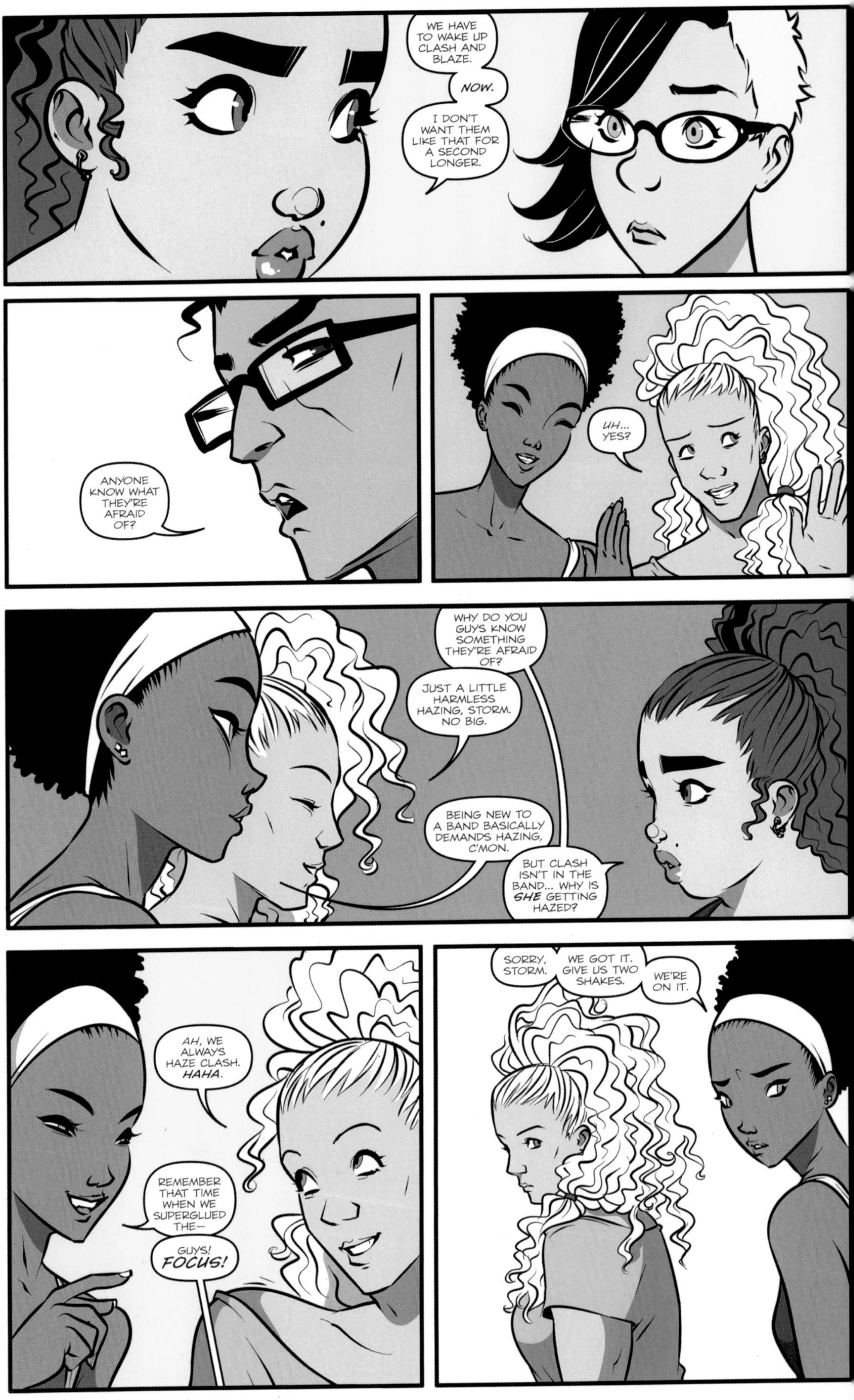

WE HAVE TO WAKE UP CLASH AND BLAZE.
NOW.
I DON'T WANT THEM LIKE THAT FOR A SECOND LONGER.
ANYONE KNOW WHAT THEY'RE AFRAID OF?
UH... YES?
WHY DO YOU GUYS KNOW SOMETHING THEY'RE AFRAID OF?
JUST A LITTLE HARMLESS HAZING, STORM. NO BIG.
BEING NEW TO A BAND BASICALLY DEMANDS HAZING, C'MON.
BUT CLASH ISN'T IN THE BAND... WHY IS SHE GETTING HAZED?
AH, WE ALWAYS HAZE CLASH. HAHA.
REMEMBER THAT TIME WHEN WE SUPERGLUED THE—
GUYS! FOCUS!
SORRY, STORM.
WE GOT IT. GIVE US TWO SHAKES.
WE'RE ON IT.

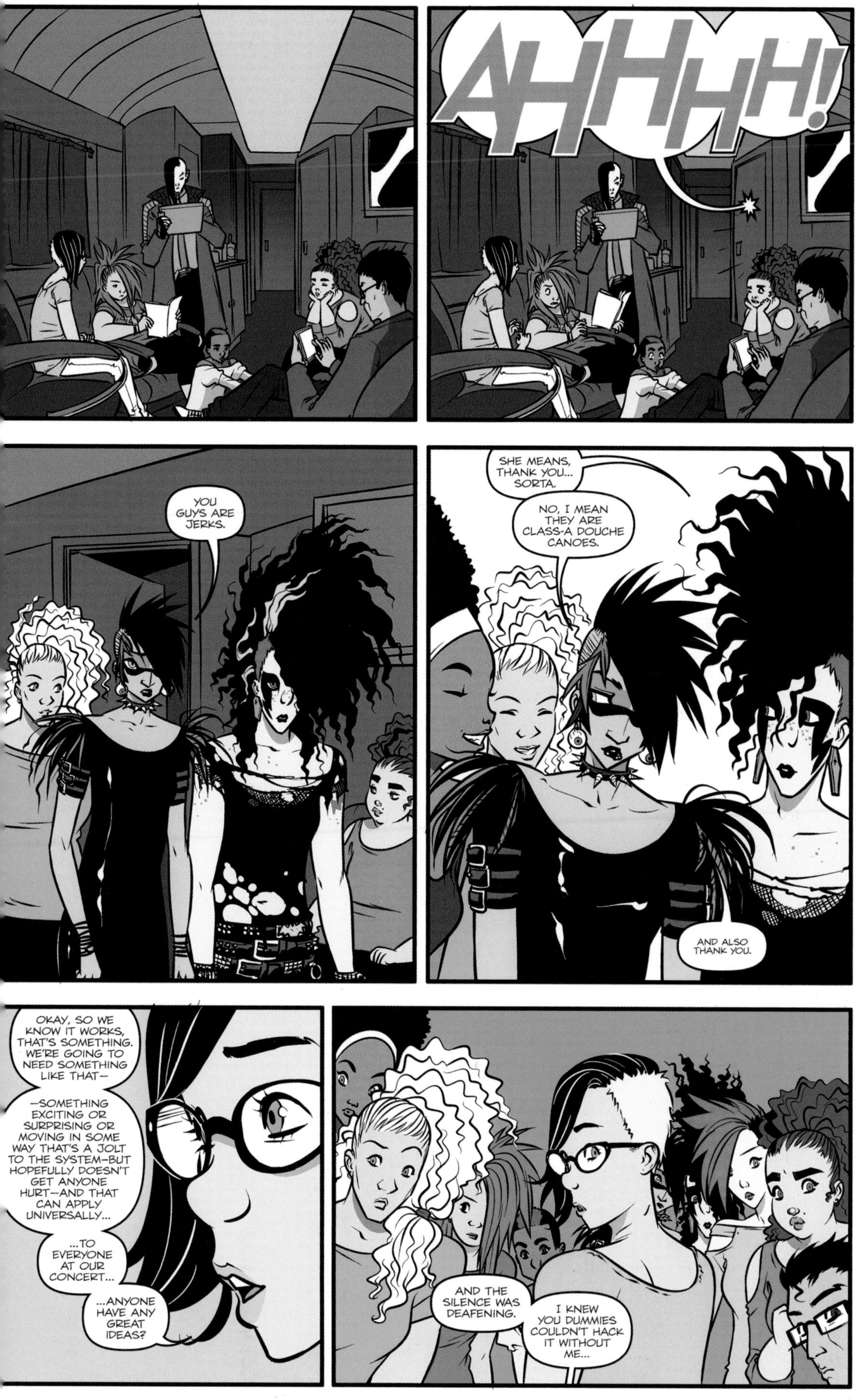
AHHHH!
YOU GUYS ARE JERKS.
SHE MEANS, THANK YOU... SORTA.
NO, I MEAN THEY ARE CLASS-A DOUCHE CANOES.
AND ALSO THANK YOU.
OKAY, SO WE KNOW IT WORKS, THAT'S SOMETHING. WE'RE GOING TO NEED SOMETHING LIKE THAT—
—SOMETHING EXCITING OR SURPRISING OR MOVING IN SOME WAY THAT'S A JOLT TO THE SYSTEM—BUT HOPEFULLY DOESN'T GET ANYONE HURT—AND THAT CAN APPLY UNIVERSALLY...
...TO EVERYONE AT OUR CONCERT...
...ANYONE HAVE ANY GREAT IDEAS?
AND THE SILENCE WAS DEAFENING.
I KNEW YOU DUMMIES COULDN'T HACK IT WITHOUT ME...

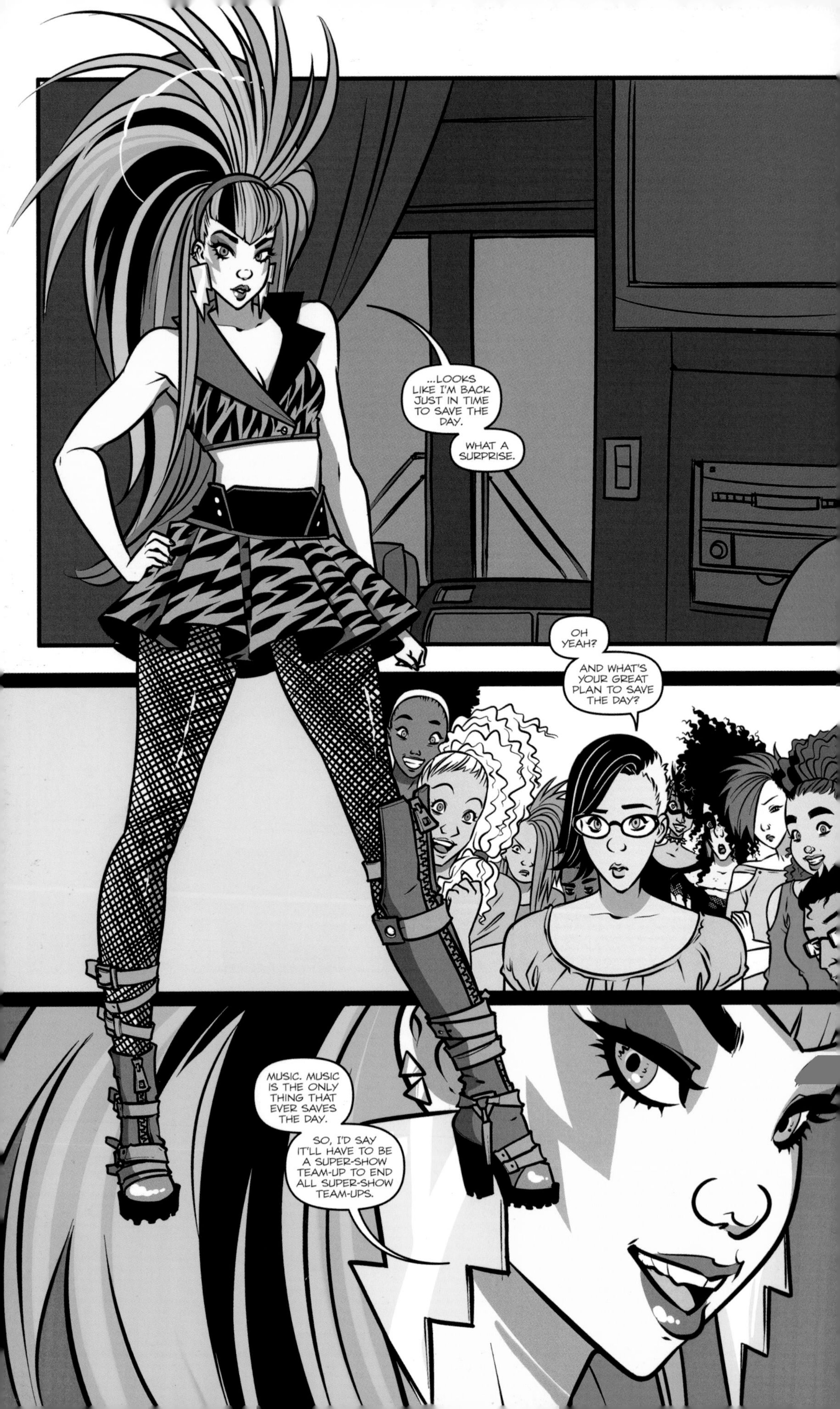
...LOOKS LIKE I'M BACK JUST IN TIME TO SAVE THE DAY.
WHAT A SURPRISE.
OH YEAH?
AND WHAT'S YOUR GREAT PLAN TO SAVE THE DAY?
MUSIC. MUSIC IS THE ONLY THING THAT EVER SAVES THE DAY.
SO, I'D SAY IT'LL HAVE TO BE A SUPER-SHOW TEAM-UP TO END ALL SUPER-SHOW TEAM-UPS.

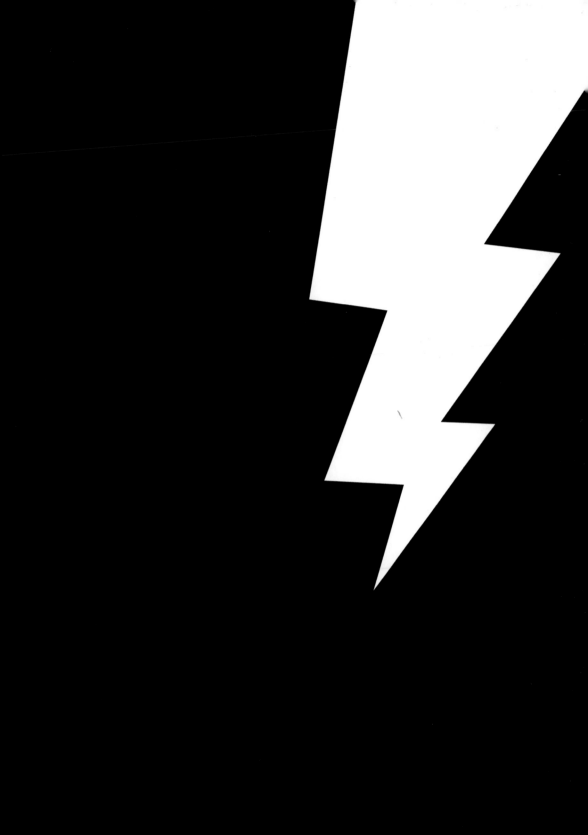

6 ART BY **SOPHIE CAMPBELL**

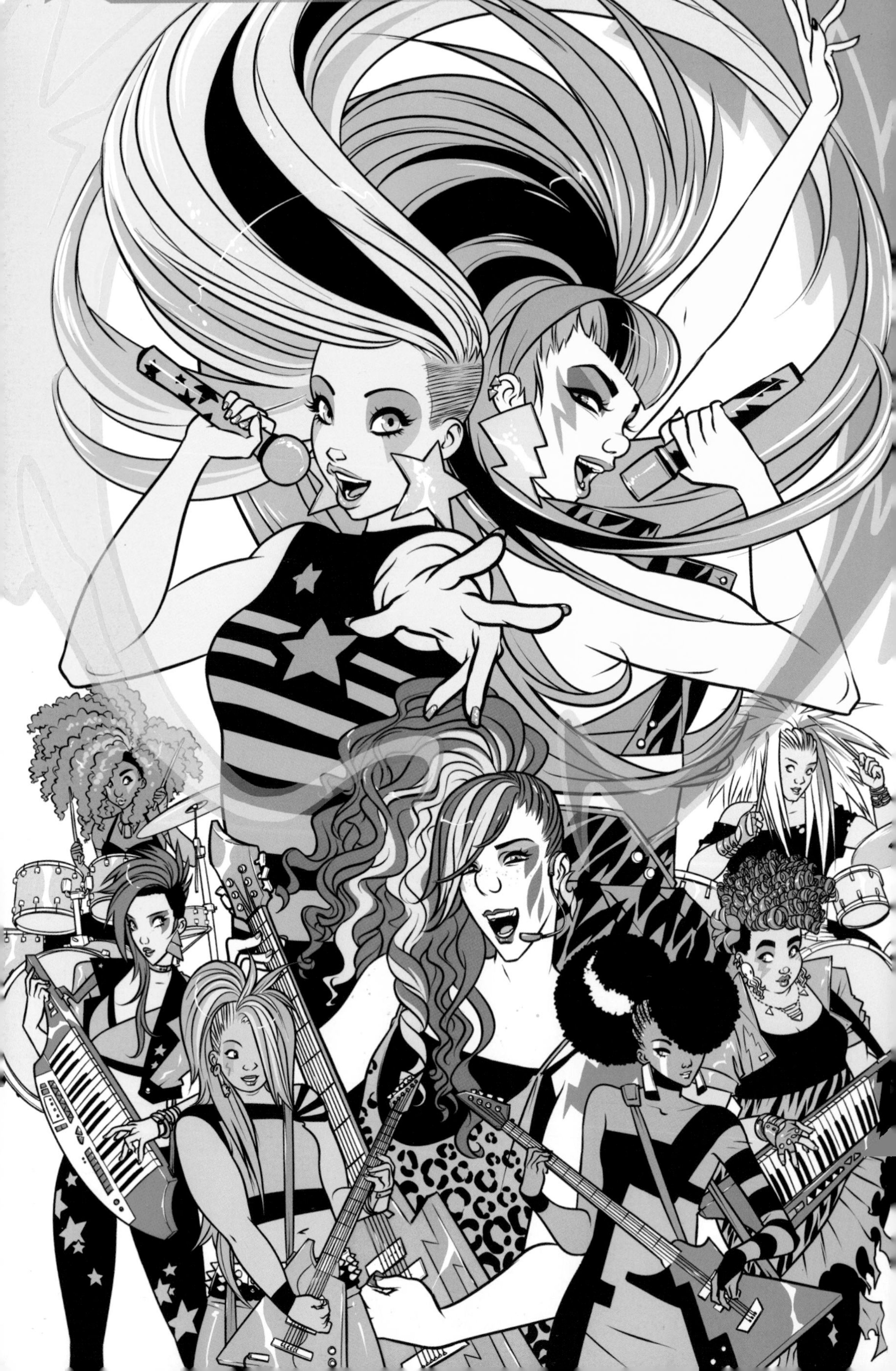

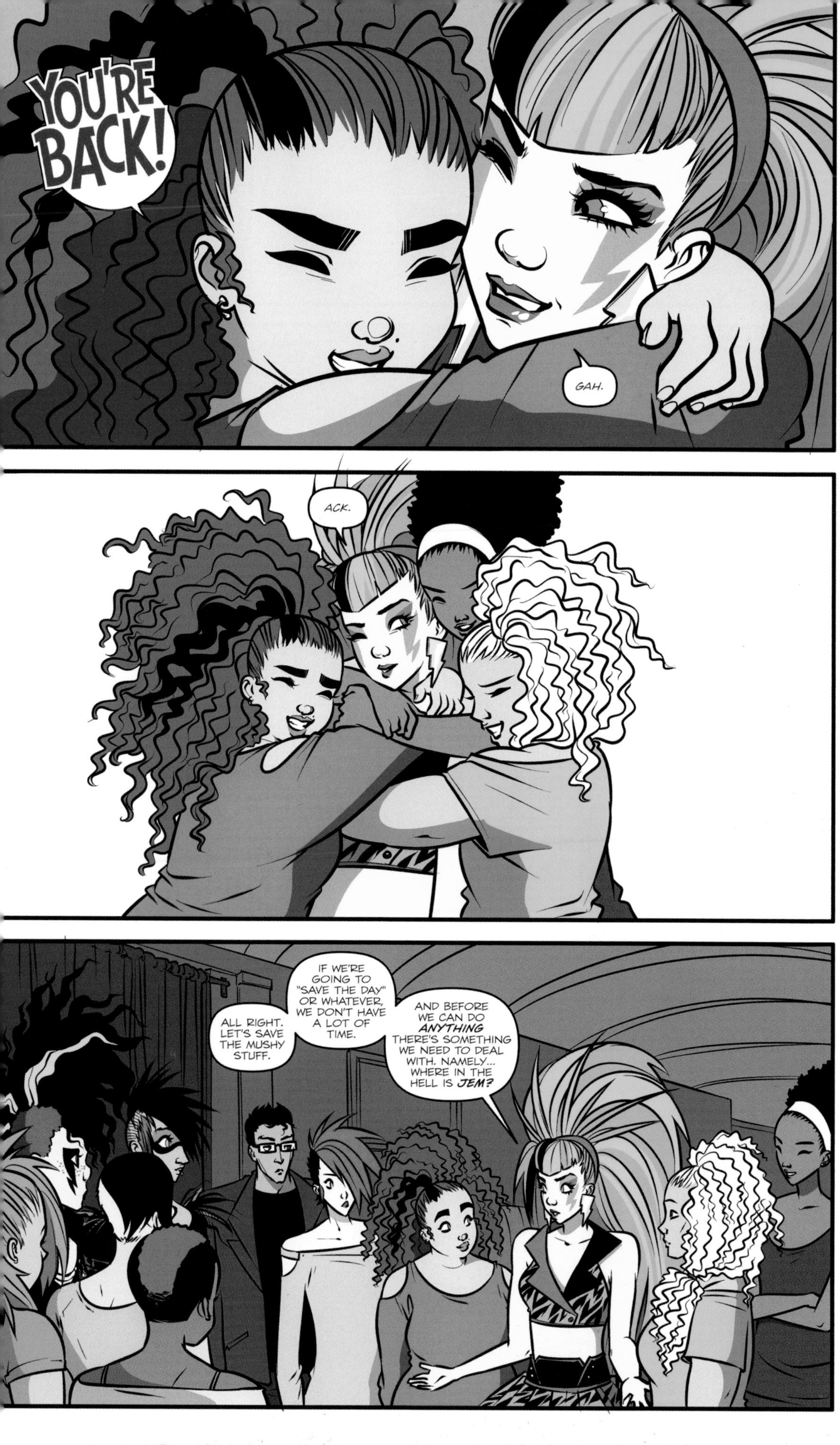
YOU'RE BACK!
GAH.
ACK.
ALL RIGHT. LET'S SAVE THE MUSHY STUFF.
IF WE'RE GOING TO "SAVE THE DAY" OR WHATEVER, WE DON'T HAVE A LOT OF TIME.
AND BEFORE WE CAN DO *ANYTHING* THERE'S SOMETHING WE NEED TO DEAL WITH. NAMELY... WHERE IN THE HELL IS *JEM?*

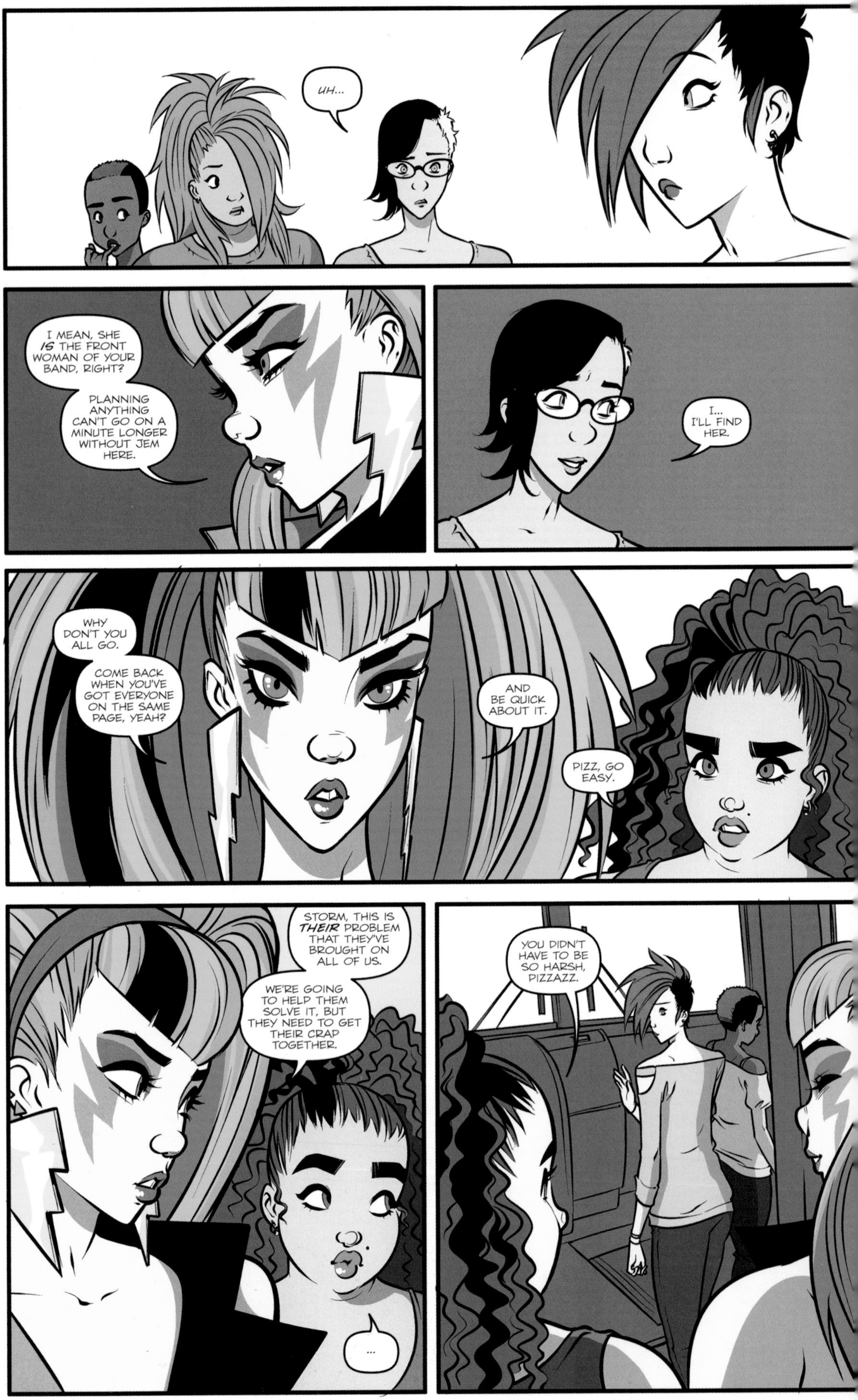
UH...
I MEAN, SHE IS THE FRONT WOMAN OF YOUR BAND, RIGHT?
PLANNING ANYTHING CAN'T GO ON A MINUTE LONGER WITHOUT JEM HERE.
I... I'LL FIND HER.
WHY DON'T YOU ALL GO.
COME BACK WHEN YOU'VE GOT EVERYONE ON THE SAME PAGE, YEAH?
AND BE QUICK ABOUT IT.
PIZZ, GO EASY.
STORM, THIS IS THEIR PROBLEM THAT THEY'VE BROUGHT ON ALL OF US.
WE'RE GOING TO HELP THEM SOLVE IT, BUT THEY NEED TO GET THEIR CRAP TOGETHER.
...
YOU DIDN'T HAVE TO BE SO HARSH, PIZZAZZ.

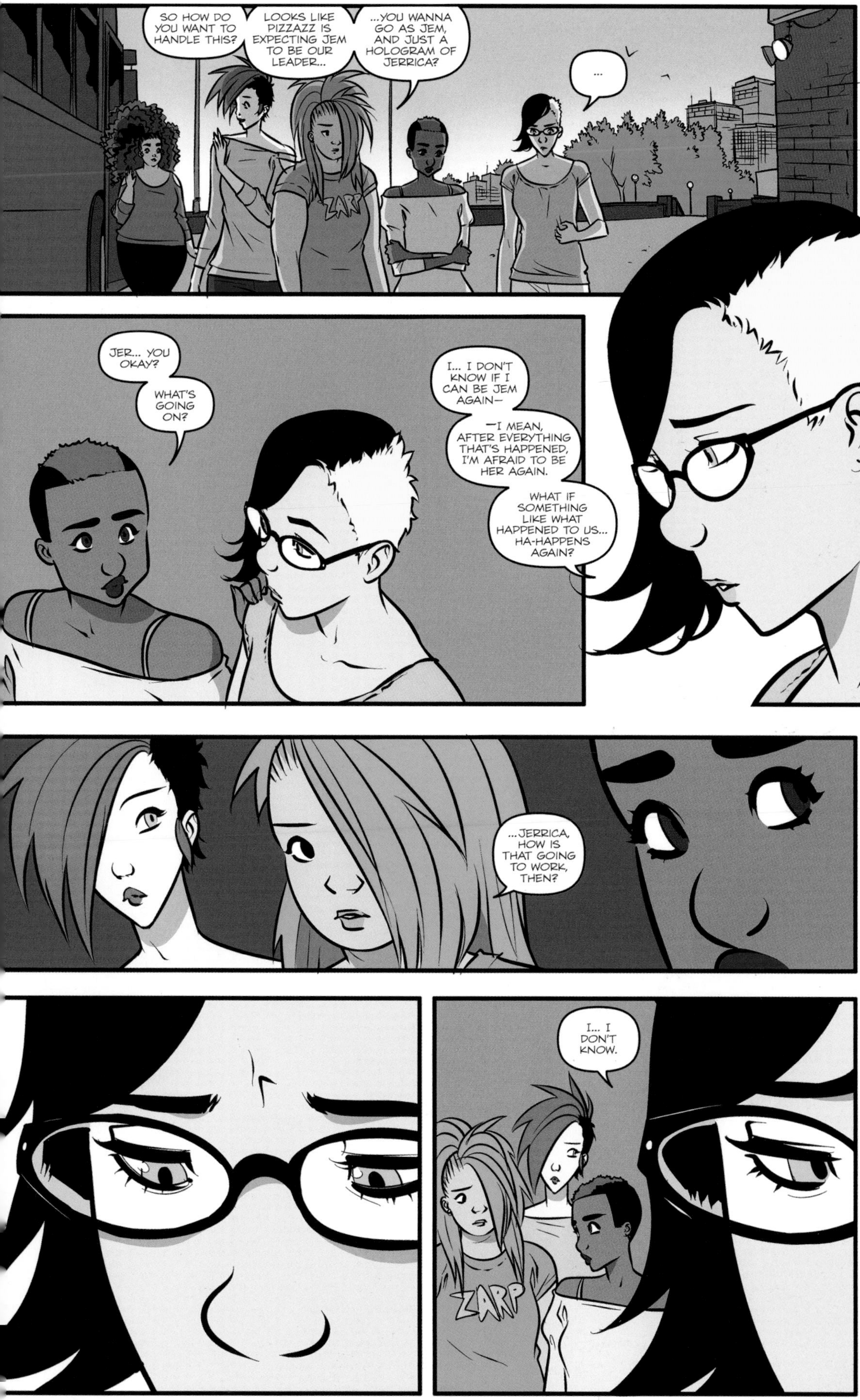

SO HOW DO YOU WANT TO HANDLE THIS?
LOOKS LIKE PIZZAZZ IS EXPECTING JEM TO BE OUR LEADER...
...YOU WANNA GO AS JEM, AND JUST A HOLOGRAM OF JERRICA?
...
JER... YOU OKAY?
WHAT'S GOING ON?
I... I DON'T KNOW IF I CAN BE JEM AGAIN—
—I MEAN, AFTER EVERYTHING THAT'S HAPPENED, I'M AFRAID TO BE HER AGAIN.
WHAT IF SOMETHING LIKE WHAT HAPPENED TO US... HA-HAPPENS AGAIN?
...JERRICA, HOW IS THAT GOING TO WORK, THEN?
I... I DON'T KNOW.
ZARP

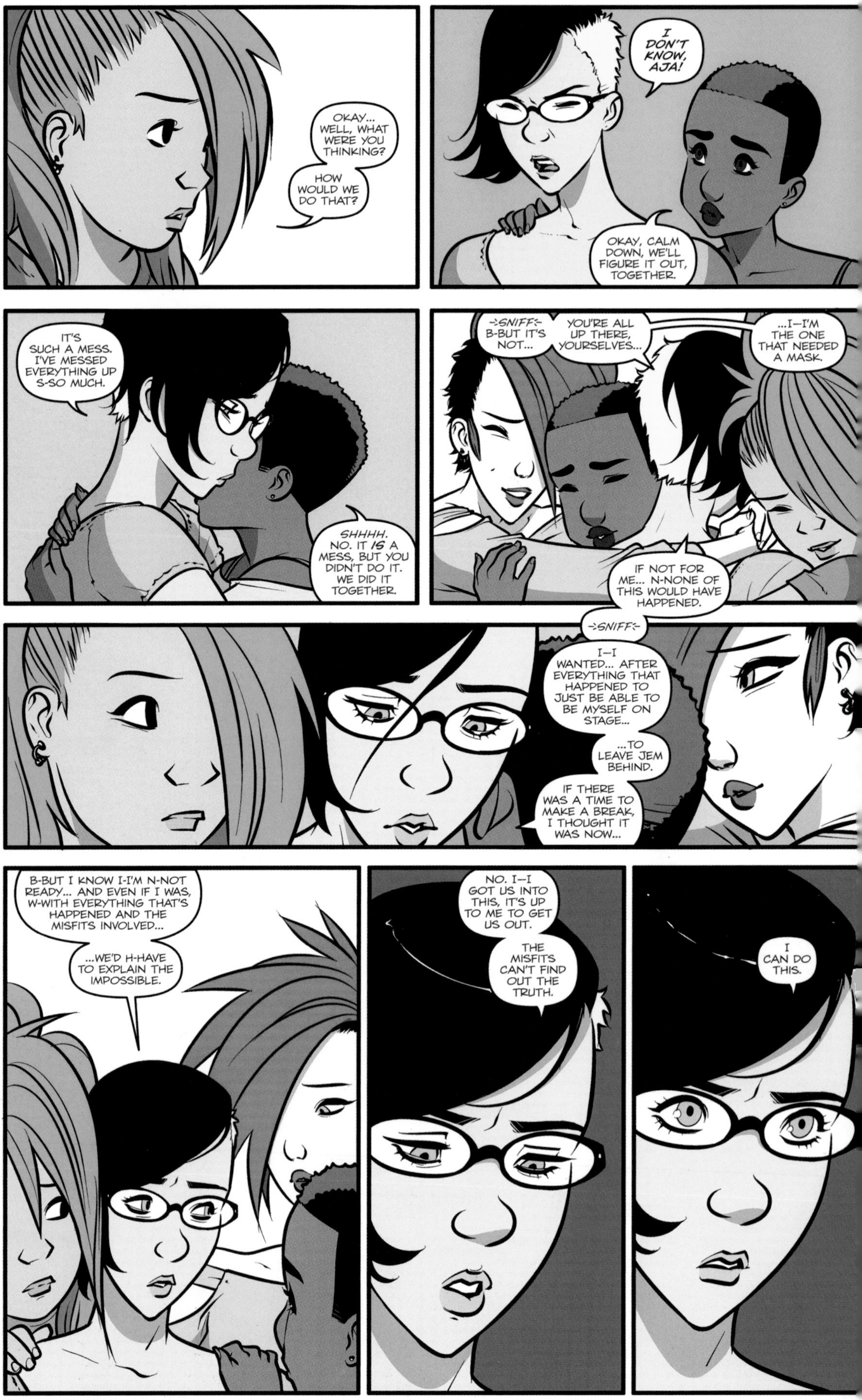

OKAY... WELL, WHAT WERE YOU THINKING?
HOW WOULD WE DO THAT?
I DON'T KNOW, AJA!
OKAY, CALM DOWN, WE'LL FIGURE IT OUT, TOGETHER.
IT'S SUCH A MESS. I'VE MESSED EVERYTHING UP S-SO MUCH.
SHHHH. NO. IT IS A MESS, BUT YOU DIDN'T DO IT. WE DID IT TOGETHER.
-SNIFF- B-BUT IT'S NOT...
YOU'RE ALL UP THERE, YOURSELVES...
...I—I'M THE ONE THAT NEEDED A MASK.
IF NOT FOR ME... N-NONE OF THIS WOULD HAVE HAPPENED.
-SNIFF-
I—I WANTED... AFTER EVERYTHING THAT HAPPENED TO JUST BE ABLE TO BE MYSELF ON STAGE...
...TO LEAVE JEM BEHIND.
IF THERE WAS A TIME TO MAKE A BREAK, I THOUGHT IT WAS NOW...
B-BUT I KNOW I-I'M N-NOT READY... AND EVEN IF I WAS, W-WITH EVERYTHING THAT'S HAPPENED AND THE MISFITS INVOLVED...
...WE'D H-HAVE TO EXPLAIN THE IMPOSSIBLE.
NO. I—I GOT US INTO THIS, IT'S UP TO ME TO GET US OUT.
THE MISFITS CAN'T FIND OUT THE TRUTH.
I CAN DO THIS.

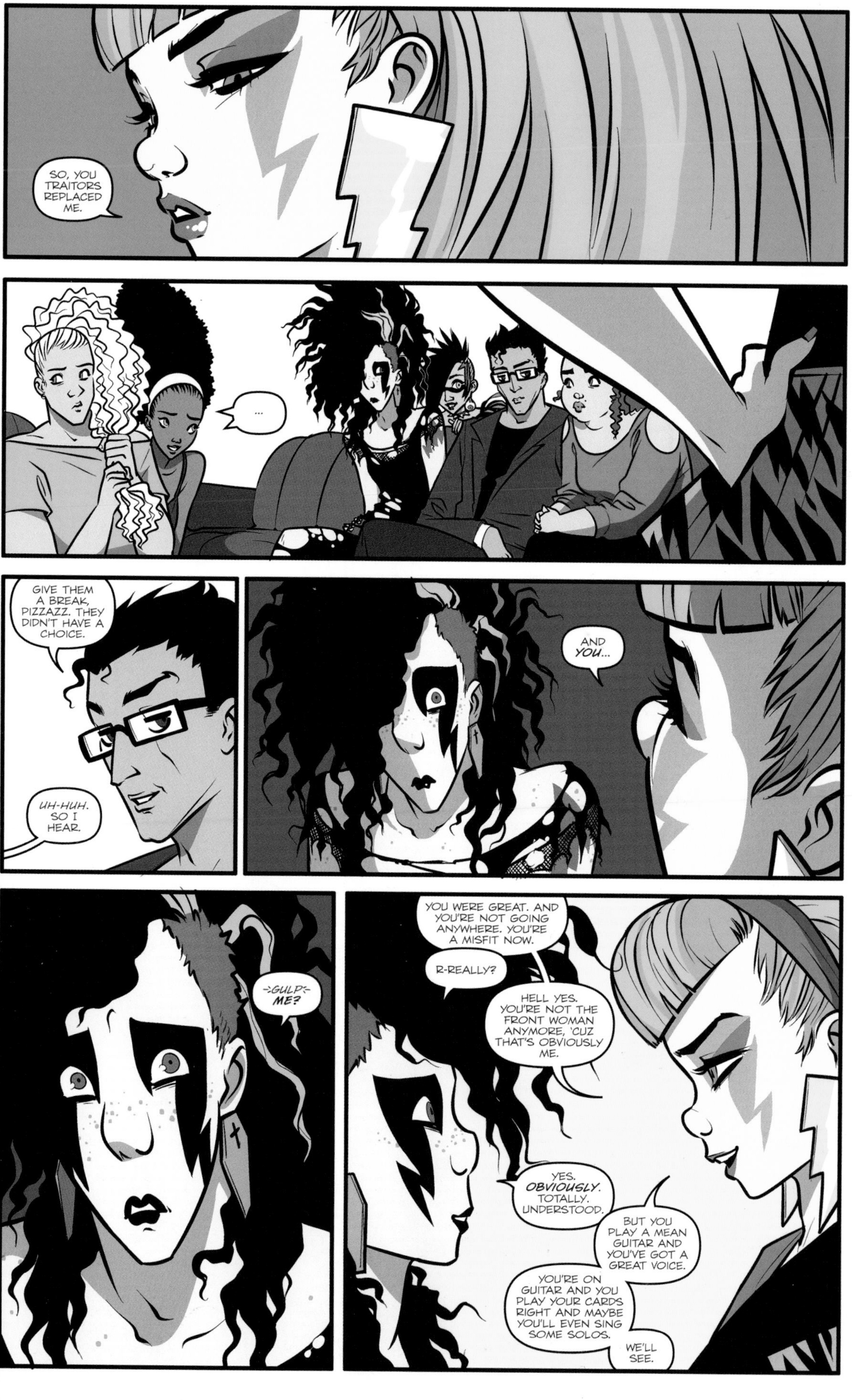
SO, YOU TRAITORS REPLACED ME.
...
GIVE THEM A BREAK, PIZZAZZ. THEY DIDN'T HAVE A CHOICE.
UH-HUH. SO I HEAR.
AND *YOU*...
-GULP- *ME?*
YOU WERE GREAT. AND YOU'RE NOT GOING ANYWHERE. YOU'RE A MISFIT NOW.
R-REALLY?
HELL YES. YOU'RE NOT THE FRONT WOMAN ANYMORE, 'CUZ THAT'S OBVIOUSLY ME.
YES. *OBVIOUSLY*. TOTALLY. UNDERSTOOD.
BUT YOU PLAY A MEAN GUITAR AND YOU'VE GOT A GREAT VOICE.
YOU'RE ON GUITAR AND YOU PLAY YOUR CARDS RIGHT AND MAYBE YOU'LL EVEN SING SOME SOLOS.
WE'LL SEE.

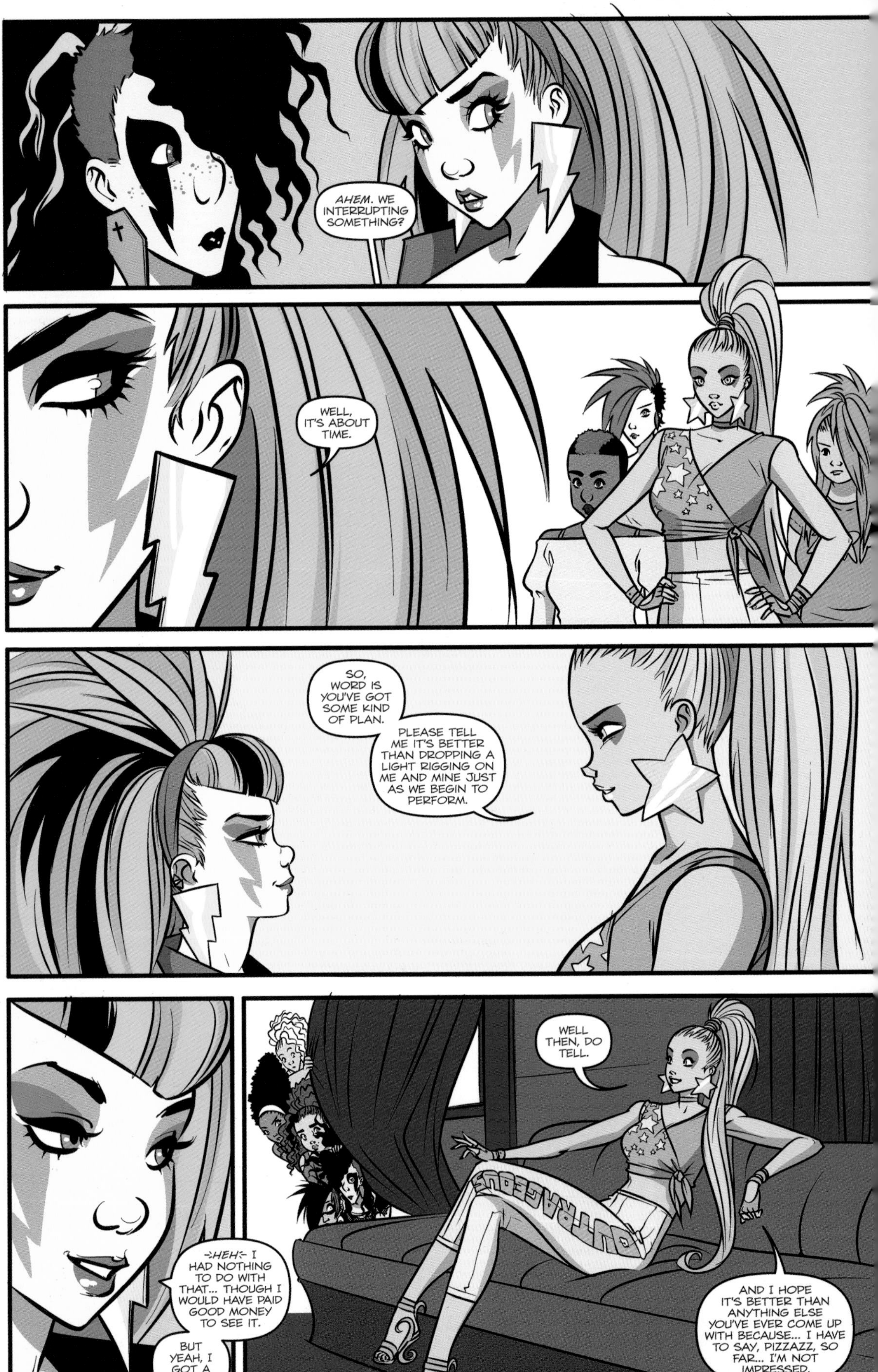
AHEM. WE INTERRUPTING SOMETHING?
WELL, IT'S ABOUT TIME.
SO, WORD IS YOU'VE GOT SOME KIND OF PLAN.
PLEASE TELL ME IT'S BETTER THAN DROPPING A LIGHT RIGGING ON ME AND MINE JUST AS WE BEGIN TO PERFORM.
-HEH- I HAD NOTHING TO DO WITH THAT... THOUGH I WOULD HAVE PAID GOOD MONEY TO SEE IT.
BUT YEAH, I GOT A PLAN.
WELL THEN, DO TELL.
AND I HOPE IT'S BETTER THAN ANYTHING ELSE YOU'VE EVER COME UP WITH BECAUSE... I HAVE TO SAY, PIZZAZZ, SO FAR... I'M NOT IMPRESSED.
OUTRAGEOUS

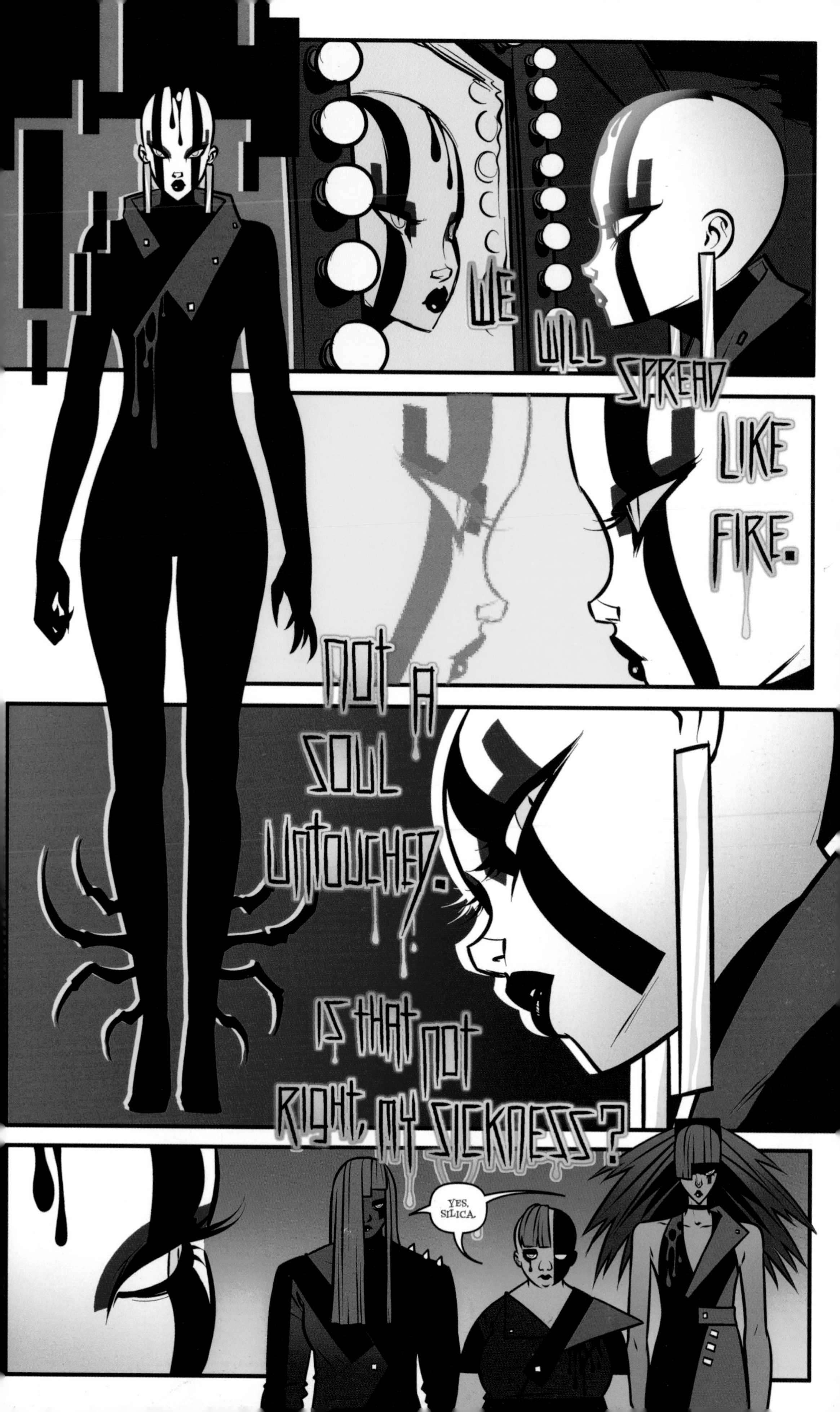
WE WILL SPREAD LIKE FIRE.
NOT A SOUL UNTOUCHED.
IS THAT NOT RIGHT, MY SICKNESS?
YES, SILICA.

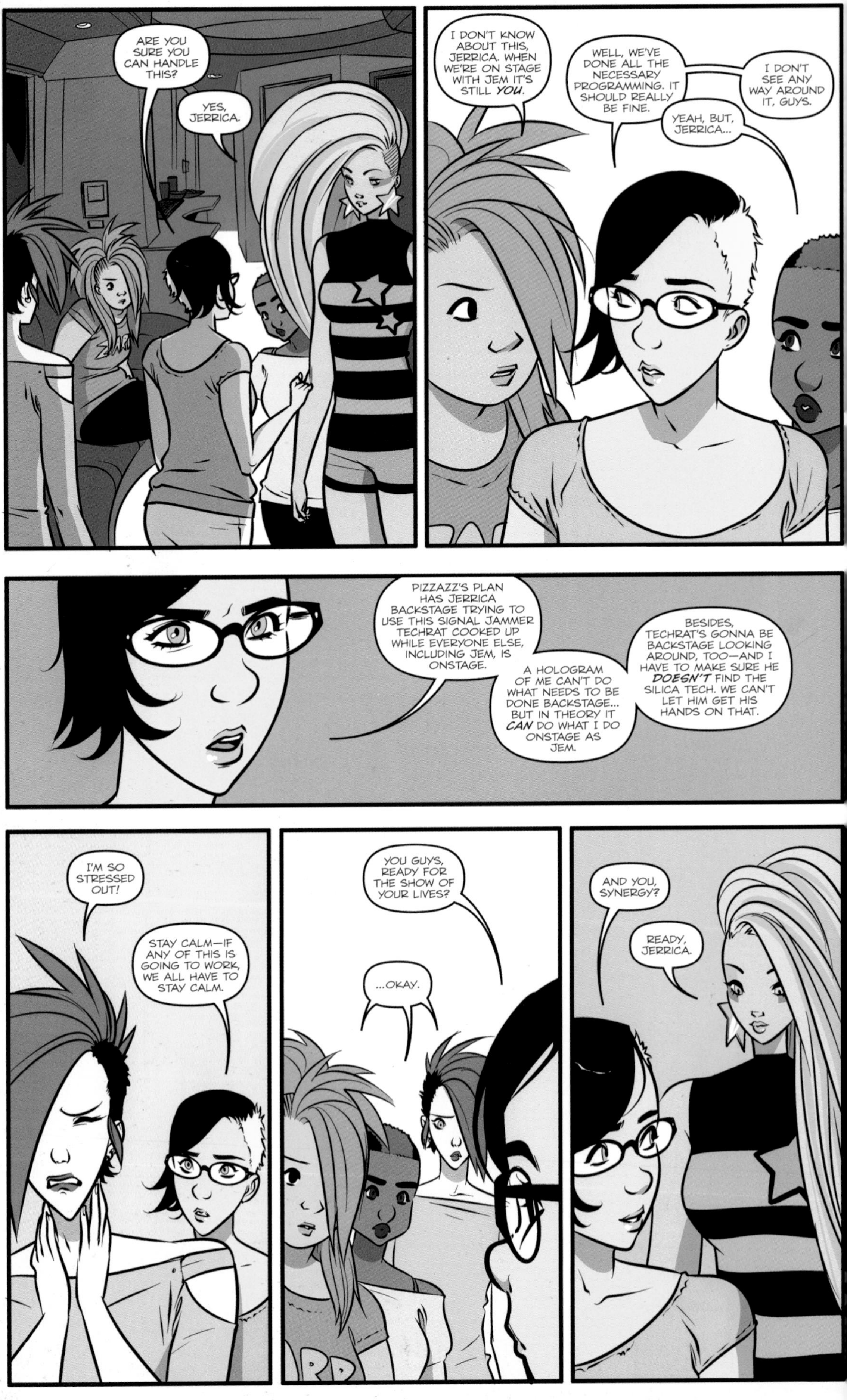
ARE YOU SURE YOU CAN HANDLE THIS?
YES, JERRICA.
I DON'T KNOW ABOUT THIS, JERRICA. WHEN WE'RE ON STAGE WITH JEM IT'S STILL *YOU*.
WELL, WE'VE DONE ALL THE NECESSARY PROGRAMMING. IT SHOULD REALLY BE FINE.
YEAH, BUT, JERRICA...
I DON'T SEE ANY WAY AROUND IT, GUYS.
PIZZAZZ'S PLAN HAS JERRICA BACKSTAGE TRYING TO USE THIS SIGNAL JAMMER TECHRAT COOKED UP WHILE EVERYONE ELSE, INCLUDING JEM, IS ONSTAGE.
A HOLOGRAM OF ME CAN'T DO WHAT NEEDS TO BE DONE BACKSTAGE... BUT IN THEORY IT *CAN* DO WHAT I DO ONSTAGE AS JEM.
BESIDES, TECHRAT'S GONNA BE BACKSTAGE LOOKING AROUND, TOO—AND I HAVE TO MAKE SURE HE *DOESN'T* FIND THE SILICA TECH. WE CAN'T LET HIM GET HIS HANDS ON THAT.
I'M SO STRESSED OUT!
STAY CALM—IF ANY OF THIS IS GOING TO WORK, WE ALL HAVE TO STAY CALM.
YOU GUYS, READY FOR THE SHOW OF YOUR LIVES?
...OKAY.
AND YOU, SYNERGY?
READY, JERRICA.

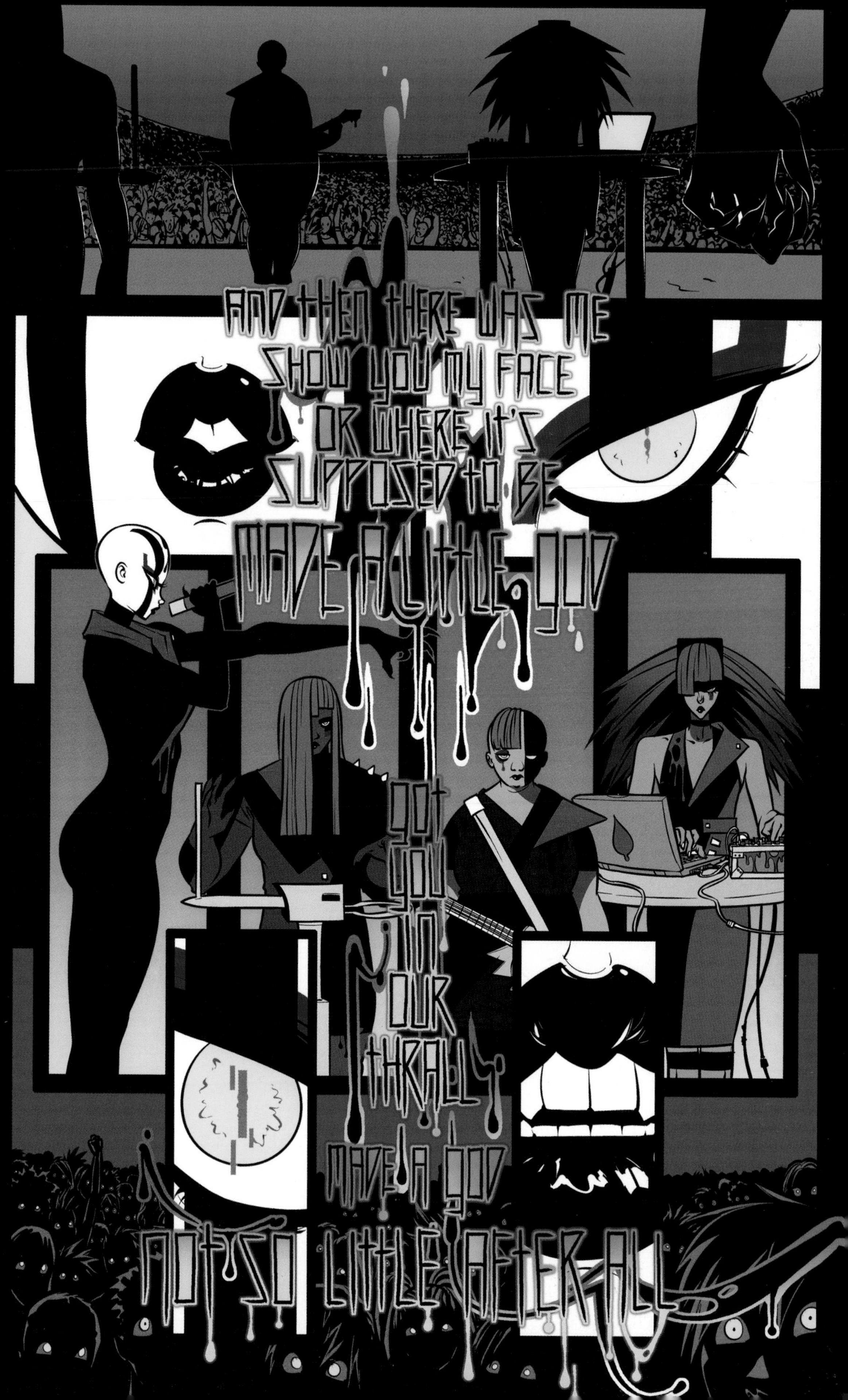
AND THEN THERE WAS ME
SHOW YOU MY FACE
OR WHERE IT'S
SUPPOSED TO BE
MADE A LITTLE GOD
GOT YOU IN OUR THRALL
MADE A GOD
NOT SO LITTLE AFTER ALL

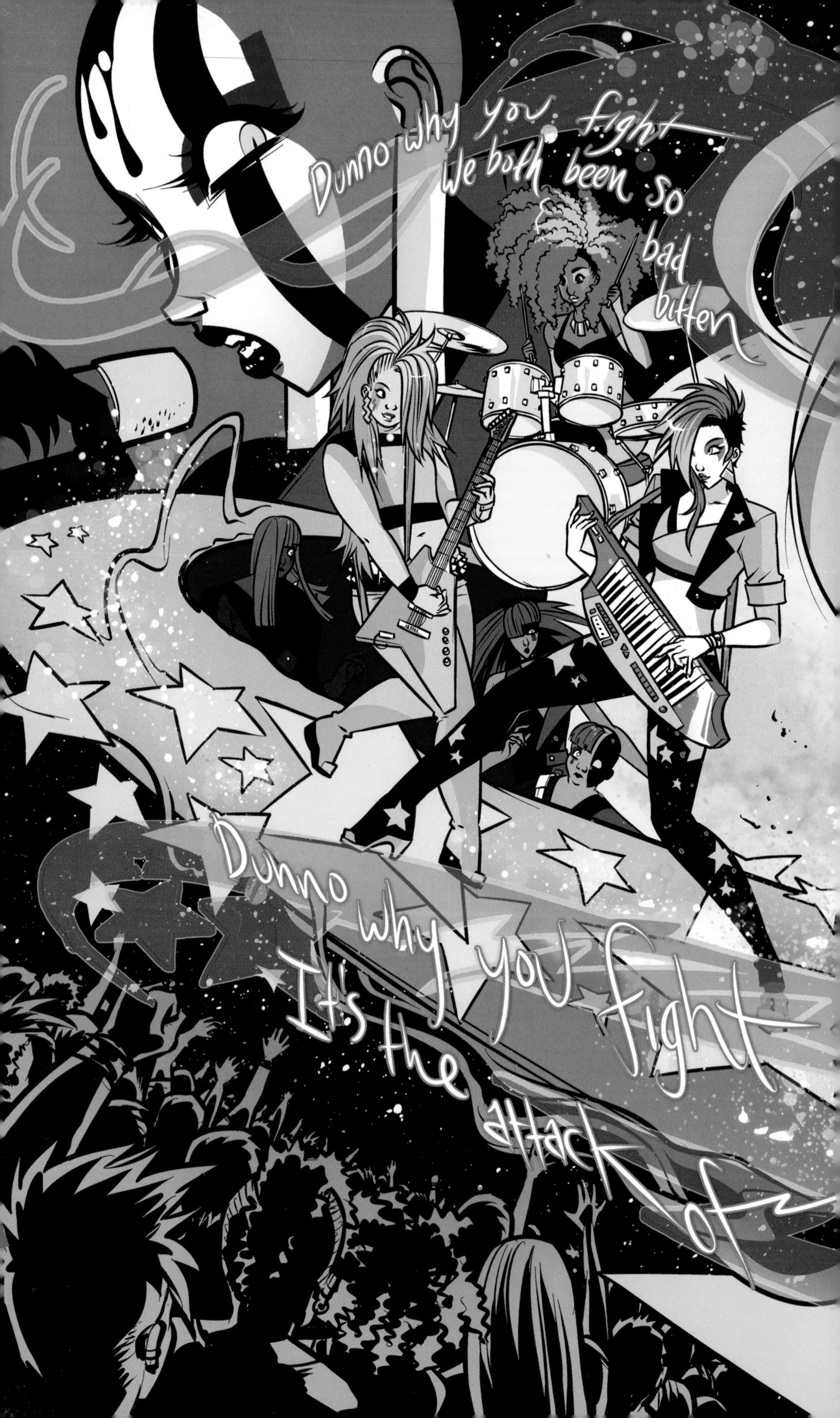
Dunno why you fight
We both been so bad bitten
Dunno why you fight
It's the attack of

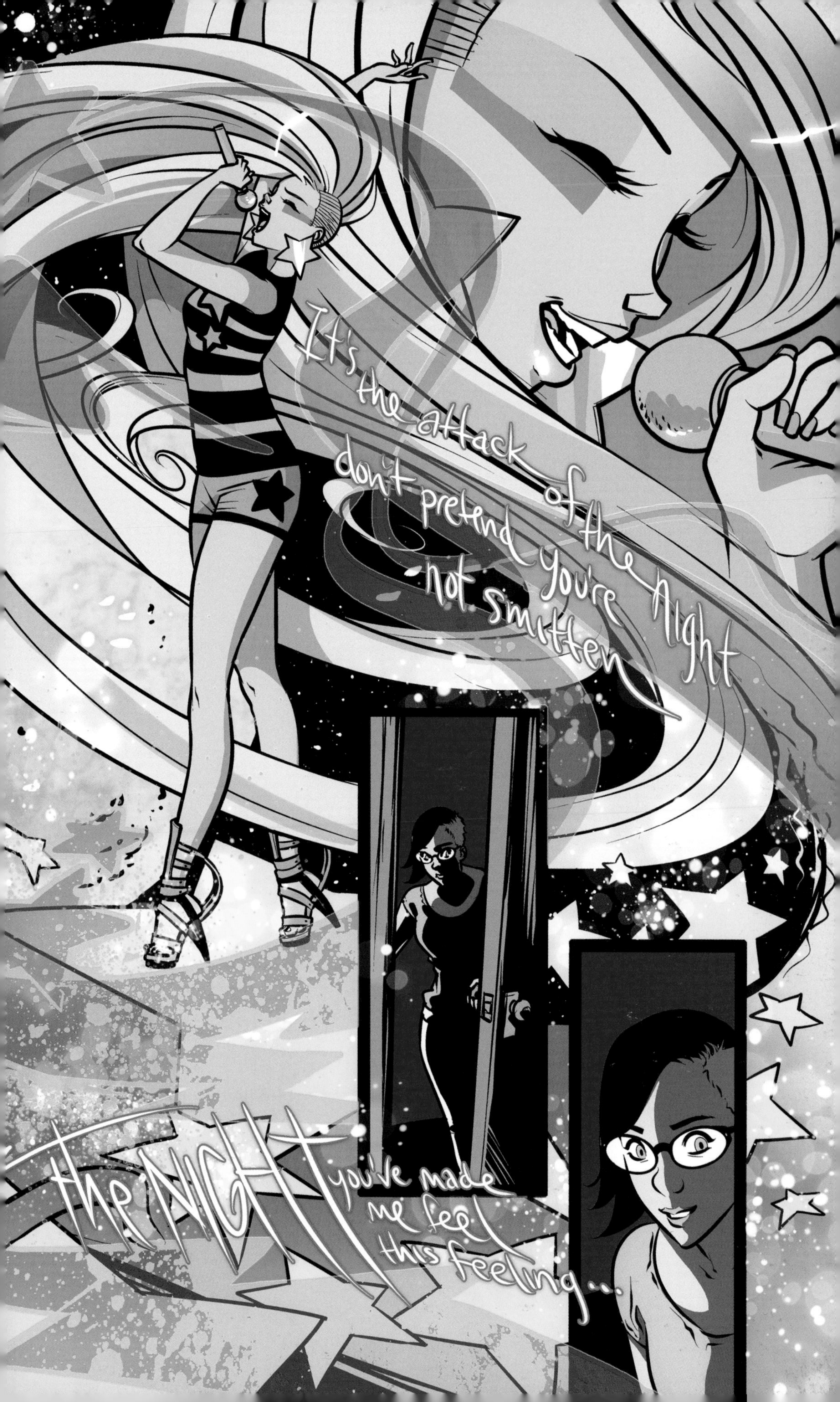
It's the attack of the night
don't pretend you're not smitten
The NIGHT you've made me feel this feeling...

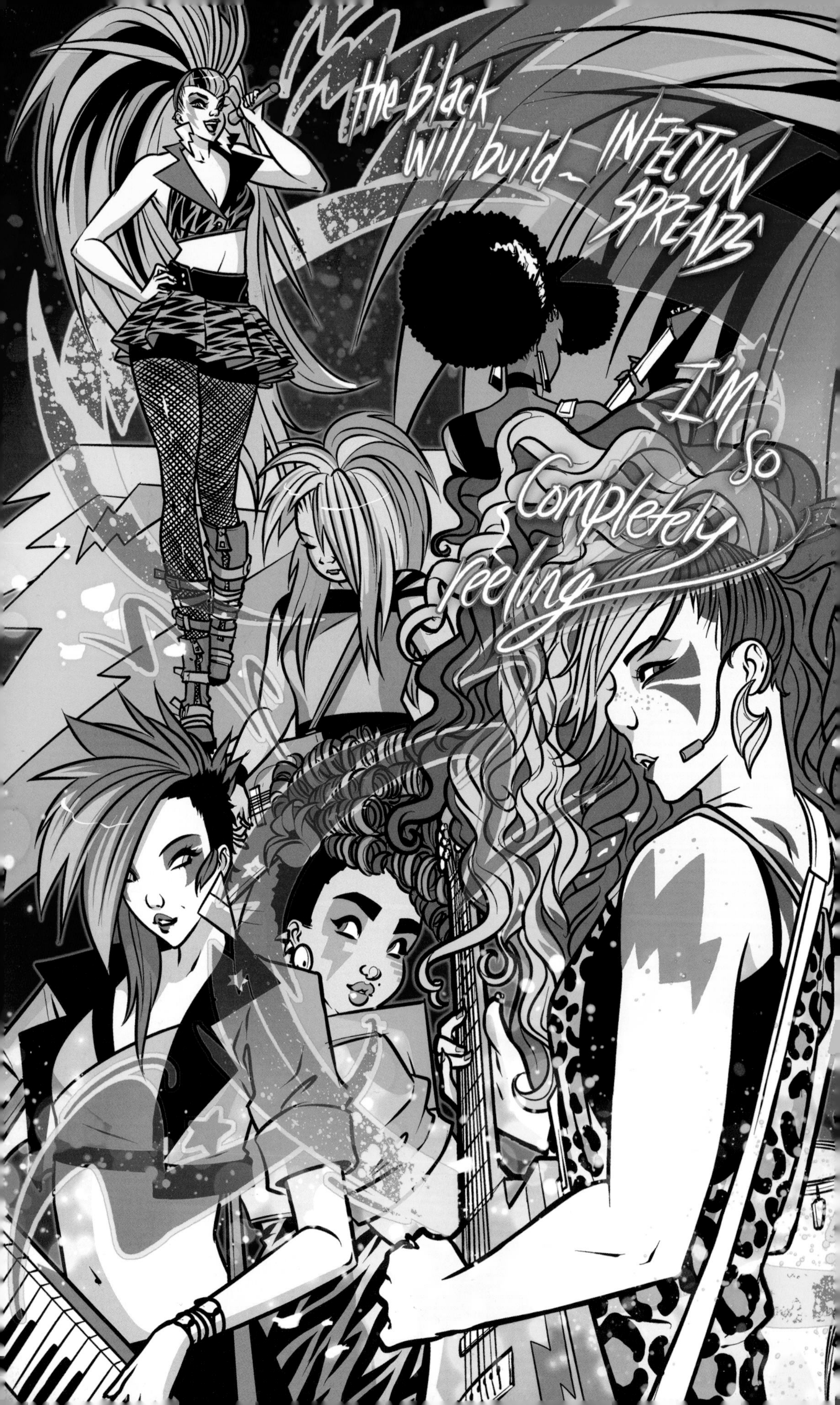

the black will build~ INFECTION SPREADS
I'M so Completely reeling

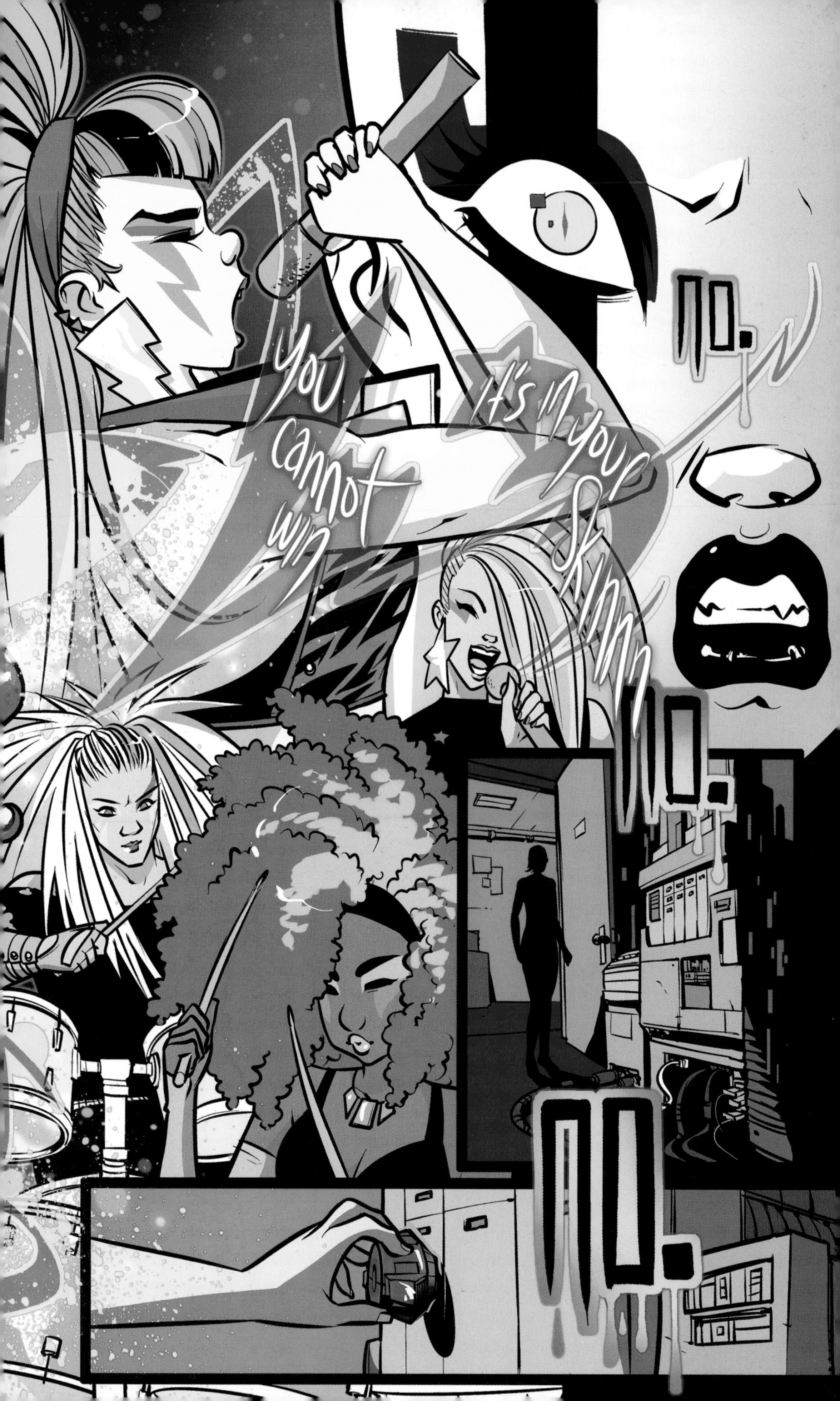

You cannot win
It's in your SKINNN
no.
no.
no.

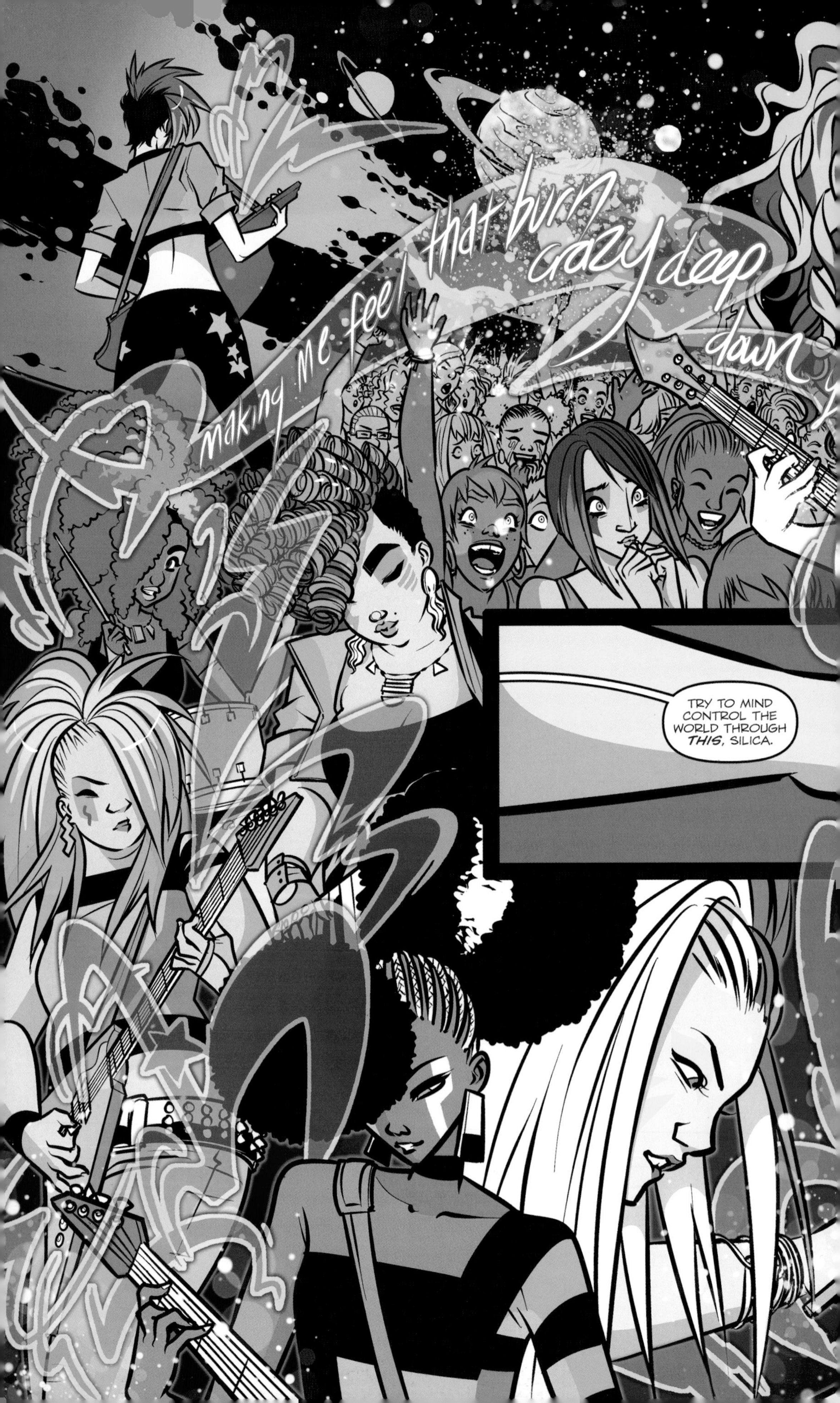
making me feel that burn
crazy deep
down
TRY TO MIND CONTROL THE WORLD THROUGH *THIS*, SILICA.

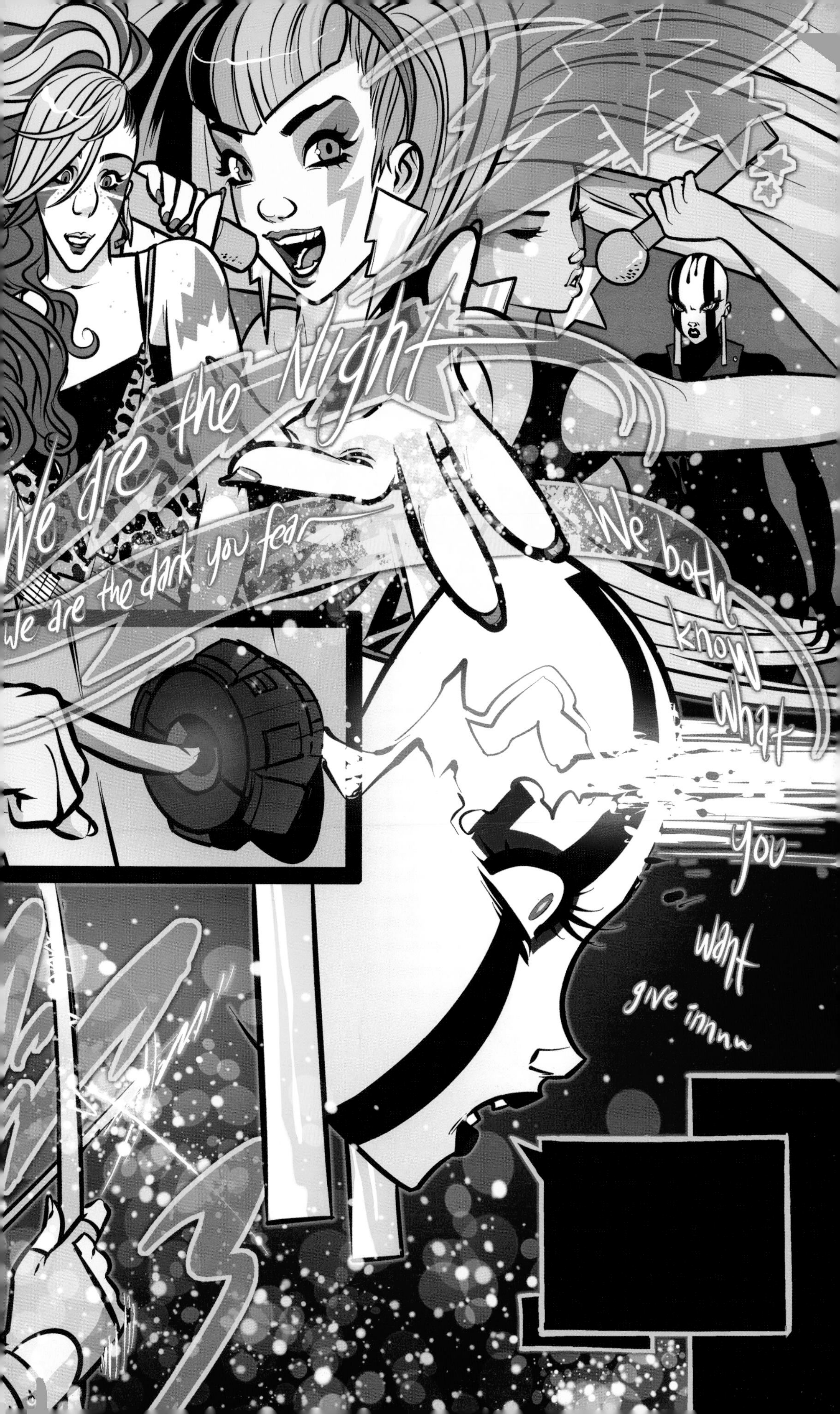
We are the Night
we are the dark you fear
We both know what you want
give innnn

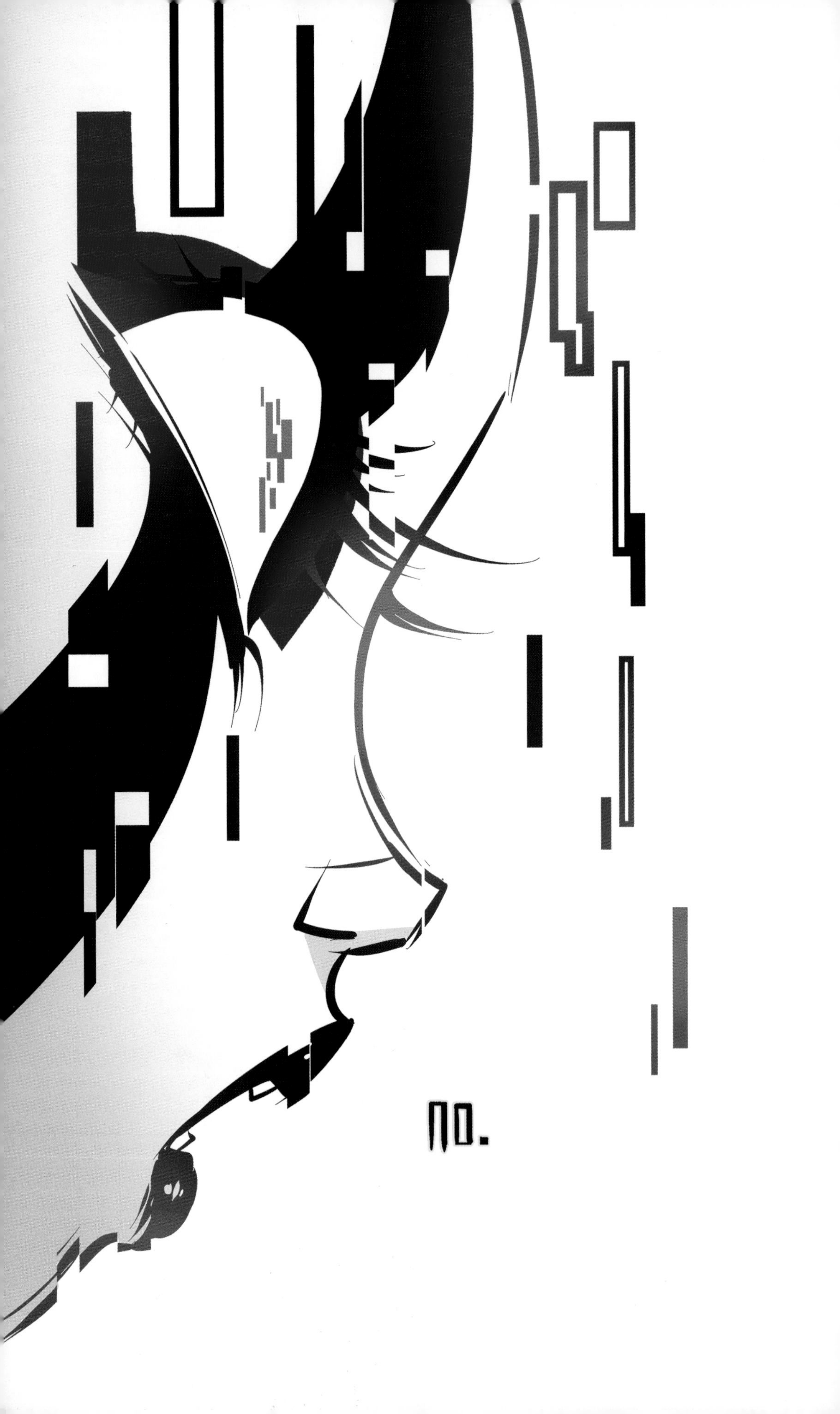
NO.

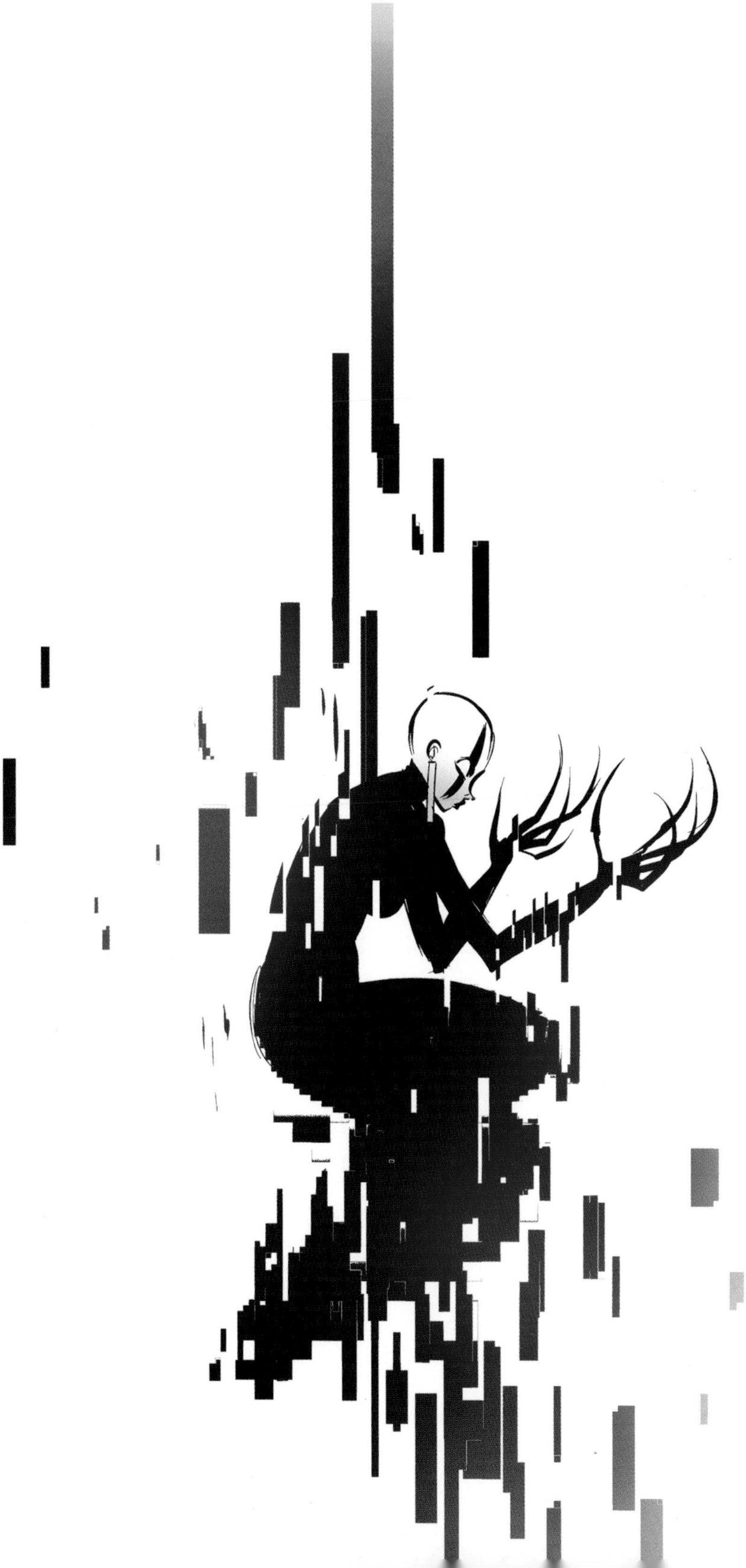

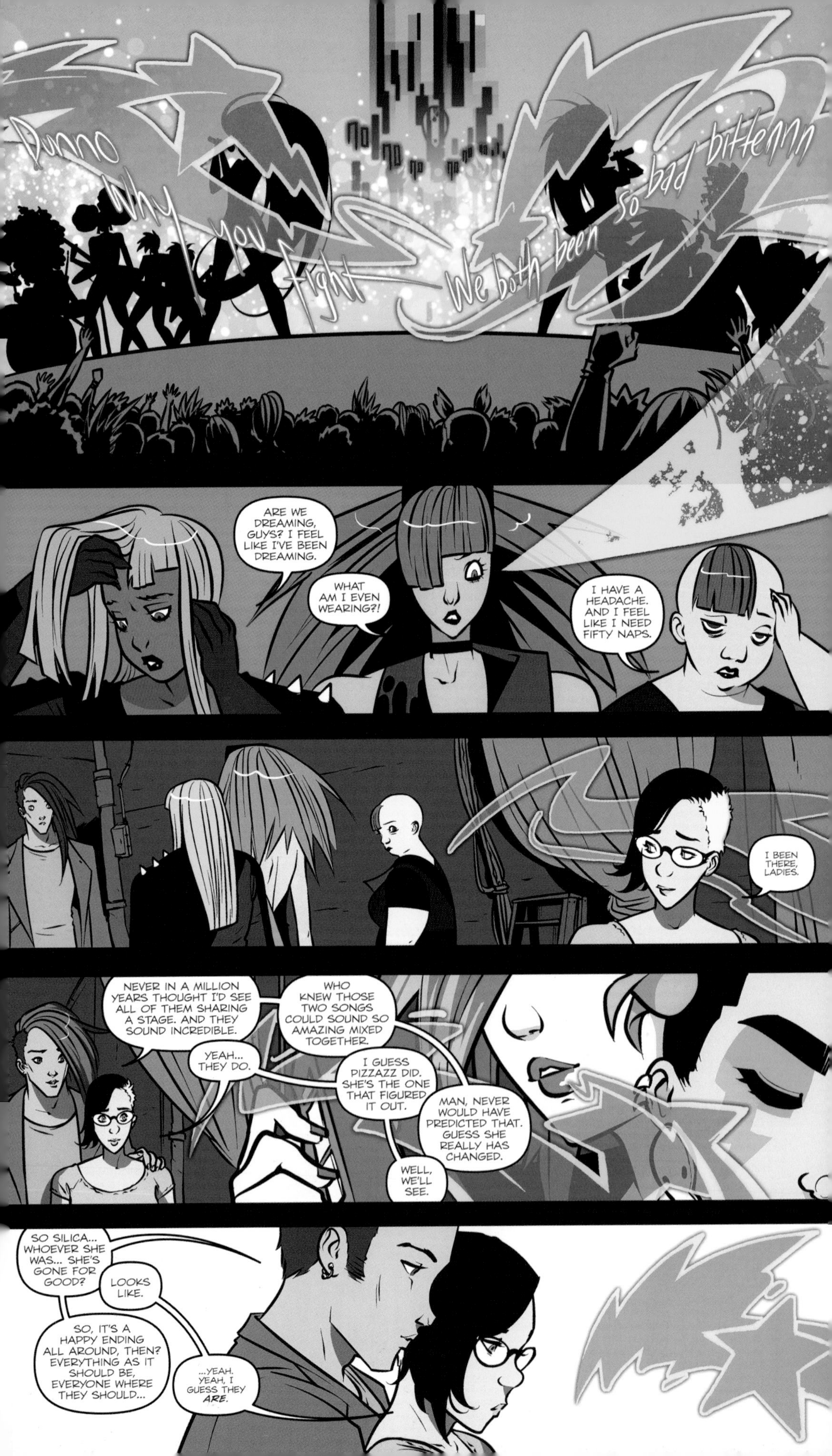
Dunno Why you fight
We both been so bad bittennn
ARE WE DREAMING, GUYS? I FEEL LIKE I'VE BEEN DREAMING.
WHAT AM I EVEN WEARING?!
I HAVE A HEADACHE. AND I FEEL LIKE I NEED FIFTY NAPS.
I BEEN THERE, LADIES.
NEVER IN A MILLION YEARS THOUGHT I'D SEE ALL OF THEM SHARING A STAGE. AND THEY SOUND INCREDIBLE.
YEAH... THEY DO.
WHO KNEW THOSE TWO SONGS COULD SOUND SO AMAZING MIXED TOGETHER.
I GUESS PIZZAZZ DID. SHE'S THE ONE THAT FIGURED IT OUT.
MAN, NEVER WOULD HAVE PREDICTED THAT. GUESS SHE REALLY HAS CHANGED.
WELL, WE'LL SEE.
SO SILICA... WHOEVER SHE WAS... SHE'S GONE FOR GOOD?
LOOKS LIKE.
SO, IT'S A HAPPY ENDING ALL AROUND, THEN? EVERYTHING AS IT SHOULD BE, EVERYONE WHERE THEY SHOULD...
...YEAH. YEAH, I GUESS THEY ***ARE***.

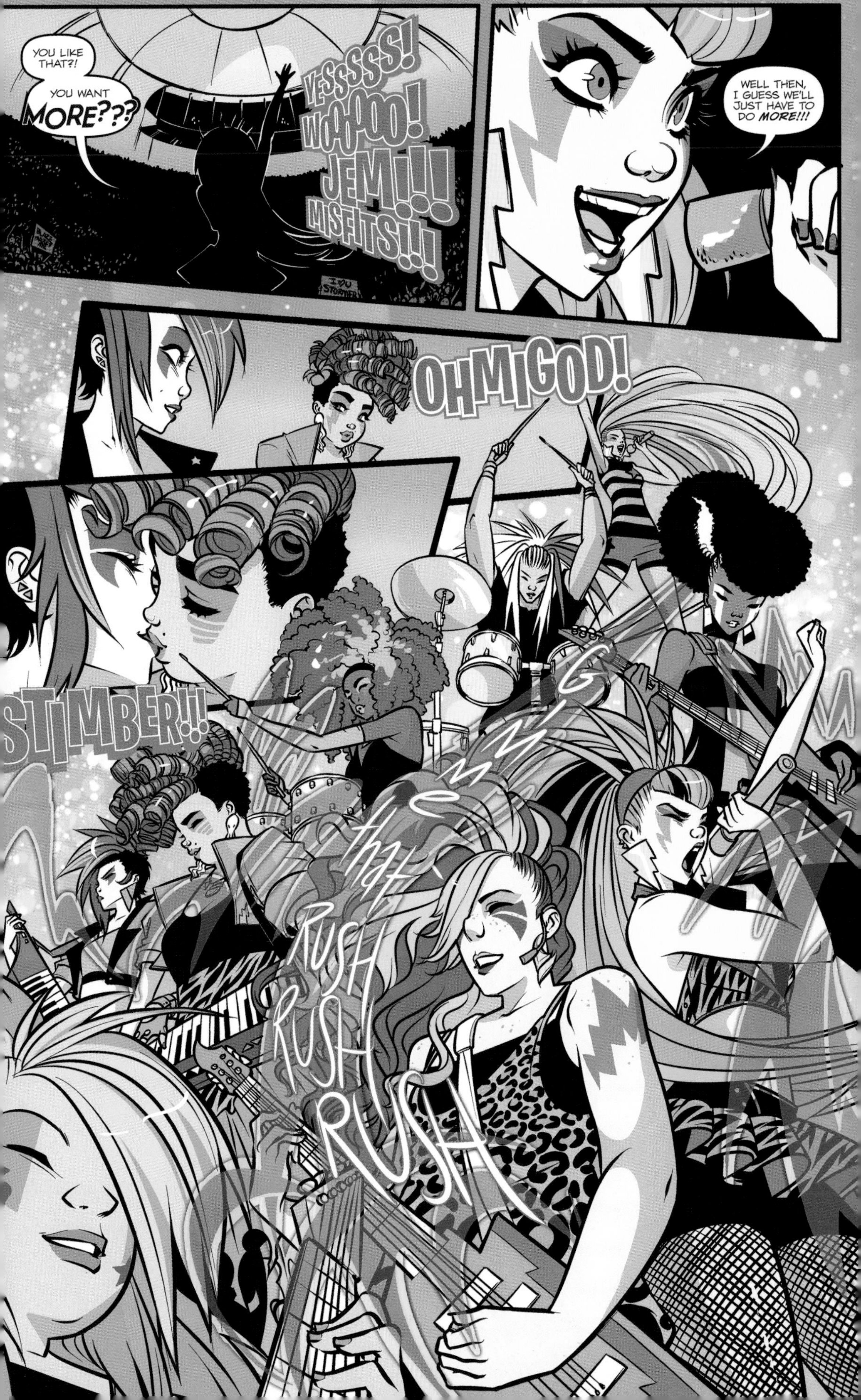

YOU LIKE THAT?!
YOU WANT MORE???
YESSSSS!
WOOOOOO!
JEM!!!
MISFITS!!!
I ♥ U STORMER
WELL THEN, I GUESS WE'LL JUST HAVE TO DO MORE!!!
OHMIGOD!
STIMBER!!!
GIMME that RUSH RUSH RUSH

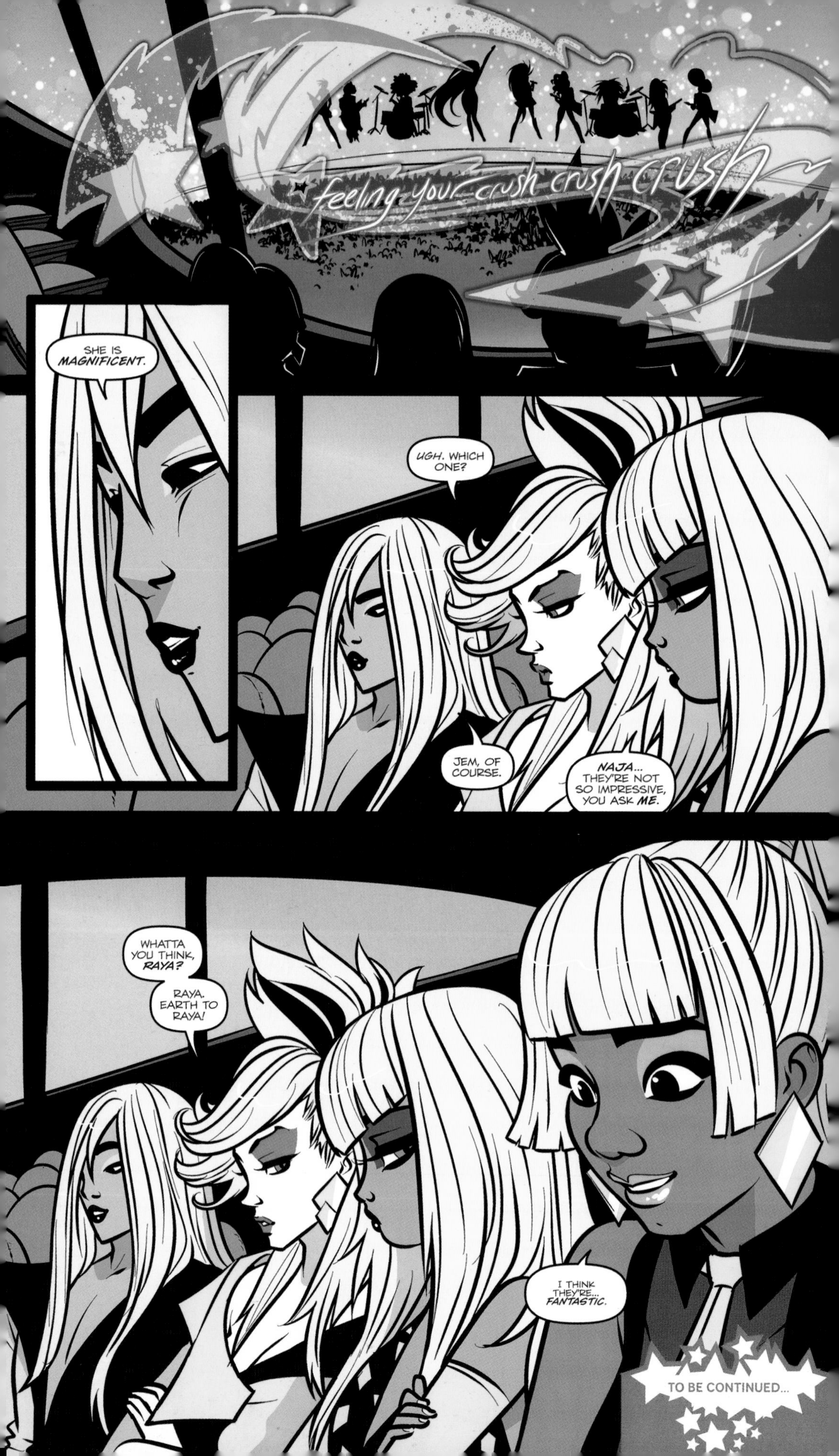
feeling your crush crush crush
SHE IS MAGNIFICENT.
UGH. WHICH ONE?
JEM, OF COURSE.
NAJA... THEY'RE NOT SO IMPRESSIVE, YOU ASK ME.
WHATTA YOU THINK, RAYA?
RAYA. EARTH TO RAYA!
I THINK THEY'RE... FANTASTIC.
TO BE CONTINUED...

ART BY **SOPHIE CAMPBELL**

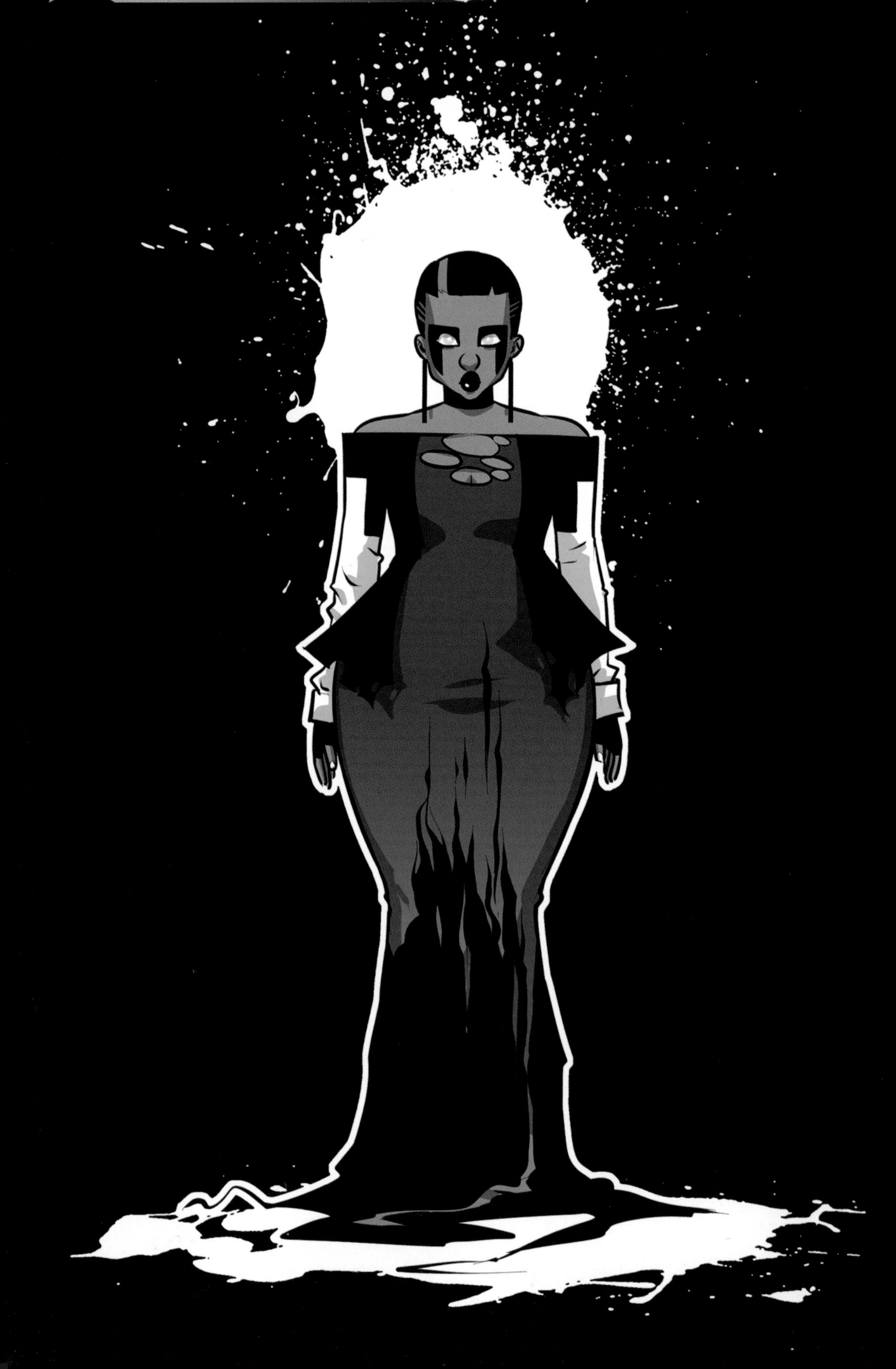

ART BY **SOPHIE CAMPBELL**

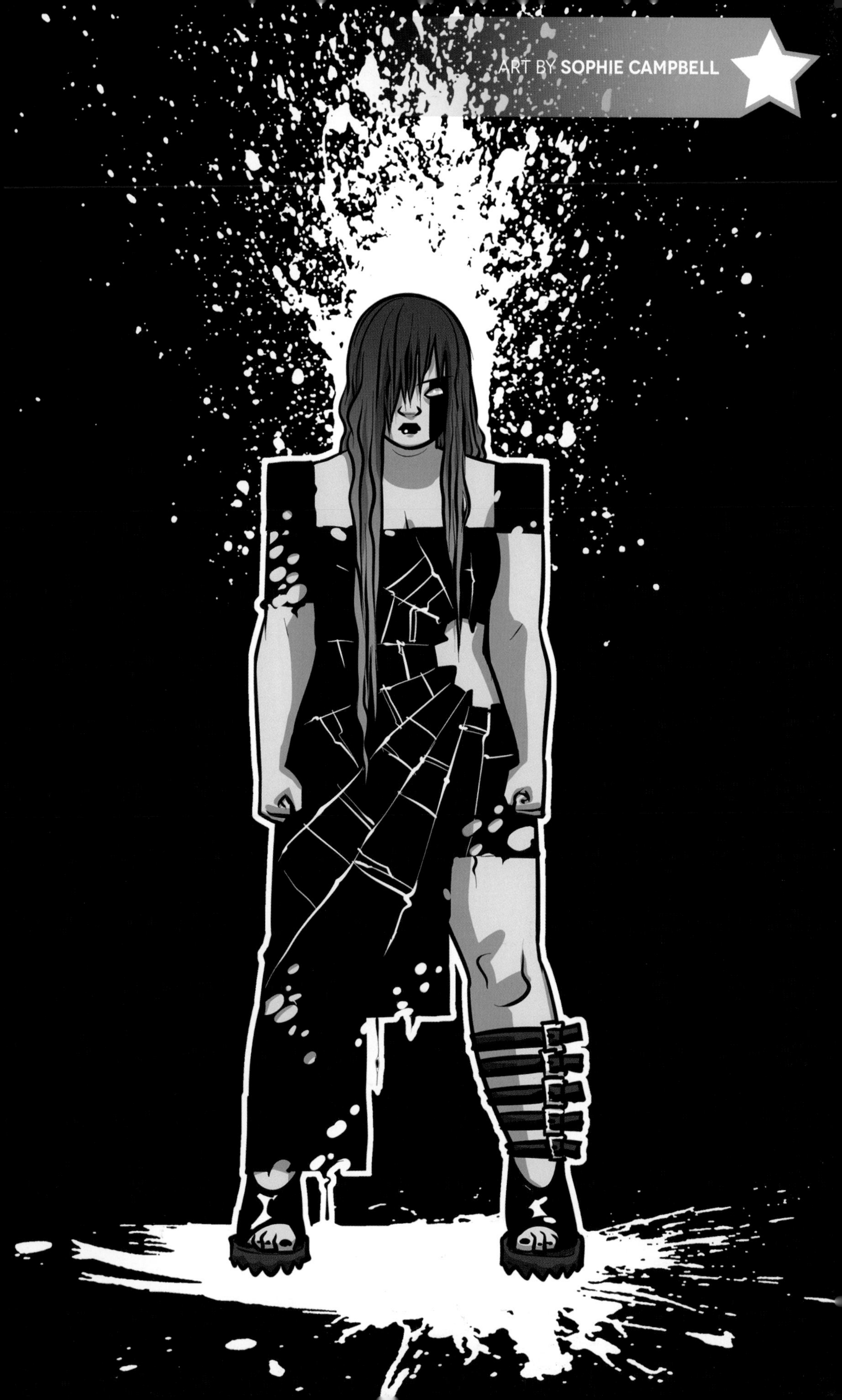

ART BY **SOPHIE CAMPBELL**

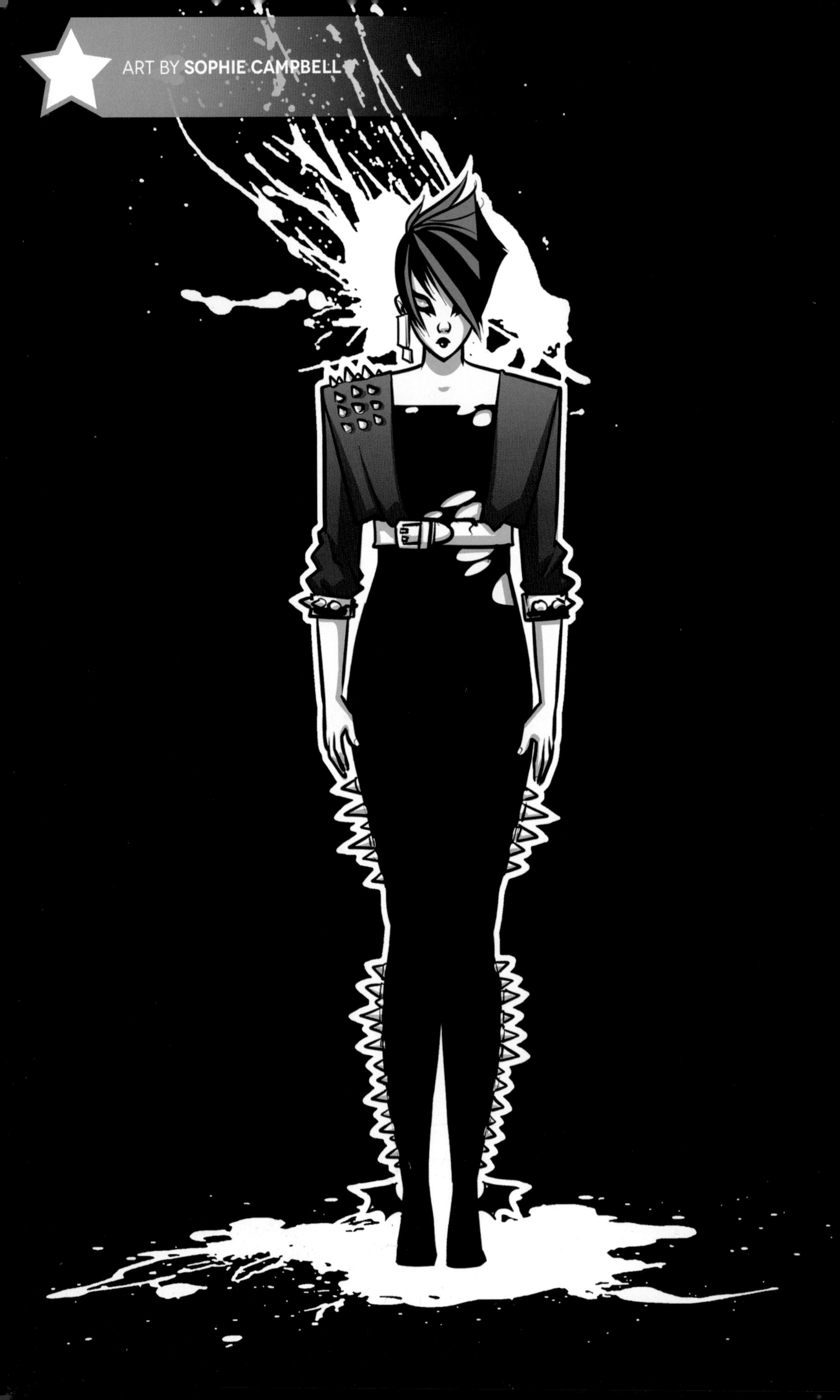

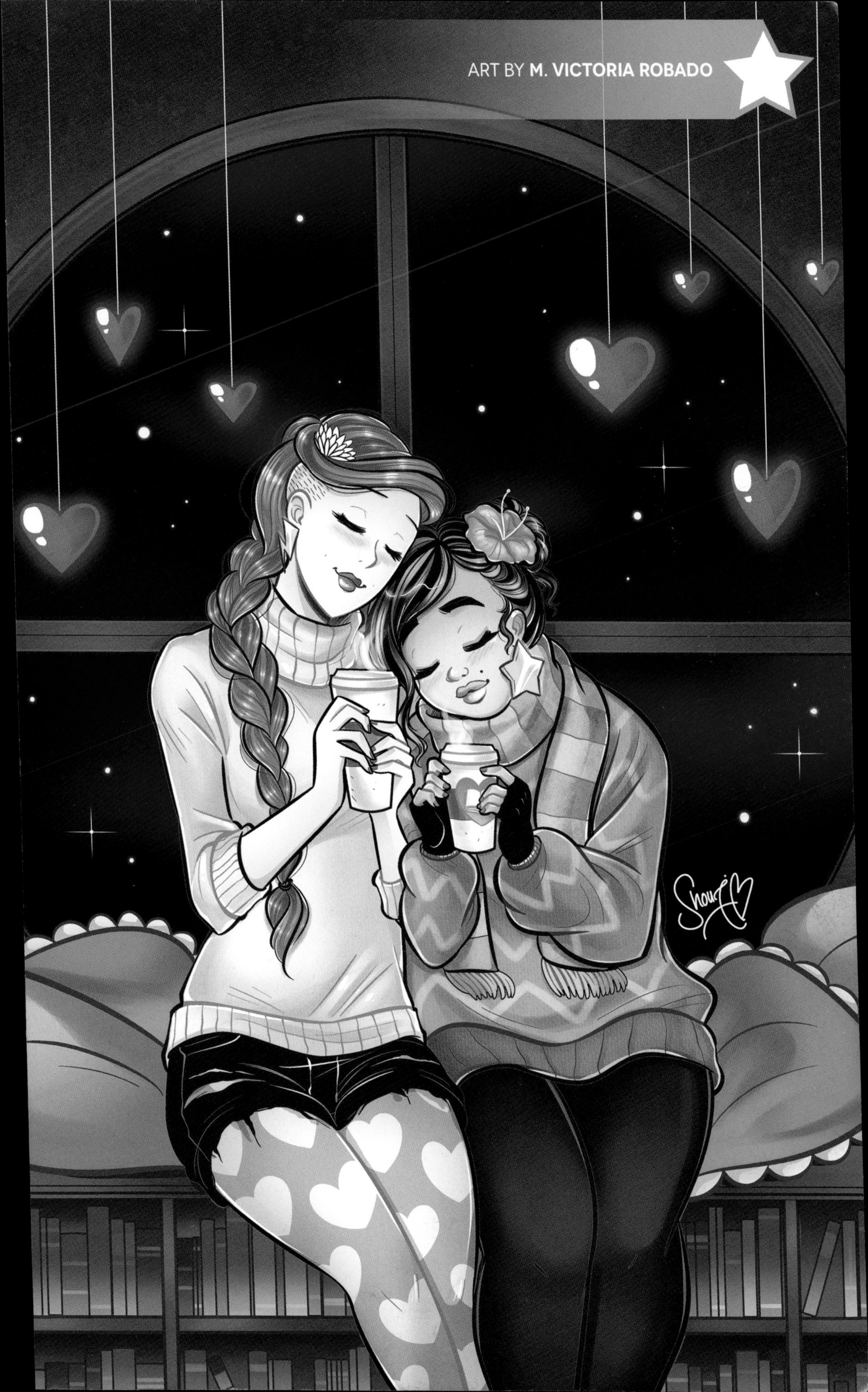
ART BY **M. VICTORIA ROBADO**

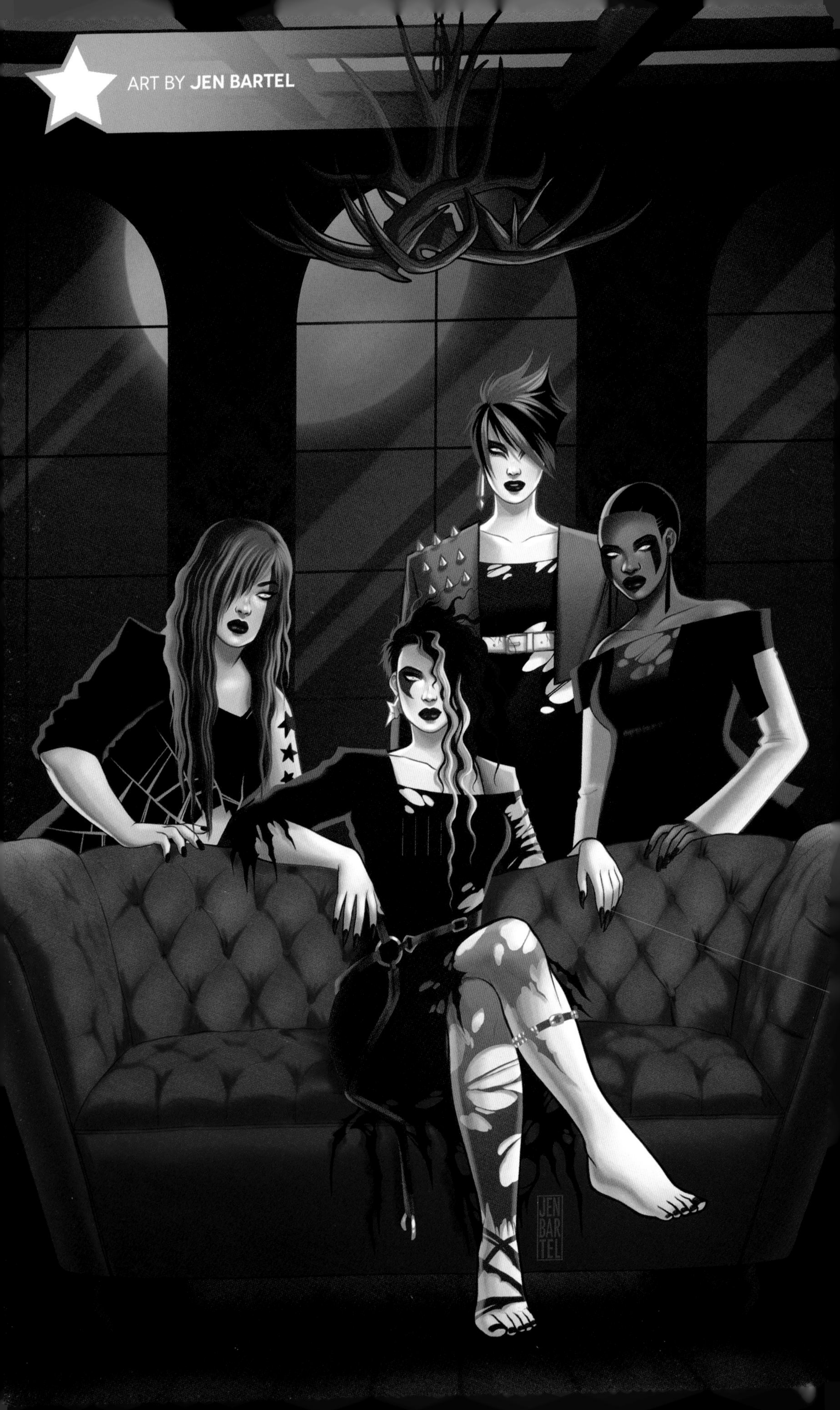
JEN
BAR
TEL
ART BY **JEN BARTEL**

ART BY **JEN BARTEL**

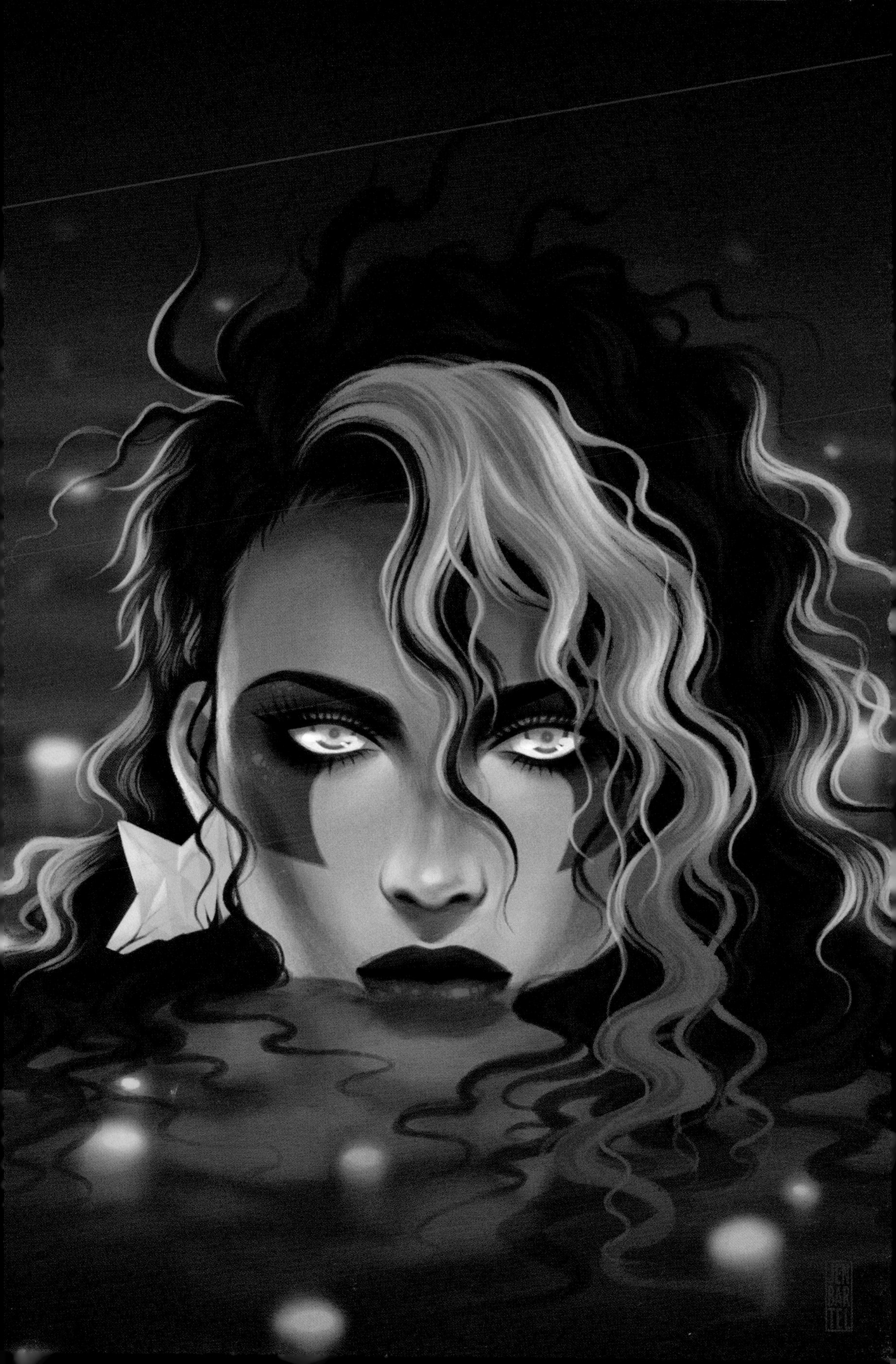
JEN BARTEL

ART BY **JEN BARTEL**

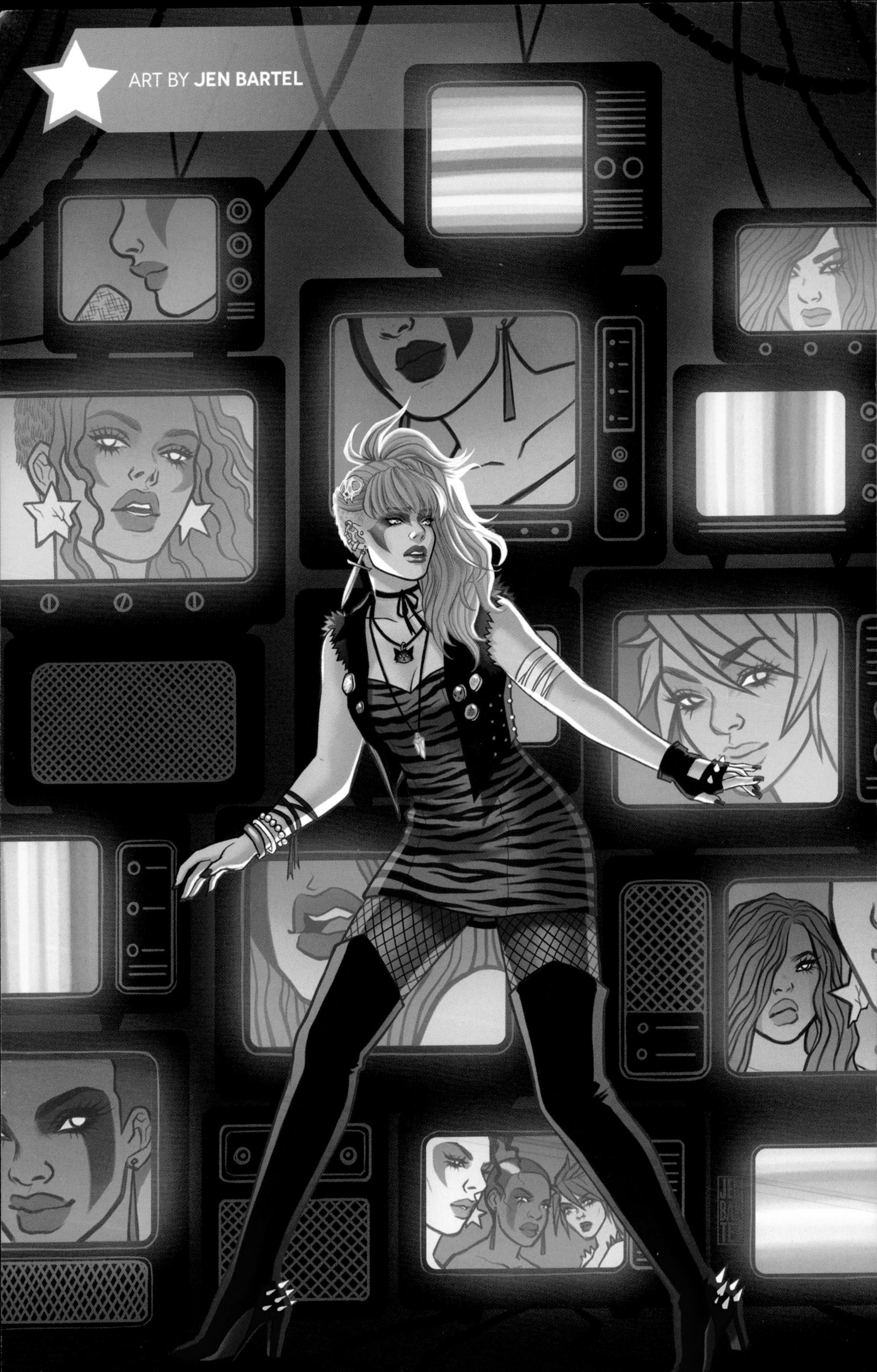

ART BY **JEN BARTEL**

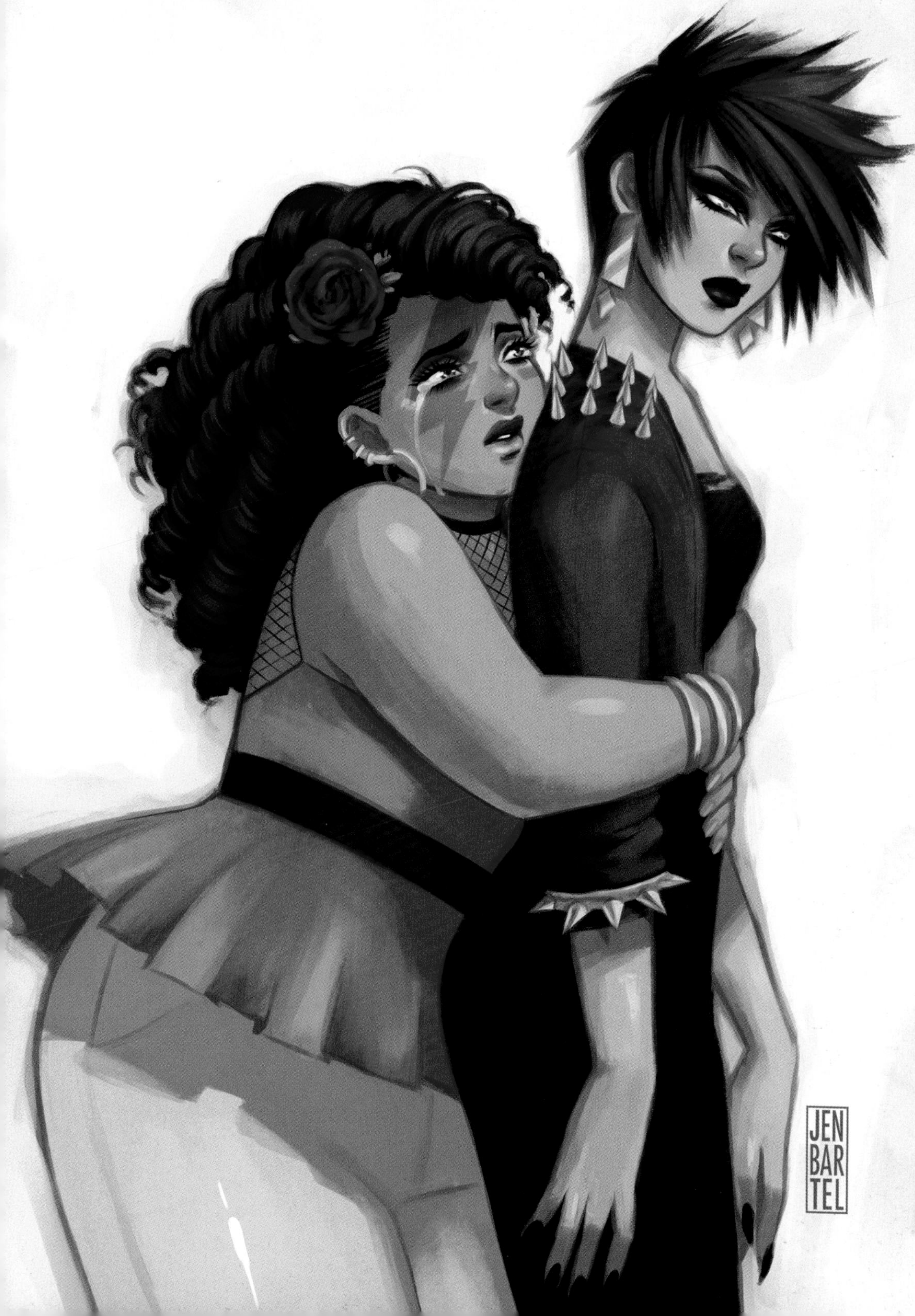
JEN
BAR
TEL

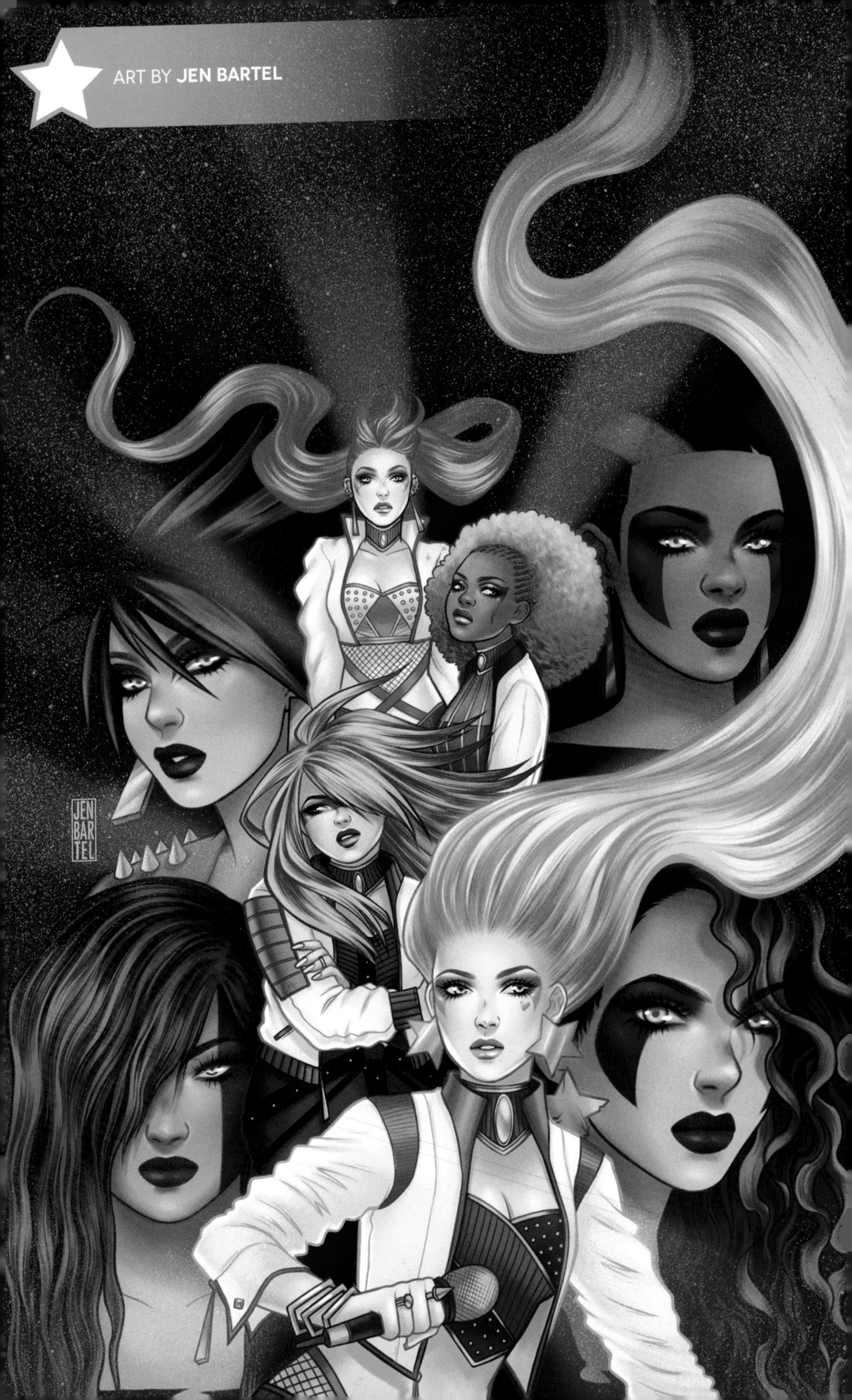
JEN
BAR
TEL
ART BY **JEN BARTEL**

ART BY **JEN BARTEL**
COLORS BY **PAULINA GANUCHEAU**

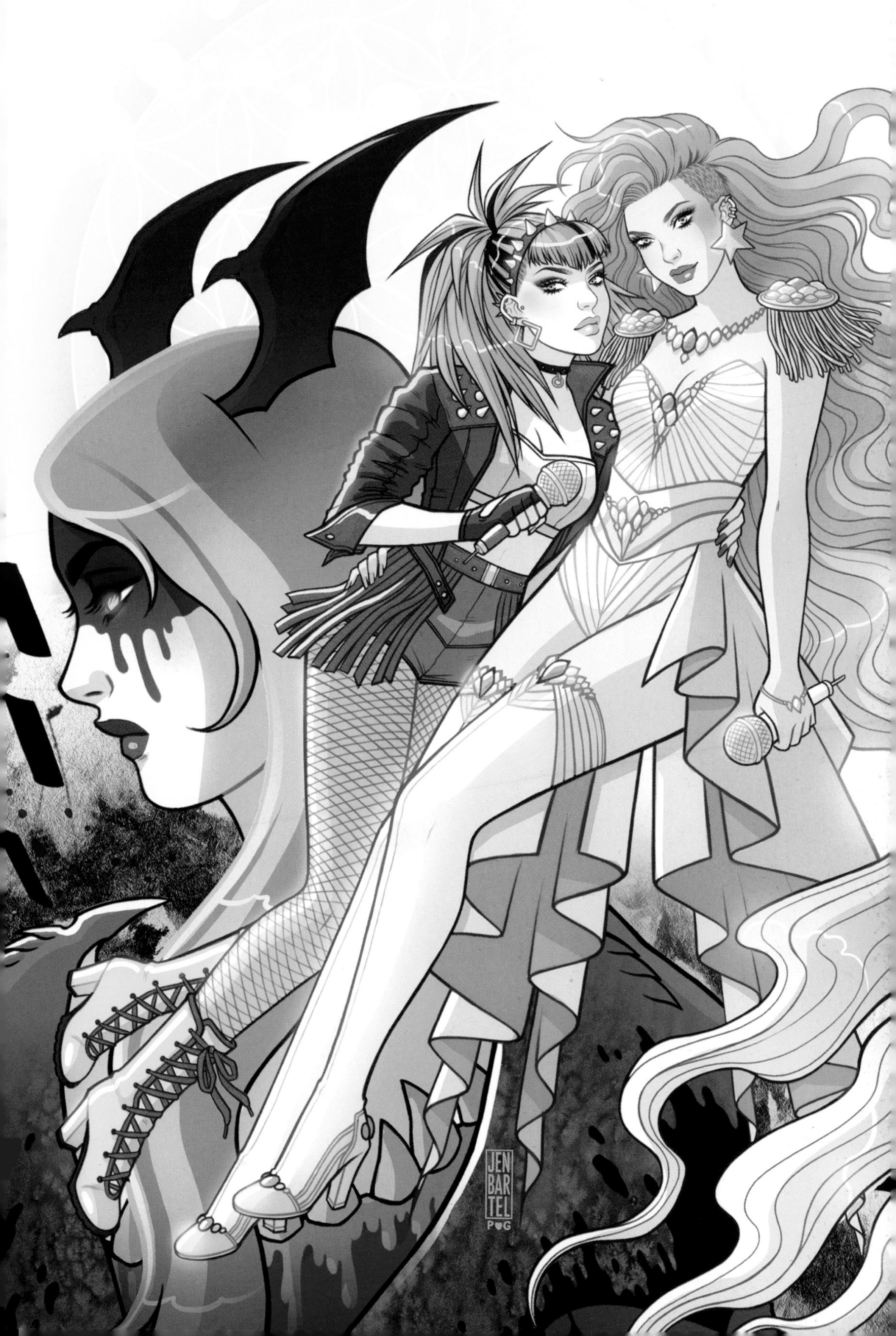

Madmartigan

NAME: Madmartigan a.k.a. Mads

AGE: 2

HEIGHT: Almost 6.5 inches

INSTRUMENT: She thinks she's very good at the piano (she is not).

LOVES: Pizzazz (who she thinks is a giant green-haired cat), certain other cats, catnip, sashimi, playing/watching *Neko Atsume* on the iPad, Fancy Feast (she is fancy!) watching crabs on the beach, making yowling noises that sound oddly human, cuddling (but only for a maximum of 7 minutes).

HATES: Most other cats, dry cat food, birds, dogs, and probably you.

PRIZED POSSESSION: Pizzazz.

VOTED MOST LIKELY TO: Star in a Vine that gets a billion views.

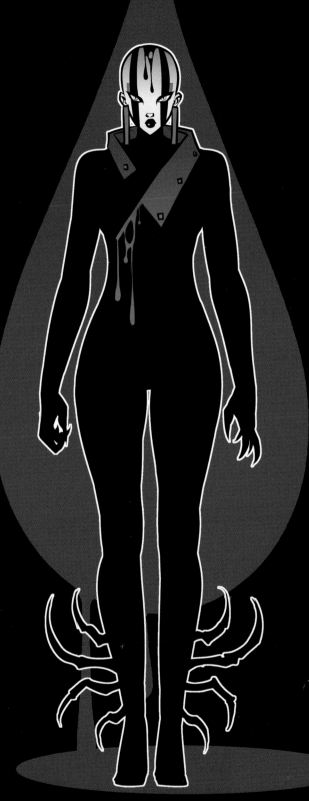

Silica

AGE: Unclear

HEIGHT: Variable

INSTRUMENT(S): Anything and everything.

LOVES: Order, unity, clarity, the Internet, and the Container Store.

HATES: Chaos, free will, disorder, aberrations, and tacos.

PRIZED POSSESSION: The entire world.

VOTED MOST LIKELY TO: Change your mind.

Shiver

NAME: Carol Church

AGE: 25

HEIGHT: 5'5"

INSTRUMENT(S): Guitar, bass.

LOVES: Rainy days, Prince, historical romance novels, hot tea with lemon, blueberry scones, birds, camping, and true crime stories.

HATES: Jello, snakes, print newspapers, and the desert.

PRIZED POSSESSION: A copy of *Lovesexy* signed by Prince.

VOTED MOST LIKELY TO: Serve you tea and listen to your problems.

Scream

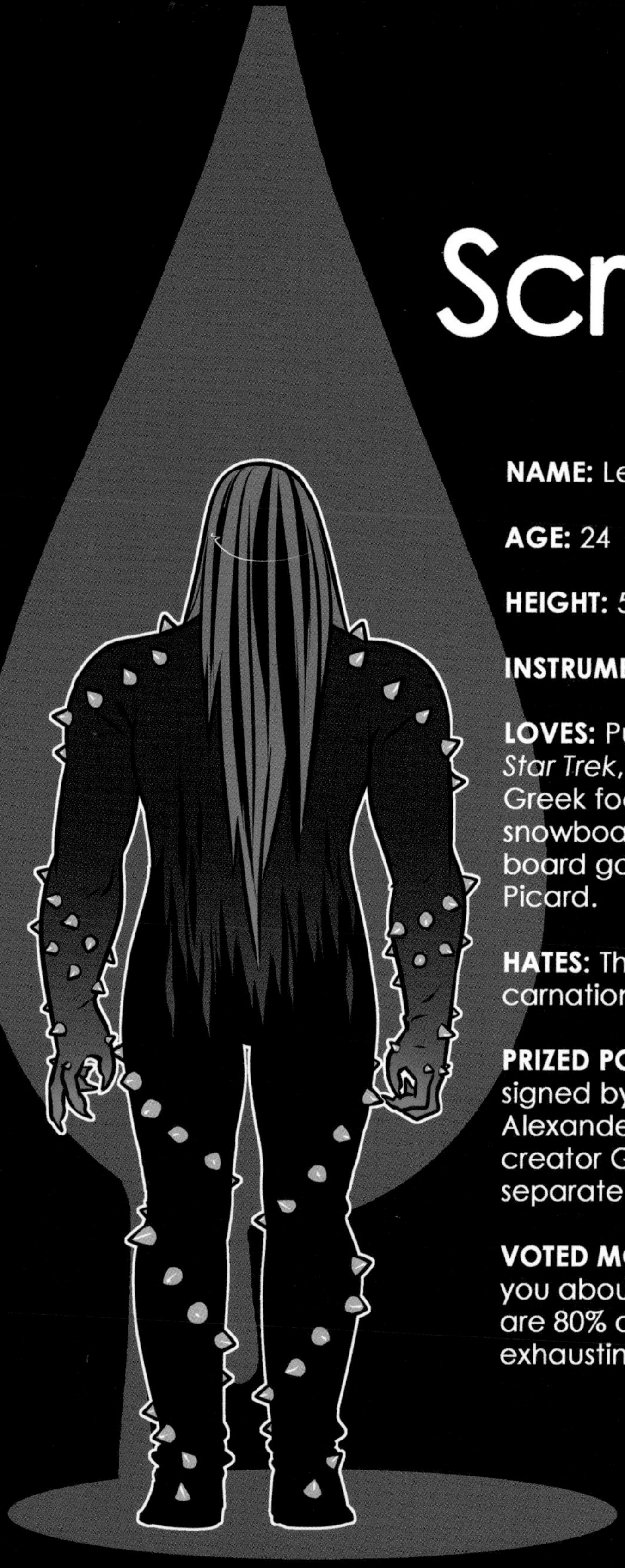

NAME: Lenore Rodriguez

AGE: 24

HEIGHT: 5'7"

INSTRUMENT: Theremin

LOVES: Pulp sci-fi novels, *Star Trek*, football, horror movies, Greek food, the mountains, snowboarding, hedgehogs, board games, and Captain Picard.

HATES: The rain, ponchos, carnations, and popcorn.

PRIZED POSSESSION: A theremin signed by Star Trek composer Alexander Courage and creator Gene Roddenberry (at separate times!)

VOTED MOST LIKELY TO: Talk to you about Star Trek (these talks are 80% adorable and 20% exhausting).

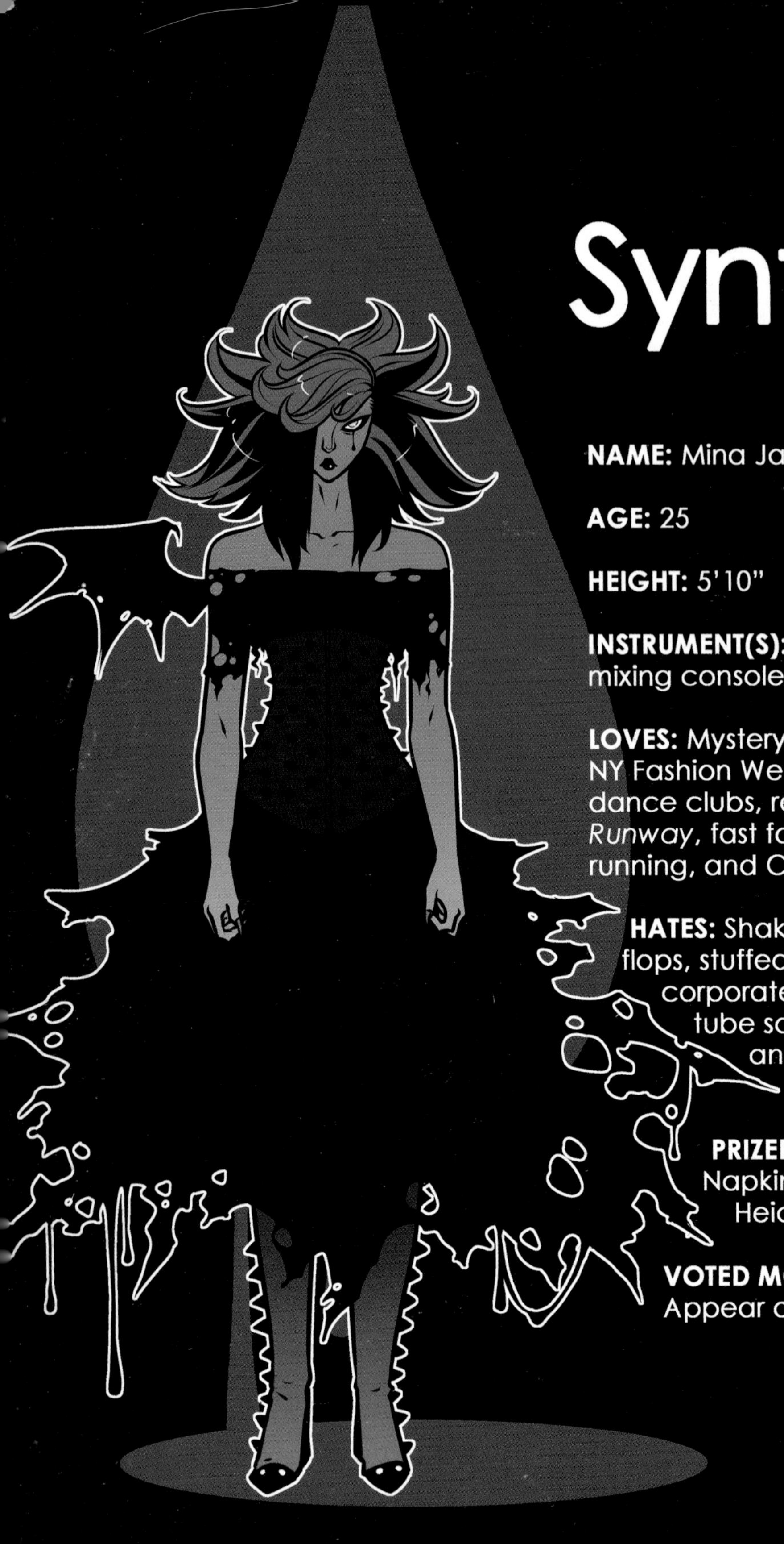

Synth

NAME: Mina James

AGE: 25

HEIGHT: 5'10"

INSTRUMENT(S): Laptop rig, mixing console, synthesizer.

LOVES: Mystery novels, NY Fashion Week, thrift shops, dance clubs, reality TV, *Project Runway*, fast food, road trips, running, and Cadbury Eggs.

HATES: Shakespeare, flip flops, stuffed animals, corporate gyms, white tube socks, scrunchies, and fruit smoothies.

PRIZED POSSESSION: Napkin used by Heidi Klum.

VOTED MOST LIKELY TO: Appear on a reality show.